THE QURAN'S CHALLENGE TO ISLAM

KHALID SAYYED

CheckPoint
Press

Copyright © 2011 by Khalid Sayyed.

All rights reserved. Printed in the United Kingdom and/or the USA / Europe or Australia. No part of this publication may be reproduced, stored in a retrieval system, or transmitted, in any form or by any means, electronic, mechanical, photocopying, recording, or otherwise, without the prior written permission of the publisher and/or the author, [as per contract terms]; except in the case of reviewers who may quote brief passages in a review.

The Quran's Challenge To Islam
(paperback version, indexed)
ISBN-13: 978-1-906628-25-3
Published by CheckPoint Press, Ireland

CHECKPOINT PRESS, DOOAGH, ACHILL ISLAND, CO. MAYO,

REPUBLIC OF IRELAND

TEL: +353 (0)98 43779

EMAIL: EDITOR@CHECKPOINTPRESS.COM

WEBSITE: WWW.CHECKPOINTPRESS.COM

(This book is also available in 7x10 hardback from all major booksellers ISBN: 9781-906628-14-7)

DEDICATION

To Pir Rashid-ud-Daula, who lit in me the torch of knowledge,

and

to Ghulam Ahmed Pervez who taught me to think objectively

Acknowledgements

I am deeply indebted to the following without whose support this work would not have seen the light of day:
- My dear friends Dr. S Azfar Husain, for his valuable suggestions and moral support; Mr. Sharif Din, who put his well-stocked library at my disposal; and Mr. Maqbool Farhat for his consistent encouragement.
- All the learned authors – past and present – who taught me.
- All the scientists who have developed the technology which has made writing so very pleasurably easy.
- Mr. Rahil Ahmed, for lovingly designing the cover; and above all..
- My family – Masooma, Pakeeza and Imran, and of course their mother, my dear wife and closest friend Billo, for their unflinching confidence and support.

Personal Description and Background

Originally from Pakistan, I have been a naturalised British citizen since 1974. A teacher by profession, I have taught English as a first, as well as a second language in the UK, Saudi Arabia and Pakistan. Currently, I am teaching ESOL (English for Speakers of Other Languages) at Leicester College. I hold the degrees of B. Sc., B. Ed., MA (English Language and Literature), PGCE and M Ed (Applied Linguistics).

Intellectual and critical inquiry into comparative religion, Islam and the Quran in particular, has always been my major academic interest. While teaching in Saudi Arabia for nearly a quarter of a century I gained fluency in Arabic, which equipped me for meaningful study of primary Islamic sources.

I have written extensively in English and Urdu. My articles have been published in Pakistan as well as Britain in magazines and newspapers. I have translated, from Urdu to English and vice versa, numerous articles and even a complete book. I regularly deliver talks on religious topics to seminars and conferences around the UK.

During my time in King Saud University, Riyadh, I regularly wrote and spoke on local cricket in the Saudi media (newspapers, radio and TV). For *Riyadh Daily,* I covered the 2000 Cricket World Cup as a columnist.

About My Book

Due to sectarian differences in my family, sceptic curiosity regarding religion was aroused early in life. My research interest spans 40 years with active contributions to the area since 1976. I bring this wealth of research and advanced skills as a trained, professional linguist to this proposed work.

My book is a frank academic study of the Muslim scripture, the Quran and its comparison to the early extra-Quranic literature of Islam - highlighting the differences and contrasts between the two. I go on to analyse the Muslim holy book itself from a linguistic perspective and explore its unconventional interpretation based upon the principle that in all Islamic matters, the last and definitive word is that of the Quran. It is not my intention to justify the doctrines of the Quran as the Eternal truth. Rather, that the traditional view of Islam (based upon the infallibility of Hadith and Muslim scholars of early Islam) does not accurately reflect the reality of the Quran.

I invite Muslims (as well as non-Muslims) to make an unbiased study of the Quran by a new methodology and give credit wherever due. I plead with Muslims to recognise real problems in their authentic literature, to exercise self-restraint in the face of criticism and refrain from responding with a *fatwa.*

To the Western world, I ask not to paint all Muslims with the same brush. A few thousand – or more – militants who believe in terrorism do not represent the entire billion-strong Muslim community of today's world anymore than the few thousand slave traders of the 18th century colonialism represent the entire Judeo-Christian world. Indeed, the Muslim faith, Islam, has sprung from the same original source of Semitic monotheism of Abraham as have Judaism and Christianity; and, strangely enough, suffers from the same problems of misrepresentations perpetuated through the centuries since its appearance.

TABLE of CONTENTS

PREFACE..10
FOREWORD..11
A BRIEF INTRODUCTION TO ISLAM...13

PART ONE: OVERVIEW
Chapter 1: THE EXTRA-QUARANIC LITERATURE of ISLAM..........18
    1.1. INTRODUCTION...18
    1.2. SECONDARY SOURCES of ISLAM...20
    1.3. A CRITIQUE OF HADITH..23
    1.4. THE WORD OF MOUTH...26
    1.5. CONFUSION AND CONTRADICTION.....................................27
    1.6. THE UNRELIABILITY OF HADITH..29
    1.7. OTHER SOURCES...32
    1.8. THE SUCCESSION CONFLICT..33
    1.9. A CRITIQUE OF HISTORICAL RECORDS..............................34
    1.10. CONCLUSION...36

Chapter 2: PROBLEMS: LANGUAGE, TRANSLATION & INTERPRETATION. 39
    2.1. INTRODUCTION...39
    2.2. TRANSLATION...40
    2.3. INTERPRETATION / EXPOSITION...44
    2.4. LANGUAGE AND CULTURE..44
    2.5. THE PRINCIPLE OF REPETITION...45
    2.6 A BRIEF INTRODUCTION TO ARABIC....................................46
    2.7. SOME SALIENT FEATURES OF ARABIC...............................47

Chapter 3: GLOSSARY of CONCEPTS and DOCTRINES of the QURAN............51

PART TWO: THE QURANIC ISLAM
Chapter 4: MAN, GOD AND THE SUPERNATURAL..........................76
    4.1. IS THERE A GOD OR NOT?..76
    4.2. ATTRIBUTES OF GOD..78
    4.3. CREATION OF MAN..80
    4.4. THE QURAN'S WORLD-VIEW..80
    4.5. THE STORY OF 'ADAM'...82
    4.6. HUMAN NATURE..88
    4.7. WITHER MAN?...89
    4.8. DEATH AND THE HEREAFTER..90
    4.8. THE DAY OF JUDGMENT..92
    4.9. PRE-DESTINY...93

Chapter 5: THE QURANIC POLITICAL SYSTEM..97
    5.1. INTRODUCTION..97
    5.2. SECTION ONE: THE HUMAN ENDEAVOUR...............................98
    5.3. WHAT THE QURAN SAYS..100
    5.4. A CRITIQUE OF DEMOCRACY..102
    5.5. MORALITY OF ETHICS..103
    5.6. SOCIALISM..104
    5.7. NATIONALISM 105
    5.8. INTERNATIONALISM 106
    5.9. SECTION TWO: THE QURANIC PRESCRIPTION.....................107

Chapter 6: THE ECONOMIC SYSTEM of the QURAN.....................................113
    6.1. CAPITALISM..113
    6.2. SOCIALISM..113
    6.3. THE QURANIC ECONOMIC SYSTEM......................................114
    6.4. THE CONSTITUTIONAL FRAMEWORK..................................118

Chapter 7: WOMEN, SEX & MARRIAGE..121
    7.1. MARRIAGE IN TODAY'S CONTEXT..121
    7.2. WHAT IS MARRIAGE?..122
    7.3. THE LOGISTICS..123
    7.4. DOWRY / GIFTS..124
    7.5. RIGHTS AND RESPONSIBILITIES..124
    7.6. RIGHTS AND RESPONSIBILITIES WITHIN MARRIAGE.............126
    7.7. DIVORCE – ONE OR THREE?..127
    7.8. DIVORCE IN TRADITIONAL ISLAM.......................................128
    7.9. SOME CONFUSING POINTS CLARIFIED................................129
    7.10. POLYGAMY...131
    7.11. REASONS FOR TAKING MULTIPLE WIVES 132
    7.12. MULTIPLE WIVES IN 'TRADITIONAL' ISLAM....................132
    7.13. THE AMOROUS MESSENGER..133
    7.14. POINT OF ORDER – GENDER DISCRIMINATION 133
    7.15. FORBIDDEN RELATIONS (INCEST).....................................134
    7.16. BASIC PHILOSOPHY: IS SEXUAL URGE INVOLUNTARY?.....135
    7.17. THE WEDDING NIGHT / HONEYMOON 136
    7.18. SEX AND SOCIETY..139
    7.19. INCEST..139
    7.20. SEX AND CULTURE...140
    7.21. PERMANENT VALUES AND TEMPTATION.........................141
    7.22. THE STORY OF JOSEPH 141

Chapter 8: 'MIRACLES' IN THE QURAN..143
    8.1. THE LINGUISTIC ASPECT...143
    8.2. THE QURANIC STANDPOINT ON MIRACLES.........................145
    8.3. MUHAMMAD'S 'MIRACLE' 145
    8.4. SOME 'MIRACULOUS' EVENTS REPORTED IN THE QURAN...146
        8.4.i Abraham and the birds..146
        8.4.ii Moses...148
        8.4.iii David and Solomon...150
        8.4.iv Jesus Christ...153
    8.5. 'MIRACLES' OF MOHAMMED..154
        8.5.i The Moon rent asunder..154
        8.5.ii Ascension to Heaven..155
    8.6. CONCLUSION 156
    8.7. MIRACLES - TO WHAT END? 158

Chapter 9: RITUALS in ISLAM...161
    9.1. *As-Salaa* (PRAYER)..162
    9.2. *Al-Hajj* (THE PILGRIMAGE) 164
    9.3. *Az-Zakaa* (THE POOR TAX, OR THE DUES OF THE STATE?).....166
    9.4. *As-Siyaam* (FASTING)..168
    9.5. FASTING AND THE QURAN..170
    9.6. SIGNIFICANCE OF RAMADAN..171
    9.7. AN IMPORTANT QUESTION – THE TIMING.........................173
    9.8. *Ash-Shahaada* (THE TESTIMONY)..173

Chapter 10: TERRORISM OR JEHAAD?...175
    10.1. 'HOLY WAR'..178

Chapter 11: THE PERMISSIBLE (*halaal*), THE FORBIDDEN (*haraam*)..............181
    11.1. THE PERMISSABLE (*halaal*)..181
    11.2. THE FORBIDDEN (*haraam*)..182
    11.3. SLAUGHTER OF ANIMALS (*Al-Hajj*)...................................183
    11.4. THE LOGIC OF IT 185

AFTERWORD..187
NOTES AND REFERENCES..189
BIBLIOGRAPHY...211
INDEX..217

PREFACE

Although I do not have any hand in the composition of this book, yet I take pride in its publication because I have mercilessly exhorted Mr. Khalid Sayyed to begin the work, to continue it, and finally to complete it despite every obstacle of diffidence and over work in other fields. Sayyed has worked exceedingly hard in odd hours of the day and night. I must say that at times when he had already worked from dawn till dusk and leisure and recreation had been fully earned, I stood darkly in the background, cracking my whip. There were two very important reasons for this. First, a book on this topic was a necessity of the hour. Secondly, in my opinion, Mr. Khalid Sayyed was pre-eminently suited to write such a book. I have known the author of this work for more than three decades now. During this period he has earned my respect as a colleague and my friendship as a person.

To my mind, what makes THE QURAN'S CHALLENGE TO ISLAM most welcome is the author's desire to avert clashes caused by misunderstandings about Islam today. Illustrating the author's ground-breaking research, this unusual piece of work convincingly acquaints the Muslim as well as the non-Muslim world with what Islam is and what it really means. Sayyed very clearly highlights the differences and conflicts which the Muslim Holy Scripture has with the conventional beliefs of Islam. Although I do not wholly subscribe to every word written here, I consider this book a pioneering work because Mr. Khalid Sayyed has dealt with the subject matter coolly, calmly, rationally and extremely successfully, attempting to bridge the gulf of misunderstanding that exists between the Muslim and the non-Muslim world. He is well aware of the fact that since the Crusades at the start of the second millennium, the non-Muslim world, particularly Jews and Christians, have looked upon Muslims as global mischief-mongers and uncivilised barbarians, while the Muslims in turn have loathed them as "infidels". However, the author goes a long way to explain that it is a very small number of people who are responsible for the tragic consequences and appeals to both sides to make solemn efforts to understand each other and act wisely in order to bring about peace and harmony in the turbulent world we are living currently.

Syed Azfar Husain
MA, M Ed (Cantab), PGCAL (Edin), PhD (London),
Formerly, Visiting Professor of English,
Cambridge University,
Cambridge, U.K.

FOREWORD

The tragic and deplorable events of September 11, 2001 changed our world for ever. The terrorists, who flew the two hijacked jet planeloads of innocent men, women and children into the twin towers of the World Trade Centre in New York, incidentally triggered multiple feelings on the part of the Western world towards Muslims and Islam – shock, disappointment, fear, disdain, and a rude awakening. Anger was reflected in what may be arguably called a Freudian slip by Gorge W Bush, the president of the United States at the time, when he termed the events the start of Crusades all over again.[i] True to some extent, tensions between the Judeo-Christian and Islamic worlds had reached the peak of armed combat for the second time in history. At the same time, however, there started a renewed interest for more awareness about the faith, hopes and aspirations of about a billion human beings who call themselves Muslim. Wealthy Muslim countries like Saudi Arabia started putting more money into departments of Islamic studies in universities all over the world, especially in the West. A large number of new publications about Islam hit the bookstores. Socially, more and more conversations featured Muslims.

Inadvertently, the 9/11 hijackers forced the Orient and the Occident to start understanding one another afresh. It is high time that they do. Ever since the Crusades at the start of the second millennium, Jews and Christians have regarded Muslims as global trouble-makers and, in return, Muslims have loathed them as 'infidels'. To some, it is a clash of different ideologies (religions);[ii] to some others it springs from different civic habits or ways of life;[iii] still others regard it nothing more than a constant war of economy, a tussle to control the world's resources. In the world of literature, there has been a huge mass of Western publications mindlessly degrading Islam while Muslims have reacted with thoughtless fury even at genuine criticism.[iv] This attitude has taken the world nowhere. It is time we sat down coolly and thought rationally about the obviously very dangerous and volatile situation we all have put ourselves in.

I ask Muslims to exercise self-restraint in the face of criticism and refrain from responding with a bullet, a *fatwa* (religious decree) or an act of terrorism: before deciding upon a course of action, try to take stock of your supplies and put your house in order. Quite often the unwanted and unsightly object, pointed out by neighbours, may be found in one's own backyard. The notion of Satanic Verses was not an invention of Salman Rushdie's imagination. It can still be found in authentic Islamic literature. Practices such as misuse of the provision of polygyny, using captive female prisoners of war as sex slaves, and generally looking down upon women as inferior to men – all have their origins in the extra-Quranic literature most Muslims still regard as authentic to the point of reverence. Saucy details of the founder of Islam, Mohammed's sex life found in the Prophetic Tradition, *Hadith*, as well as in books of *sira* (the biographies of the Prophet) and *tareekh* (annals of history), have been the source of publications like *Rangeela Rasool* (The Amorous Messenger) in India during the British Raj.v Complacency and telling lies may find their justification in Islamic literature. Killing of innocents and hostage–taking are acts which can find no justification in Islam. Muslims have always held the belief, to the dismay of Christian orthodoxy, that Jesus was not Son of God but simply a man exalted by the office of prophethood; also, they have always looked down upon, and have been quite deridingly vocal about, the doctrine of Trinity. Nonetheless, I am not aware of any Christian on record to have turned hostile towards Muslims for such 'blasphemous' beliefs and statements on the pretext that they were hurting Christian sentiment. Why should Muslims pick up arms every time some criticism – even serious, scholarly and academic – is made of Islam? It is only morally fair that if Muslims derive contented pleasure over the prospect of traditional Christianity being destroyed by the discovery of the Dead Sea Scrolls, they should gracefully and academically receive the scholarly research resulting from the 1972 find of ancient fragments of the Quran from the Grand Mosque in Sana'a, Yemen.vi Apart from the philosophical and academic discussions, Muslims should get used to the place hard evidence, such as archaeological finds, occupy in the human pursuit of knowledge and truth. The Quran lays great emphasis on use of reason; therefore, echoing the appeal to rational thinking made by Mohammed himself, I beseech Muslims to pause and think.vii

Backdrop

This work is intended for the educated middle classes – young school-leavers, graduates, and generally people with an academic bend of mind who are curious to read and think about Islam seriously and critically. I am assuming some basic background information on the part of my readers about Islam and its founder, Mohammed. However, to save some of my interested readers the trouble of referring to very basic books, I here give briefly what I think should help to appreciate what I have presented in this work. Nonetheless, the following background information is in the form popular among the dominant majority of Muslims as representative of Islam. I have found it difficult to accept the entirety of it as true. Some significant parts of it are in need of critical and academic inquiry according to both internal as well as external criteria. That in fact, is exactly what I have attempted to do in this work.

A BRIEF INTRODUCTION TO ISLAM

According to the commonly accepted version of history, around the middle of 6th century CE the Middle East had two very powerful empires ruling over a vast area. To the west was the Eastern Roman Empire with its capital at Constantinople (ancient Byzantium), the present day Istanbul in modern Turkey. To the east lay the vast Persian empire of the Sassanid dynasty with its capital at Madaain (ancient Ctesiphone) not far from present day Baghdad in modern Iraq. By the middle of the 6th century, the two giants had almost exhausted themselves to near-total collapse as a result of centuries-long mutual wars. Beyond the Fertile Crescent to the south lay the vast and desolate expanse of Arabia – arid and unattractive to the outside world – inhabited by a few nomadic tribes. On the western edge of the Arabian Peninsula, running along the length of the Red Sea, was a thin area of relatively more active human settlements with a trade route extending from the fertile Yemen in the south to Syria in the north. On this trade route there was a small town,[viii] tucked within parched stone hills, housing an ancient religious sanctuary called the *Ka'ba*.[ix] It is in this town Bakka (later known as Mecca) that in circa 570 AD was born a boy to a reasonably well-to-do family of the wealthy tribe al-Quraysh. He was Mohammed, son of Abdallah, the future founder of Islam.[x]

The Founder

Mohammed was an only child of his parents, Abdallah and Aamena, who were both lost to him when he was still a very young child, in fact before he reached the age of about 4 years. He was taken care of for a while by his grandfather Abdul Muttalib, upon whose death he was raised by one of his uncles, Abu Taalib. Mohammed grew up into a quiet and sober young man who was quite different from the normal contemporary youth in that he developed a reputation for being honest and trustworthy. Following many of his elders, Mohammed became a merchant and entered the world of trade by buying and selling merchandise along the trade route already mentioned. One of his clients was a wealthy widow Khadija who commissioned him to oversee her trade caravans to Syria. She was impressed by the conduct and temperament of the young Qurayshite and offered marriage. Reportedly, Khadija was 40 and Mohammed 25 when the marriage took place in 595. They had several children – at least two boys and four girls. Both the boys died in infancy but the girls survived and grew into important figures of Islamic history; two of them - Ruqqayya and Umm Kulthoom - were one after the other married to Uthmaan ibn 'Affaan, the future third successor (*khaleefa* – Caliph) to Mohammed; the youngest and the most famous daughter, Fatima, became the wife of 'Ali ibn Abu Taalib (son of Mohammed's benefactor uncle), Mohammed's dear cousin and the future fourth Caliph of Islam. Fatima is the matriarch at the head of the

Prophet's progeny to this day; she is revered by Shiite Islam as the lady who started the long line of *imam*'s (spiritual and religious leaders) and gave her name to the well-known dynasty of caliphs of Egypt, the Fatimids.

When he was about 40, in about 610, during one of his sessions of solitary retreats in a cave just outside Mecca, Mohammed had the epoch-making experience which was to change the world for ever. It was of a vision of Archangel Gabriel, who brought down the first Divine Message to him appointing him God's Messenger. The angelic visits continued over the next 23 years of Mohammed's life till he breathed his last and the messages became what we today know as the Quran, the holy Book and the Scripture of the Muslim world. The Message called Man to believe in the One Creator God – *Allah* – in the way of the monotheistic philosophy of the great patriarch Abraham, who had been followed by several previous messengers like Moses and Jesus. Mohammed's call to the new faith angered the people of Mecca and, initially, conversions were very few. Eventually, after having suffered the Qurayshite persecution for 13 years, an opportunity arose in a town about three hundred kilometres to the north. The handful of Muslims – the converts to the new faith of Islam - migrated in about 622 to Yathrib, now renamed *Medina tun Nabi* – City of the Prophet. There, gradually, Islam grew in strength and towards his last days Mohammed was able to found the beginnings of the first Islamic state in history. Finally, the great man expired in Medina in about 632.

History

After some teething problems, the fledgling state took roots and by the end of the second caliph 'Umar's reign in 644, the Islamic Empire controlled an area of about one million square miles. The era of the first four caliphs ended with the assassination of the fourth successor 'Ali ibn Abu Taalib in circa 652 and is known as *khilaafa tur raasheda* – the Righteous Caliphate. Thereafter, the Empire digressed considerably from the established way of the Prophet and his Companions and effectively became a hereditary monarchy. The dynasty of Umayyad caliphs ruled the Muslim world for 90 odd years. During this time, the Empire extended to its farthest limits. The Umayyads were overthrown by a rival clan, the 'Abbasids, to begin a dynastic rule of around six centuries to be terminated in 1258 by the barbarian hordes of Halagu Khan, grandson of the great Mongol, Genghis Khan. The 'Abbasid era is popularly considered to have been the Golden Age in the history of Muslim civilization and culture. It produced some of the greatest academics, artists, scientists and writers of Islam. The late part of the Umayyad and the early and middle part of the 'Abbasid rule saw a huge number of literary and religious works produced by some of the greatest names of Muslim history, such as Bokhari (hadith), Abu Hanifa (jurisprudence), Jaaber bin Hayan (science), Ibn Sina (medicine), and al-Ghazali (philosophy), etc.. Modern historians have recognised the Arab contribution to the spread of human knowledge. From the learning places of the

Middle East through the universities of Grenada and Cordova in Moorish Spain, Muslims brought Greek thought into medieval Europe and lit up the Dark Age with the torch of Knowledge. xi

Mohammed did not leave behind any legacy other than the Quran. About 150 years later began the appearance of compilations of records of his sayings and deeds – the *Hadith* – literally 'something new' but also means 'talk.' A little later appeared the first biographical records of Mohammed and his times. They are known as *at tareekh* [(books of) history], *al maghaazi* [(annals of) raids (and battles)], *sira* – short for *sira tar Rasool Allah* (biography of the Messenger of God), and *tafseer* – literally 'explanation and elaboration' – [(books of the Quranic) exegeses]. These earliest works from Islamic history formed, along with the Quran, the traditional sources of Islam, which were used by great jurists to compile books on Islamic jurisprudence. xii As a consequence of all these historical events, the Muslim world split into several factions (sects) quite early in their march through Time. The dominant mass of Muslims is known as *Sunni* – people who follow the *sunna* (way) of the Prophet. They are further divided into four sub-sects. The other big faction is called *Shia* – from *Shi'aan Ali* (Partisans of Ali) who are further subdivided into several smaller sects. The Shia maintain that, at Mohammed's death, his cousin and son-in-law Ali ibn Abu Taaleb should have succeeded him as caliph as he was the Messenger's rightful and divinely-appointed heir; they further hold that Ali's God-given *imaama* (spiritual as well as temporal leadership of the Muslim nation) carried on in his descendents. xiii There are close to a billion Muslims in the world today living in an area stretching from Morocco in northern Africa to Indonesia in the east and from Turkey in the north to Mauritania and the Sudan in the south. There are also several sizable populations of Muslims around the world in non-Muslim countries like the USA, the UK, Canada and many European countries.

Philosophy

The Quran's message, Islam, is not a religion in the conventional sense of the word - not in the sense as the West takes it with reference to Judaism or Christianity. The Western mind takes religion to be a personal discipline, which is a private relationship of an individual with the Creator with the main emphasis on spirituality. The more mundane matters of human life on Earth are left to the state.xiv The Quran, in comparison, presents a set of values on which is based a comprehensive system of social existence for human societies in the present form of life with an aim to develop the human personality so that it is equipped to be transformed to the next stage of existence in the march of evolution. The social system prescribed by the Quran is explained with the help of examples from the Arabian culture at the time and illustrated by instances from prior history. It encompasses all aspects of individual as well as collective human existence – politics, economy, education, welfare, relationships, etc. Theologically, the Quran believes in the one Creator God, who is intelligent and compassionate and has created the Universe according to firm, permanent physical as well as social laws. God created Man different from the rest of His creation in one important aspect – freedom of choice. To help Man choose the best value system of his own volition, God established a system of periodically sending his suggested Message to mankind through specially appointed men – Messengers of Allah, such as Noah, Abraham, Moses and Jesus. Mohammed is the last and final messenger in this long chain. Essentially, it is the same message which was given to these men. Prior to Mohammed, the Message used to get corrupted, or lost, due to various reasons, chief among them was men's greed and ulterior motives. But, with the Quran, God vowed to look after the preservation of the Message Himself guaranteeing its incorruptibility till the end of Time. Hence, the finality of Mohammed's mission – there would be no new messenger after him because there is no need of any – the eternal Message of God is forever preserved and enshrined in the book in the Arabic language called the Quran. It has the last word in all matters.

Practically, in everyday life, Muslims are normally expected to: offer five ritualistic prayers every day – at dawn, noon, late afternoon, sunset and late night – individually or (preferably) in congregation in a mosque; observe one month of fasting [abstain from consuming any food and sexual intercourse during daylight hours] in Ramadan, the 9th month of the Islamic (lunar) calendar; contribute regularly to charity; and make at least one pilgrimage in one's life to the holy city of Mecca in the first week of the 12th Islamic month.[xv] By observing these rituals, and also by generally trying to live as the Quran demands, Muslims hope to find favour with God on the Day of Judgment (*al qiyaama*) and enter Paradise for an eternal existence of pure bliss. That day, occurring at the end of Time when the Universe will be rolled up, will see each and every single human being ever created brought back to life to be made accountable for their deeds to God, who will preside over the proceedings and send the bad to Hell and the good to Paradise.

Let me now invite my readers to the book proper.

Editorial note:
In all instances I have used Abdulla Yousuf Ali's translation of the Muslim holy book titled *The Holy Quran – English translation of the meanings and Commentary*, unless otherwise stated. Where I have departed from the translation, I have indicated it.

Reference to the Quranic verses have been made in numbers, with the first figure denoting the number of the *sura* (chapter) and the second (after the colon) referring to the verse(s). Thus 2:219 means verse 219 in the second chapter.

Part 1

OVERVIEW

Chapter 1

THE EXTRA-QUARANIC LITERATURE OF ISLAM

1.1 INTRODUCTION

Traditionally, what we know as Islam has a multiple of sources. The primary source is of course the book known as the Quran while the category of secondary sources comprises of a variety of a great mass of literature mostly authored during the 8th, 9th, and 10th centuries, CE (3rd, 4th, and 5th centuries, Hijra). It is our task to examine the secondary sources of Islam in this chapter. I shall deal with the Quran in the second part of this book.

The question 'What is Islam?' has been asked thousands of times and appears to be ridiculously simple. In reality, however, it is not as easy to answer as many of my readers might like to think. As has been realistically - even if in a derogatory tone - observed by some writers, one might distinguish THREE Islams:

First, the Islam contained in the Quran; second, the Islam as interpreted and developed by theologians through the Prophetic Tradition (*Hadith*); it includes what is known as the *Sharia* as well as *fiqh* [the Islamic jurisprudence (law)] for legal purposes; and third, the Islam reflected in the deeds and achievements of Muslims through history as well as the present day.[1]

In my personal view, however, this is too fine a distinction. What Muslims have done and achieved throughout their history, and still do, has largely been on the basis of second Islam in our list. At least, they have tried, and still do, to find a justification for most of their actions in Traditional Islam–the conventional view of Islam based upon an amalgam of *Hadith* (records of the sayings and deeds of Mohammed), *Taareekh* [historical records like *kutub al-maghaazi* (annals of raids and battles), *Sira tur Rasool* (biographical records of Mohammed)], *Tafseer* (the Quranic exegeses), as well as *Fiqh* (treatises on Jurisprudence). That has prompted some writers to come up with works such as *Do Islam* (Two Islam's) and *Do Quran* (Two Quran's).[2]

Practically, that means that there is the Scripture (the Quran) and there is the interpretation of it (the extra-Quranic literature).[3] At times, the two sources are at odds with one another and present different – sometimes, contradictory – views about a given subject. The result has been scores of brands and definitions of Islam solidifying those different views, over more than fifteen centuries, into as many sects of Islam. The logic commonly accepted and adhered to by the dominant majority of Muslims is as follows:

1. The Quran, the Divine Message, was revealed to Mohammed.
2. He had the duty to transmit, as well as explain and interpret, the Message.
3. Mohammed fulfilled his prophetic duty to the full by honestly transmitting God's Word (the Quran) to the people of Hejaz (whose duty in turn it was to spread the Message to the rest of the world); also, he explained and interpreted the Divine Message by his deeds as well as utterances.
4. Mohammed's explanations and interpretations were recorded by very able compilers, under the title *Hadith*, after extremely careful and hard work that is almost flawless.
5. No one can ever understand God's Message better than the Messenger himself, who was directly guided by God. Therefore, in a way, *Hadith* is God's own explanation and interpretation of His Word.
6. It follows logically that if one finds a discrepancy between the Quran and Hadith,
    i   the problem lies with the reader's understanding,
    ii the Hadith view overrides the Quranic view (because the reader's conception of the Quranic view is a misunderstanding in the first place and therefore faulty.

The problem is compounded by another term often used by Muslims – the *Sunna* (the Prophetic Model). Short for *Sunna tar Rasool Allah* (the way of the Messenger of Allah) or *Sunna tan Nabi* (the way of the Prophet), it is almost invariably used in conjunction with the term *Quran*. Most Muslims thinkers, on the individual as well as the collective level, assert that Islamic laws must be based upon 'the *Quran* and the *Sunna.*' But, there we come up against a problem. In response to the question 'What / where is the *Quran*?' one can point to a particular volume in a pile of books and say, 'Here is a volume in the Arabic language, consisting of 114 chapters, revealed to the Prophet Mohammed in 6th/7th century Arabia.' No one is likely to dispute that statement. But, the answer to the question 'What / where is the *Sunna*?' is not that easy to provide. The response is very likely to be: 'Well, the *Sunna* is contained in the various authentic compilations of *Hadith*, reliable records of *Taareekh* and *Sira*, and of course, the *Quran.*' So, the *Sunna* has to be compiled from all these sources. There have been scores of such compilations in various languages throughout the history of literature on Islam. The diversity of these sources has meant the appearance of differing versions of the Prophetic Model simply because of the inconsistencies of the source material. The result has been a very conspicuous absence of one authentic compilation of the *Sunna* unanimously agreed upon by Muslims. A more unfortunate consequence has been the division of the *umma* (the Muslim nation) into literally scores of sects believing in versions of Islamic philosophy and conduct based upon the Prophetic Model vastly different from - at times, opposite to – each other. In fact, Islamic sects have been at such variance from one another that each and every sect in history has been branded a *kafir* (infidel) with a proper *fatwa* (religious decree) issued against it.[5] Sadly from a literary, and tragically from the Muslim, point of view, this lack of a united standpoint on the immensely important question of *Sunna* has been clumsily justified as God's Will by none other than the Prophetic Tradition (*Hadith*) itself. The Messenger of Allah (Mohammed) is reported to have said:

> 'There are going to be 72 sects in my *umma*, but only one of them is destined for Paradise.' [6]

That should help a good deal in explaining why today there are so many different Islamic systems in operation even in non-secular Muslim countries professing to have the Law of Islam in place. Saudi Arabia and Iran are two examples in this regard. Saudi Arabia operates strict Wahaabism (named after Mohammed ibn Abdul Wahaab, the late 18th century revivalist from Nejd, central Arabia) under the influence of the Hanbali school, itself a sub-sect of the greater Sunni sect. Iran follows the other big division of Islam, the Shia sect. Countries like Egypt and Algeria are trying to go down the Shafe'i or the Maliki roads, which are the other Sunni sub-sects. If Pakistan ever becomes a theocratic state (after hopefully having resolved the Sunni-Shia differences), it is very likely to adopt the Hanafi jurisprudence, the philosophy of the biggest of the four major Sunni sects. Since these sectarian divisions have existed for the most of the Muslim history, it has forced some thinkers to admit the gravity of the problem. Abul A'la Maudoodi, the founder of *Jamaat e Islami* in the sub-continent of India and Pakistan, one of the most influential Islamic scholars in modern times, wrote:

> 'It is not possible to arrive at an interpretation of Islam based upon the Quran and the Sunna that may be acceptable to all sectarian divisions in Islam.' [7]

In view of this confused state of affairs it is desirable for us to attempt to appraise these sources of Islam critically and rationally from an academic standpoint. The most important of all is decidedly the Quran, which we shall take up later. First, let us look at the extra-Quranic material.

1.2 SECONDARY SOURCES OF ISLAM / HADITH

Historically, the most widely accepted as authentic compilations of *Hadith* by Sunni Islam are the *Sahaah Sitta* (the Six Authentic Ones): [8]

1. *Al-Jaame as Saheeh* by Mohammed bin Ismail Bukhari (d. 256 AH/870 AD) of Bokhara, in central Asia. He is reported to have selected around 2,700 – 3000 reports out of an estimated original collection of 600,000.

2. *As-Saheeh* by Muslim bin Al-Hujjaj (d. 261/875) of Neishapour, in Iran. He selected 4,000 items to report from about 300,000.
3. *As-Sunan* by Abu Dauood (d. 275/888) of Seestan, in Iran. He recorded a selection of 4,800 reports from nearly 500,000.
4. *As-Sunan* by Abu Abdallah bin Maajja (d. 273/887) of Quzwain, in Iran. He selected 4,000 out of an original 400,000.
5. *Al-Jaame'* by Abu Eesa Mohammed Tirmadhi (d. 279/892) of Tirmadh, Itan. He reported about 2,100 items out of 300,000.
6. *As-Sunan* by Abdur Rahman Al-Nisaaee (d. 303/915) of Nisaa in Khurasaan, Iran. He selected 4,300 items to report out of 200,000.

In addition to these six major works, some minor ones are:
    1. *Muwatta* by Malik bin Anas (d. 179/795), and
    2. *Musnad* by Ahmed bin Hanbal (d. 241/855).

Drawing upon all the above works, Wali ad-Din al-Tibrizi wrote

    3. *Mishkaat al-Masaabeeh* in the 8th/14th century.

Shia Islam believes in a Hadith selection of their own. They are:

    1. *Al-Kaafi* by al-Kulayni (d. 329/941).
    2. *Man la yahduruhu al-faqih* by Shaykh al-Saadiq, also known as Babawayh (d. 381/991).
    3. *Al-Istibsar* by Mohammed bin Hasan al-Tusi (d. 460/1067), and
    4, 5. *Tahdheeb al-ahkaam* and *Wasai'l al-Shia* by Al-Hurr al-Amili (d. 1104/1692).

In addition to *Hadith,* information about Islam, its founder, and early days is also obtained from three important early works of history. The principal accounts of the life of Mohammed were written in about 100 years from 750 to 850 AD. They are:

    1. *Sira tar Rasul Allah* (Life of the Messenger of Allah) by Muhammad ibn Is-haaq (d. 150/767).
    2. *Maghaazi* (Battles/Raids) by Muhammad bin 'Umar al-Waqidi (d. 207/823).
    3. *Tabaqaat* (Dynasties) by Muhammad bin Sa'd (d. 230/ 845).

The Shia have;

    4. *Sharh Nahj al-Balaagha* [Explanation of 'The Mature Path'] by Ibn Abi al-Hdid (d. 656/1258). It is a commentary on the letters and sayings of 'Ali ibn Abi Talib, the Prophet's cousin and the fourth caliph of Islam.

Also, among the classical works, we find some biographical dictionaries on Mohammed's Companions by people like Ibn 'Abd al-Barr (d. 463/1070), Ibn al-Athir (d. 630/1233) and Ibn Hajar al-Asqalani (d. 852/1449). Yet another useful source on early Muslim conquests is *Kitab al-Ghazawaat* ('The Book of Raids') by the Andalusian Ibn Hubaysh (d. 584/1188).

Some important works on history are:

> 1. *Tarikh* ('History') by al-Yaqubi (d. 283/897).
> 2. *Al-Akhbar al-Tiwal* by Abu Hanifa al-Dinwari (d. 281/894)
> 3. *Kitab al-Ma'arif* ('Book of Information') by Ibn Qutayba (d. 276/889).
> 4. *Muruj al-Dhahab wa Ma'adin al-Jawher* ('Golden Ways and Mines of Precious Stones') by Al-Masudi (d. 345/956).

But, doubtlessly, the crucial historical works of the late 9th and early 10th centuries – and the most respected and influential in the Muslim world – are:

> 1, 2. *Ansab al-Ashraaf* ('Genealogies of the Elite') and *Futuh al-Buldaan* ('Conquest of Countries') by Ahmed bin Yahya al-Baladhuri (d. 279/892), and, 3, 4; *Al-Tarikh al-Rusul wa al-Muluk* ('The History of Prophets and Kings'), and, *Jaame al-Bayaan 'an Taweel al-Quran* ('Comprehensive Report on the Interpretation of the Quran'), an exegetical treatise, by Abu Ja'far Muhammad ibn Jarir al-Tabari (d. 310/923).

The last two authors mentioned drew upon older collection of historical material which had been written down roughly a century before in the decades around 800 AD. They often narrate not structured and connected events but report from a series of discrete anecdotes known as *akhbar* (singular, *khabar*). [9]

As mentioned earlier, the various sects of Islam take their credence from these extra-Quranic sources. Islamic sects follow their preferred *fiqh* (jurisprudence) as taught by learned scholars [*fuqahaa* (lawyer or legal experts, sing. *faqeeh)*] of yesteryears. That is the basis of the four major Sunni sects:

- The **Hanafi** school of *fiqh* was founded by No'maan bin Thaabet, an *'ajamy* (non-Arab) scholar, who is better known as Abu Hanifa (d. 150 H/765 AD) in Kufa, Iraq. The followers of the Hanafi tradition are the most numerous and are spread mostly in Asia and the Middle East.
- The **Maliki** school takes its name from Malik bin Anas (b.93 H/680 AD–d.179 H/796 AD) of Medina. He is the compiler of the earliest collection of *hadith*, titled *al Mu'atta*.
- The **Shafe'i** school comes from Muhammad Idris As-Shafi'i (b.150 H

/767 AD – d.204 H / 820 AD) from Gaza, Palestine. His followers are mostly found in Egypt.
- The **Hanbali** school was founded by Ahmed bin Muhammad bin Hanbal (b. 164 H / 780 AD – d. 241 H / 857 AD) from Merv in Iran. A revivalist movement in the Nejd (now Saudi Arabia) in late 18th century by Muhammad bin Abdul Wahaab (d. 1787) founded an offshoot of the Hanbali school. It is known as the **Wahaabi** Movement.

The Shia follow the system of jurisprudence formulated by Ja'far al-Saadiq, their sixth *imam* (religious leader) in the line of twelve direct descendents of 'Ali ibn Abi Talib, the fourth Caliph. 10

1.3. A CRITIQUE OF HADITH

The dominant majority of Muslims hold the view that most of these extra-Quranic works, especially the *Hadith,* are essential sources of Islam along with the Quran. Support for this view is primarily derived from the Quran :

> '... We have sent among you a Messenger of your own, rehearsing to you Our Signs (*aayaatenaa*), and purifying you (*yuzakeekum*), and instructing you in Scripture (*alkitaab*) and Wisdom (*alhikma*) and in new knowledge.' (2:151) 11

If 'Wisdom' (*al-hikma*) in this verse is to be taken to mean *hadith* (the extra-Quranic utterances and deeds of the Messenger), we are faced with a dilemma. As we know for a fact that Mohammad died around 630 AD/10 H; another fact is that there is no legacy of his available other than the Quran (the earliest compilation of *hadith* did not appear till about 150 years *after* his death). In other words, Mohammed did *not* compile and leave behind a collection of his sayings as he did the Word of God. If his sayings were essential for true understanding of, and were complementary to, the Quran, he should have done that duty. The fact that he did not do so can only mean one of two things: he either did not fully carry out his responsibilities as a teacher, or he was not supposed to, and never intended to do so. From the Quranic point of view, the latter appears more likely to have been the case rather than the former. Evidence to this effect is found in the Quran. The Book claims that it has taken care of *all* that needed to be said (16:89 - ...*al-Kitaabe tabyaanan le kulle shaye*), and has omitted *nothing* (6:38 – *ma farratnaa fil kitaabe min shaye*). Also, he (the Prophet Mohammed) transmitted all he was supposed to (87:6 – *sa nuqruka fa la tansaa*). To emphasize that the Book is self-sufficient for the purposes of teaching what God wanted to, it poses the rhetorical question: 'And is it not enough for them that We have sent down to thee the Book which is rehearsed to them?...' (29:51). The task of transmitting God's Word, as well as explaining the entire system (*ad-Deen*), to its primary audience was successfully completed in the last days of Mohammed's life. It is popularly agreed that the occasion of the Last Pilgrimage was the time when the last verse of the Quran was revealed:

> al yawma akmaltu lakum deenakum –'...this day I have perfected your religion for you...' (5:3).

Outside of the Quran, we find similar evidence: 12

1 A report from *Musnad* by *Imam* Ahmed ibn Hanbal says:
'We used to write down whatever we heard from the Messenger of Allah. One day, the Messenger happened to come to us and asked, "What is that you write?" We said, "Sir, whatever we hear from you." He said, "A book parallel to the Book of God? Keep the Book of God clean and pure and free of all confusion." Then we gathered all that material in a field and burnt it.'

2 *Imam* Zahbi reports in *Tazkera tal Haffaaz Zahbi* about the First Caliph:
'Hazrat Abu Bakr Siddiq gathered the people after the death of the Messenger of God and said, "You narrate reports from the Messenger which differ from each other. People in future will become firmer in such differences. Therefore, do not attribute any saying to the Messenger. If asked, you should say, 'We have the Book of God in our midst.' So, follow the criterion of *halaal* (permissible) and *haraam* (forbidden) as given in the Book."'

3 *Tabaqaat ibn Sa'd* reports about the Second Caliph:
'When *ahaadith* [Prophetic Tradition Reports] proliferated in Umar's time, he put people under oath and forced them to surrender all collections to him. Then he ordered them all burnt.'

4 Above all, ironically enough, one authentic report says that the Messenger said:

> 'Do not write anything from me other than the Quran; and whosoever has written anything other than the Quran, erase it.' 13

Another verse, among several, of the Quran in support of this idea of the Quran-Hadith partnership is as under:

> 'O ye who are convinced! Obey Allah, and obey the Messenger, and those charged with authority among you..' 14 (4: 59)

The three distinctly separate spheres of obedience identified by Muslims in this verse [the Quran (*obey Allah*), Hadith (*obey the Messenger*) and, the law of the government of the day (*those charged with authority among you*)] do not synchronize with the general teachings of the Quran for the following reasons.
God's Law (the Quran) was transmitted to men through the Messenger. He is to be obeyed because he is the honest guardian of the Divine Message

(81:21). The Messenger asks Muslims to obey God alone through the Quran (5:48; 6:156; 7:3) *not* his own self (4:35; 39:24). That clearly means that obedience of the Messenger is but that of God's. During the lifetime of the Messenger, he was the central authority for Muslims to obtain Quranic judgment on any given matter (4:59). Indeed, as it says in the Quran: "He who obeys the Messenger, obeys Allah..." (4:80). After his death, this responsibility passed on to his rightful and righteous successors. They too asked citizens to follow God's Law (the Quran). There was no question of obedience of the Messenger as different from that of God's because he had not left behind any collection of his sayings/instructions. Every successor must have regarded the judgments of his predecessors, and those of the Messenger, but as precedence only because nothing can supersede God's Word! That is why Muslims are asked by the Quran to make decisions through consultation (42:38). Even the Messenger was asked to consult Muslims (3:159). In fact, according to the Quran, principles and values are more important than persons or personalities:

> "Mohammed is no more than a Messenger; many were the Messengers that passed away before him. If he died or were slain, will ye then turn back on your heels..." (3:144)

That is exactly what Abu Bakr, the first caliph meant when he said to mourners at Mohammed's demise,

> 'If you worshipped (followed) Mohammed, be informed that he is dead; but if you worship (follow) Allah, be informed that He never dies!' 15

And that is why, on the same occasion, 'Umr bin Al-Khattab, the future second Caliph, made an historical utterance: '*husbunaa kitaabAllah*'–The Book of God suffices for us. 16

Therefore, in essence, obedience is only for God's Law (the Quran). Clearly, the rulers are to be obeyed only if they enact laws according to the Quran (10:35; 5:77, 25:52; 26:151). Even parents are not to be obeyed if they ask you to go against God's Law (29:8; 31:15). Obedience and loyalty is only to be for one who has the appropriate knowledge (10:89), and refers to God's Law for judgment (31:15).

That is why Abu Bakr, on appointment as the first successor to the Messenger, said in his inaugural address,

> 'Support me as long as I abide by God's Law; if I digress, remove me.' 17

Secondary support for this standpoint is taken by the dominant majority of Muslims from the following argument:

The Quran gives principles, general guidelines and boundaries. It does not contain detailed instructions for, for instance, very essential and basic pillars of Faith like Prayer *(salaa)* and Fasting *(sowm)*. It was the Messenger's duty to provide those details and he did it quite comprehensively. His *sunnah* (his way of putting Quranic principles into practice) is available in the compilation we know as *Hadith*. If we did not have *Hadith,* it would have been impossible to arrive at the true meanings of the Quran.18

This argument does not hold much water when subjected to critical analysis. Firstly, contrary to the sweeping generalization, the Quran *does* give considerable details on the common rituals. Fasting (*as-Siyaam*), for instance, has detailed instructions on the time of the year (*Ramadan,* the ninth month of the Muslim lunar calendar), exemptions and penalties in verses 2:185 – 186; and about the exact timing of starting and breaking a fast, etc in verse 2;187. *Az-Zakaa* (commonly known as poor-tax or alms) is dealt with in great detail throughout the Scripture save for the rate of payment.19 The annual ritual of pilgrimage (*al-Hajj*) to the Ka'ba in the Grand Mosque at Mecca (now in Saudi Arabia) has an entire Quranic chapter devoted to it – Sura *al-Hajj*, numbered 22. Even *as-Salaa* (daily ritual prayer) has instructions on preparation for the ritual – *wudoo* (ablution) in verse 5:6, the direction Muslims have to face in prayer (2:150), the general etiquette (4:43) and specific mode in travel (4:101) and in battle (4:102) for performing the ritual. Even timing has been dealt with in 62: 9, 10 for the congregational performance on Fridays and also in 11: 114 and 17:78 for the daily prayers.

Secondly, one cannot help wondering, if the detailed instructions and guidance provided by *Hadith* were originally meant to be an integral and essential part of the Islamic system, why did Mohammed not take any steps to preserve it for posterity? How did the hundreds of thousands – if not millions – of Muslims in the vast empire managed to perform their rituals during the 150 years before the first compilation of *hadith* made its appearance?

1.4. THE WORD OF MOUTH

Logically, the unreliability of the word of mouth and its capacity to lose accuracy in no time is quite well known (it is still with us in the form of expressions like 'the Chinese whisper'). For example, according to Bokhari's own statement, he gathered the huge pile of reports that he did from scraps of paper, old records and mostly by word of mouth. Remember that he was working almost two hundred years after Mohammad's death. 20 To raise doubts about the accuracy of these reports is not out of place because Bokhari, and all the other compilers did it. They sifted through the material they had obtained, and decided to accept the reports that they did, on certain criteria. They may have been very meticulous in their work and their sincerity was beyond doubt. Nonetheless, the fact remains that they did not get those reports directly from the Messenger himself. They duly quote their references in a chain of transmitters (*isnad*) going back to Mohammed. They could not have obtained their material *directly* from the second - and possibly not even the third - generation of transmitters *after* the Prophet because they must have all been dead. They had to rely on their own academic judgment, which was by no means flawless, given the fact that they were all human – they were not divine or even Divine-appointed for this task! If *they* had the right to look critically at that material – and they certainly did – everyone else has the same right. Surely, scholars *have* exercised this right. Abu Hanifa, the great scholar who has given his name to the biggest Sunni sect, the Hanafis, is well known to have made extensive use of his academic discretion in choosing and making use of Hadith while compiling his *fiqh* (jurisprudence). Most recently, Abul Ala Maudoodi in Pakistan is known to have done the same. These scholars were academically in the right when they looked at all that material with a critical eye. Evidence of the use of discretion on the part of the *hadith* compilers remains available in the very work they did. Most of the reports in Hadith open with the words '*qaala Rasool Allah*' ('The Messenger of God said') and close with '*ow kamaa qaala Rasool Allah* ('or whatever like this said The Messenger of God'). Therefore, the element of doubt and inaccuracy in *Hadith* is inherent and intrinsic to it was admitted and acknowledged by the great compilers themselves.

1.5 CONFUSION AND CONTRADICTION

An impartial, critical examination of Hadith reveals differences not only between various reports on the same subject but also between Hadith and the Quran. I present just a few examples:

1. *Mut'a* (temporary marriage) is forbidden according to some reports while according to others it is permissible.21
The Quran, however, does not sanction it; the Quranic marriage is intended for life in a loving and caring environment for both partners (30:21).

2. According to Hadith, the punishment for fornication is 100 lashes for the single (unmarried) and stoning to death for the married.22
The Quran makes no such distinction and prescribes 100 lashes regardless.

> 'The woman and the man guilty of fornication, flog each of them with a hundred stripes;...'   (24:2).

Incidentally, the same verse continues to say:

> 'Let not compassion move you in their case, in a matter prescribed by Allah, if ye believe in Allah and the Last Day:...'

But, *Hadith* does exactly the opposite and recommends compassion for the sick and the old, suggesting using a stick with 100 branches to be struck just once 'to satisfy the requirements of the law.' 23

3. The Messenger is reported to have said that his *umma* will have 72 sects, and that differences among them are God's blessing (*al-ikhtelaaf fi ummati rahma*).

The Quran emphatically disowns factionalism and sectarianism:

> 'And for those who divide their religion and break up into sects, thou hast no part in them in the least...' (6:160, 3:102, etc).

4. Ritual prayer is one of the 'Five Pillars of Islam' and *Hadith* is credited with complementing the Quran on this immensely important and basic aspect of a Muslim's life. Sadly, *Hadith* has caused factions and sects to arise as a result of different reports on the subject. A few examples:

a. *takbeer tahreema* – raising ones hands to start prayer

Tirmadhi – The Prophet used to raise his hands up to the shoulder level.
Abu Dawood – He [the Prophet] raised them up to his ear-lobes.
Tirmadhi, Abu Dawood, Nisaai – The Prophet raised his hands only once at the start of prayer and not after that during the entire prayer.
Bokhari, Muslim – He used to raise his hands at the start as well as during prayer.

b. placing one's hands during prayer

Sunan Shaf'ai and *Musnad Ahmed Hanbal* – The Prophet folded his hands over his chest.
Muwatta – He [the Prophet] used to leave his arms hanging.

c. recitation during prayer

Tirmadhi, Abu Dawood, Nisaai – The Prophet allowed prayer if nothing else but *subhaan Allah* (God is Exalted) and *la ilaaha il Allah* (There is no god but Allah) was recited.
Bokhari, Muslim, Muwatta, Ibn Maajja – No prayer is complete without recitation of *Sura Al-Fateha* (chapter 1 of the Quran).
Muslim – After starting prayer (*takbeer tahreema*), the Prophet used to recite *Al-Fateha*.
Bokhari – He used to recite a short prayer (*Allahhumma ...*) *before* reciting *Al-Fateha*.
Abu Dawood – He used to recite *a'oozu be Allah e min ash-Shaitan*
Nisaai - He used to recite *inn as-salaati wa nuseikee....*
Tirmadhi, Ibn Maajja – He recited *subhaanak Allah humma....*

5. Bokhari reports that the great monotheistic patriarch Abraham was guilty of lying blatantly THREE times in his life. [24]

The Quran emphatically deplores falsehood and the practice of lying and reports all prophets to have been truthful individuals. About Abraham it is

Part One: Chapter One

very specific in Sura *Maryam* (Mary):

> "(Also) mention in the Book Abraham: he was a man of truth, a prophet [*innahu kaana siddiqan nabbiya*]." (19:41).

6. The difference – rather, contrast – between *Hadith* and the Quran is perhaps nowhere else more obvious and glaring than in the field of human sexuality. The subject has been dealt with in detail elsewhere in this work. Here, just one example should suffice. The Quran categorically prohibits sexual intercourse (*baashara* in 2:187) during menstruation (2: 222), during ritual fast (2:187), and during Retreat [*e'tekaaf* – a planned isolation at specific times for specific purposes and duties (2: 187)].

But, *Hadith* reports on the authority of Ayesha that Mohammed himself used to do it during menstruation as well as during fasting. [25]

1.6. THE UNRELIABILITY OF HADITH

It is not surprising therefore that we see so much confusion and difference of opinion among Muslims as to what Islam really is and what it stands for. They have gone from one extreme of relying totally on the Prophetic Tradition (such as in Wahaabism) to the other of completely disregarding everything other than the Scripture proper, the Quran. Thus we witnessed, not long ago, the birth in the sub-continent of India-Pakistan-Bangladesh of a mini sect called *Ahl al Quran* (People of the Quran). This group was led by Abdallah Chakraalewi and Maulvi Charaagh Ali, among others. They proposed total reliance on the Quran for principles as well as laws and sub-laws formulated on the basis of those principles. For example, they practised only three ritual prayers during a day as this is all that can be derived from various verses of the Book. They rejected *Hadith* totally in its entirety. [26]

A careful look at the historical evolution of that vast mass of literature known as Hadith raises important questions. The fact is that nearly the entire body of Hadith made its appearance approximately two centuries *after* the death of the founder of Islam; another significant fact is that it was mostly done during the late Umayyad and early Abbasid periods of Islamic history. It is not entirely impossible that a considerable part of this literature was deliberately designed, in the first place, to suit certain social attitudes and practices, which had become standard Muslim behaviour over the previous two centuries, and in the second place, to condone and lend legitimacy to the authoritarian and dictatorial regimes of the day. In short, the socio-politico-cultural needs of the time must have been the impetus and incentive for such a proliferation of Prophetic sayings. That the vast majority of these reports were spurious is undeniable – it is inherent in the records of the numbers of items collected by various compilers before selecting what they deemed as authentic (please see above). As it has been noted by the Hungarian scholar Ignaz Goldziher (1850-1921):

> The Hadith will not serve as a document for the history of the infancy of Islam, but rather as a reflection of the tendencies which appeared in the community during the mature stages of its development. 27

So confusing and contradictory were these reports that they confound even the very important and basic question of the actual time of their being written down, or worse, if they were written down at all at a particular time in history. One tradition cites 'Abdullah bin 'Amr reporting:

> 'I used to write everything that I heard from the Prophet, intending to commit it to memory. (On some people taking objection to this) I spoke about it to the Prophet who said: "Write down, for I only speak the truth."' 28

Another report cites the famous Abu Hurairah recording:

> 'None of the Companions preserved more traditions than me, but 'Abdallah ibn 'Amr is an exception, for he used to write and I did not.' 29

Yet, the same Abu Hurairah reports:

> 'The Prophet of God came to us while we were writing traditions and said: "What is this that you are writing?" We said: "Sayings which we hear from you." He said: "What! A book other than the Book of God?"'

Now only one of the two following possibilities could have been the case. Either Mohammed gave mutually conflicting guidance about writing his sayings down, or one of these reports is definitely a fabrication.

Some authors dealing with the issue of the Prophet authorizing the recording of his sayings have gone to extraordinary lengths of argumentation touching the borders of absurdity. Fazlur Rahman, definitely of the opinion that no Tradition was written down in the Prophet's lifetime, opines:

> The delay in compiling Hadith must have resulted from the fear that if the extra-Quranic speech of Mohammed was formally recorded, it could have easily been confused with the text of the Quran (both came out of Mohammed's mouth). One could have been taken for the other. 30

Maulana Muhammad Ali, a prominent and highly respected scholar of the Ahmediya sect of Islam, however, maintains that at least some of the Prophetic tradition *was* written down in his lifetime:

> 'It is, however, a fact that the sayings of the Prophet were not generally written down, and memory was the chief means of their preservation.' 31

But then he goes further and appears to make it as if the non-writing of Tradition was deliberate and, in fact, attempts to put it across as a positive point in the evolution of Islam:

> Memory was by no means an unreliable mode for the preservation of Tradition, for the Quran was safely preserved in the memory of the Companions of the Prophet in addition to being committed to writing.

Resting his strange theory on the 'wonderfully retentive memory of the Arab,' he then makes the following mind-boggling statement:

> In fact, had the Quran been simply preserved in writing, it could not have been handed down intact to future generations. 32

Why not? How can the written word interfere with the preservation of the spoken?

Such claims are made in the face of the fact that the Quran itself has laid down considerable emphasis on the importance of the written word (2: 282) – the Quran calls itself *al-Kitaab* (2:2), which means 'written down.' It is needless to say that, anthropologically, writing was invented to preserve the spoken word. There is also the commonly accepted historical fact that the first collection of the Quran was initiated by 'Umar al-Khattaab after the battle of Yamamah for fear of its being lost precisely because it had not been entirely written down. As Watt & Bell put it:

> According to this report 'Umar ibn-al-Khattab (who succeeded [Abu Bakr] as caliph in 634) was perturbed by the fact that in the battle of Yamama during the 'wars of apostasy (*ridda*)' many of the 'readers' [*qurra*] of the Quran were killed. Since these were the men who had learnt parts of the Quran by heart, 'Umar feared that, if more of them died, some of the Quran would be irretrievably lost. He therefore counseled Abu Bakr to make a 'collection' of the Quran. 33

In addition to that, as we have already seen, a large number of Tradition items start with the words *'qaala Rasool Allah'* (The Messenger of God said) and finish with *'ow kamaa qaala Rasool Allah* (or whatever like this said The Messenger of God). Also, we can find a number of items which typically mention 'three important things which the Prophet mentioned' and the narrator recounts two of those and 'forgets the third.' So much for the 'wonderfully retentive memory of the Arab'!

A large number of reports circulating in the Muslim world at the time were dubious and were produced either as a result of popular versions circulating in society courtesy of the fabled story-tellers in the *souks* (market-places) of Arabia, or fabricated for ulterior or sincere motives. This fact is accepted not only by the ancient writers, i.e. the compilers themselves but also by the most ardent defenders of the hadith genre in modern times. Maulana Muhammad Ali, writes:

> 'That there are some incredible stories even in the collections of Tradition is true...'

That explains why we find Prophetic Traditions praising the House of Abbas; it is reported that,

> 'The Messenger said, "No Muslim can be a true believer unless he/she loves (my uncle) Abbas and his progeny."'

This report gives preference to Abbas over other more important and historically illustrious uncles of Mohammed, such as Abu Talib (who protected Mohammed and raised him as his own after the Prophet had lost his parents and his grandfather and had no home) and Hamza (who reputedly became the first Muslim martyr when he laid down his life in the cause of the new Faith during the battle of Ouhud).

1.7. OTHER SOURCES

The status and value of Prophetic biographies and other works of history are no different. In fact, the situation is worse because they are not held in that high esteem special to compilations of hadith. The annals of early history of Islam, popularly accepted as authentic sources by Muslims (please refer to the short sampler list given earlier in this chapter), fare as badly, in some cases worse, as the records of Prophetic Tradition do when compared with the Scripture (the Quran). The earliest documented records of Muslim history available to us, as we have seen, date to the 3rd / 9th century and leave a void of at least 250 years since the time of Mohammed. This is about a century longer than the gap left by *Hadith*. As such, it is not entirely implausible that early Muslim historians were, at least to some extent, influenced by the available records of *Hadith*. There must have been other factors, such as the socio-politico-cultural environment of the time, at work to affect an historian's work. The historical records in question were compiled during the 'Abbasid caliphate, and it is difficult to imagine for a literary work of political importance to have survived if it was not at least neutral towards the interests and pleasure of the rulers. [34] Actually, writers were more likely to appease and please the ruling elite by toeing the official policy line. The great Muslim divide of *Sunni-Shia* [35] is a case in point. Before I attempt to highlight the point under discussion, however, a glimpse at the commonly accepted version of the relevant part of Muslim history is desirable.

1.8. THE SUCCESSION CONFLICT

It is reported [36] that the very first conflict resulting in a political division occurred immediately after the death (circa 632 AD) of the Messenger (by some accounts even *before* he was buried). Both the migrants from Mecca (*al muhaajeroon*) and the Medinites (*al ansaar*) aspired to Muhammad's succession, clashed and came to blows. In the words of Al-Tabari, there was enacted a scene reminiscent of *al jaaheliyya* (the age of pre-Islamic ignorance)![37] Eventually, Abu Bakr was chosen as the first *khaleefa tar Rasool* (successor to the Messenger – the Caliph). Reportedly, Ali, Muhammad's darling first cousin and husband to his beloved daughter Fatima, was not happy and considered this a violation and usurping of his declared, firm and deserved right to the succession.[38] This seed of resentment was nurtured by a series of later incidents. Among them was the third *khaleefa* Uthman's favoritism of his clan[39], the Umayyads – more particularly of Mu'aawiya ibn Abu Sufiyaan (the fifth *khaleefa*). Later, after the assassination of Uthman (656), when Ali was chosen as the fourth *khaleefa* in Medina, Mu'aawiya, who had been governor of Syria in Damascus, refused allegiance to Ali, and declared himself a contender to the Caliphate (658). There took place two big battles in the indecisive civil war. The assassination of Ali at the hands of the *kharejee*'s (the Exiters)[40] in Kufa, Iraq, made Mu'aawiya the sole master of the Muslim world. The fledgling plant of discord became a fully grown tree when Muhammad's grandson Hussain (the second son of Ali and Fatima) was killed along with most of his family by the forces of Yezeed (the sixth *khaleefa* and Mu'aawiya's son) in the butchery of Kerbala in 680. This was the origin of the biggest rift in the Islamic world and has resulted in the second largest sect–the *Shia*. The discord between the Umayyads and the Alawis – or the Hashemites [41] / Fatimids / *ahl al Bait* [42] / *Shia*s – matured into bitter rivalry over the following years, and resulted in numerous armed conflicts, assassinations, constant socio-political tension, and eventually, the full-fledged religious sect, the Shia. In time, the Hashemites found an ally in the Abbasids – descendants of Abbas, one of the Messenger's real uncles. The Abbasids saw their gain in the loss of the Hashemites and started an anti-Umayyad movement in Iran, where many Hashemites and Shias had fled to safety. One Abu Muslim Khorasaani was instrumental in pioneering this campaign.[43] The Abbasids adopted as their banner a black flag to symbolize their grief over the Umayyad's brutal mistreatment of the Messenger's progeny. The uprising used the pretext of endeavouring to rectify the wrong and install in power the rightful and true heirs of the Messenger, the House of Ali. Eventually, in 750, the Umayyads were overthrown and the Abbasid era began, depriving the Alawis yet again of the temporal leadership of the Muslim world. They continued to be oppressed by the rulers – only this time round it was the Abbasids – who considered them enemies of the state and a potential threat. This kept the Shia migration trail to Iran alive. Hence we find several of Ali's illustrious descendants buried in mausoleums in Iran. Over time, this ideology fermented into the sub-religion (sect) we know today as *Shia*ism.

It is against this background that it will be interesting to see a report from early Islamic history. Bokhari reports from Abdallah ibn Abbas (incidentally, the son of Abbas ibn Abdul Muttalib, the famous uncle of the Prophet and the ancestor of the Abbasid caliphs): 44

> During the terminal illness of the Messenger of Allah, when Ali ibn Abi Talib came out from his bedside he was asked, 'Abul Hasan, how is he this morning?' Ali said, 'Praise be to Allah. He is fine.' Abbas ibn Abdul Muttalib took him aside and said, 'By God, you will be a slave in three days. I am sure that the Messenger of Allah will not survive his ailment. I am quite familiar with the facial changes of Abdul Muttalib's progeny when they are about to die. Let us go to him and ask him who will inherit [political] power. We will find out if it is going to be us or some others. If it is someone other than us, he [Mohammed] will instruct his heir in our favour.' [Ali replied, 'Can others beside us be interested in this matter?' Abbas said, 'By God, I think yes, definitely.']. Ali said, 'By God, if we ask the Messenger of Allah and he refuses us, we will surely never be in power after his death. So, by God, I will never ask him.' 45

1.9. A CRITIQUE OF HISTORICAL RECORDS

Clearly, this report aims at portraying 'Abbas, the Prophet's uncle and ancestor of the 'Abbasid caliphs, as a friend of Ali's and making him dear in the eyes of the Alids / Alawis. Eventually, Mohammed died without nominating his successor or leaving behind any guidelines for the process save the Quranic principle that the affairs of the *umma* (the Muslim nation) should be decided upon through mutual consultation (42:38 and 3:158). The subsequent commotion for his succession that ensued at the meeting place (*saqeefa*) of Banu Sa'da has been reported in detail by early historians like at-Tabari (please see note 36 of this chapter). It portrays some Companions of the Prophet–such as Sa'd bin Ibaada, Abu Bakr and 'Umar ibn al-Khattaab– violently arguing and physically assaulting each other for the coveted position of Caliph; Ali ibn Abu Talib, who equally desired the post, sulked and regretted all along as he could not leave his exalted cousin and father-in-law unburied. A critical examination of the episode that Heikel has recorded raises notable concerns from the Quranic standpoint. A negative, i.e. contrary to the Koran, image of the Companions notwithstanding, there are important theological issues which need attention. First, it reports divisions so deep that a serious suggestion was made by Hubaab ibn Mandhar to alternate the caliphate between the Migrants and Helpers. 'Umar rejected it in his usual fiery and hostile manner. Abu Bakr calmly quoted a prophetic Tradition which says, 'Leaders shall always be from (my tribe of) Quraish.'46 Second, Ali has been reported to press his claim on the basis of his family relationship to

Mohammed. He refused and denied pledge of allegiance to Abu Bakr for six months. When pressed by 'Umar, he is quoted to have said, 'I cannot give you my allegiance as [you have convinced people of your succession on the basis of your proximity to the Prophet, and as such] I am closer to Mohammed in relationship and therefore more worthy of his succession. It should be *you* pledging allegiance to *me*!' 47 On a subsequent occasion, Ali is reported to have accused Abu Bakr of usurping his birthright to Mohammed's succession which he had because of his blood-ties with the Prophet.48

The notion of inheriting leadership solely on the basis of kinship is very clearly rejected by the Quran. As a rule, responsibility and position of authority is to be delegated on the basis of merit alone. The Quranic criterion for appointment to a responsible public office is that the candidate must have STRENGTH (the ability to do the job) and HONESTY / TRUSTWORTHINESS – *al qawi al ameen* as in Sura's *An-Naml* (27:39) and *Al-Qasas* (28:26). Delegation of responsibility shall be according to suitability as in Sura *An-Nisaa* (4:58) where Allah commands to 'render back trusts to the deserving' (*al amaanaat ila ahlehaa*), performance as in Sura *Al-Ahqaaf* (46:19), where it says 'And to all degrees according to deeds (*wa lekulle darajaatum mimmaa 'amaloo…*), and personal character being in line with the Quranic ideology as in Sura *Al-Hujaraat* (49:13). Above all, no position of authority shall be hereditary; that is clear from the example of patriarch Abraham narrated in Sura *Al-Baqara* (2:124) where God promises him leadership of people: 'I will make thee an *imam* to the people.' But, when he desired the same for his progeny (*zurriyyati*), he was denied it unless they deserved it. Not only the highest office in the land but also all the officials of the Quranic government shall be appointed on the same criteria of ability, knowledge, and character as is evident from the story of Taloot 49 in Sura *Al-Baqara* (2:247).

That brings up yet another dilemma for the educated thoughtful Muslim. Were those close Companions of the Prophet, who were his initial students and disciples, misbehaving disgracefully by so blatantly flouting the Quranic principles? Or, are these historical records of early Islam utterly untrustworthy? The Muslim intelligentsia should seriously attempt to find a way out of this quagmire if there is going to be hope of restoring real and rational confidence in Islam. The need for an intellectual and critical cool look at the sources of Islam is nowhere greater as in the genre of *Hadith* – the Prophetic Tradition. As we have seen earlier in this chapter, the commonly accepted 'correct' attitude towards *Hadith* is that a report is considered authentic on the basis of the validity of the chain of transmitters (*isnad*). The focus has to be shifted to the contents of a report instead so that it is weighed against the final authority of the Faith, the Quran, which is agreed upon by all Muslims to be the Canon, the Book of God. If Muslims continue to adhere reverently to their extra-Quranic literature of the early Islamic periods, especially *Hadith*, so uncritically as they have for centuries, scathing criticism by non-Muslim scholars of the stature of Goldziher cannot be avoided or ignored. He very rightly observed that the *isnad* is the only method available to Muslims for authenticating the *Hadith* and is wholly inadequate.

> Traditions are only investigated in respect of their outward form and judgment of the value of the contents depends on the judgment of the correctness of the isnad. If the isnad to which an impossible sentence full of inner and outer contradictions is appended withstands the scrutiny of this formal criticism, if the continuity of the entirely trustworthy authors cited in them is complete and if the possibility of their personal communication is established, the tradition is accepted as worthy of credit ...Muslim critics have no feeling for even the crudest anachronisms provided that the isnad is correct. Muhammad's prophetic gift is used as a factor to smooth over such difficulties. [50]

As far as the conventional historical records are concerned, I leave my readers with the standpoint, in his own words, of one of the most respected and renowned historians of early Islam – none other than Abu Ja'far Muhammad ibn Jarir al-Tabari (d. 310/923). In the introduction to his pioneering work *Al-Tarikh al-Rusul wa al-Muluk* he writes:

> Let him who studies this book of ours know that in everything I say about the subject which I have decided to recount here, I rely on what I transmit from explicitly identified reports (*akhbar*) and from accounts (*aathaar*) which I ascribe by name to their transmitters. I do not achieve understanding through rational proofs nor do I make discoveries by intuition (*fakr al nufus*), save to a very limited degree. For knowledge about the men of the past and current news about men of the present cannot be obtained by one who has not himself witnessed these men or whose lifetime does not reach back to theirs. [In the latter situation knowledge can be obtained only] by the statements of reporters and transmitters, not by rational deductions or intuitive references. And if we mention in this book any report about certain men of the past which the reader finds objectionable or the hearer offensive, to such a degree that he finds in it no sound purpose or truth, let him know that this is not our fault, but is rather the responsibility of one of those who has transmitted it to us. We have presented (such reports) only in the form in which they were presented to us. [51]

Tabari's reluctance to commit himself to the accuracy of his work not only reflects a cautious scholarly approach to the subject but also belies his non-conviction about the reliability of the reports he had based his work upon. Muslim scholars and writers of today should have reason to pause here and re-evaluate their heavy reliance on such works whose reliability was in doubt to their authors themselves.

1.10 CONCLUSION

In my view, the way forward for Muslims, if they desire to remove all that confusion and sectarian stances that exist, may be the following:

Part One: Chapter One

According to the Quran, the canon is the Book of God, which was given to Mohammad. His duty was to teach it to the people of his time in a manner which should make them understand it comprehensively so that they could pass it on to the rest of humanity for all times. This included their moral as well academic training, interpretation of the Message, and implementing it under the circumstances of the time. The collection of his actions and sayings is a valuable historical record which should serve as a precedent. It should be used to take guidance from as we do in taking lessons from history. They should help us to know how Mohammed and the people of his time viewed the fundamental principles of the Quran. The details in Hadith were never meant to become etched in stone for all eternity. Of all Muslim literature, only the Quran lays a serious claim to divinity, universality and eternity and as such, in the Muslim context, it should be the ultimate authority in matters of Faith. The Quran has been and still is, to countless human beings the final, unadulterated, direct Word of the Creator.

* * * * * * *

Chapter 2

THE PROBLEMS OF LANGUAGE, TRANSLATION AND INTERPRETATION

2.1 INTRODUCTION

Language is a faculty unique to mankind in the animal world on Earth, especially so when considered with the ability to conceive abstract ideas. It is the medium through which we communicate with our fellow beings either by speech or in writing. Even when we make use of gestures, we communicate in a language. It is Nature's gift to Man. It has made it easy for us to convey our thoughts to others and receive theirs. In a social context, language plays a crucial role in our lives individually as well as collectively. Language, it has been said, is power. It not only shows the power behind a discourse, but also exercises influence on the listener(s).[1] Also, language needs to adapt to the varying levels of ability of comprehension of listeners / readers. In other words, the addresser has to change language according to the needs of an addressee, that is to say, the addressee influences the style of the language used.[2] Not only that, the language used changes according to the context and the setting;[3] for instance, it borrows and adapts foreign vocabulary as is sufficiently illustrated by writers like Rudyard Kipling.

So it is with the Quran. The language of the Quran can be considered 'pure Arabic' despite having made use of hundreds of foreign (Aramaic, Syriac, Ethiopic, etc) terms and expressions; the particular vocabulary had been incorporated into the normal language of the day and the addressees were familiar with it, and that was considered the most effective way to successfully convey the intended message. We have also seen that its language changes according to the needs of the addressee and the demands of the situation. In the case of the Quran, for example, it changes from the more rhyming poetical style of the Meccan suras to the assertive imperatives of the Medinan; or, it shifts from the Second Person Singular to the Second Person Plural according to the number of addressees, and so on.

2.2 TRANSLATION

So far, it is good. But, in the case of the Quran, we come up with another difficulty which is by no means exclusive to it. Despite our wondrous advances in technology in recent times, we still have literally hundreds of languages currently in use around the world. We have not as yet come out of the Tower of Babel.4 We still need to translate a foreign language into ours to understand its meaning. Generally, the process of translation serves very well its basic function of transferring meanings of one language to another. But, more often than not, some of the original meaning is lost in the process. This is evident even in the case of the concrete. For example, if the very ordinary, everyday English word 'table' was translated into Urdu (*maze*) or Arabic (*taawala*), it will have to be specified whether the original term referred to a material article with a top and some legs or to its applied sense of either a list of items or a layer of subterranean water. The problem is much more acute in the case of the abstract, especially concepts, for the simple reason that ideas are intricately interwoven with a particular culture. Therefore, almost invariably, a simple translation of an abstract idea fails to carry the *exact* meaning of the original over to another language. This difficulty is nowhere more obvious than in the domain of religion; so it is with the Quran. It manifests itself even in the most simple and common utterances. *Allahu akbar* is a widely-known phrase, taken from the Quran,5 of the Muslim world forming a part of *azaan* (the Call for daily ritual prayers). It is invariably translated as 'God is great.' Firstly, the verb to be (*is*) is non-existent in the original phrase, which consists of only two words and, strictly speaking, should only be translated as 'God great.' Secondly, the adjective *akbar* is not in the First degree but is in the Comparative and, as such, should be translated as 'greater.'6 Thus, the phrase in question should be rendered in English as 'God (is) greater / (the) greatest.'

Very early Urdu translations done in the sub-continent were modelled on the word-for-word literal translation pattern, where the translators diligently placed the Urdu equivalents exactly under those of the Arabic regardless of the differences of the sentence structure between the two languages. The result was that works by Shah Rafiullah and Shah Abdul Qadir, for instance, were confusing to the point of being incomprehensible to the average Urdu reader.

One more example will suffice. The Arabic word *rabb*, one of the attributes of God, is normally translated as 'Lord' in most English translations.7 In English, the term is used for 'one having power and authority over others,' among other meanings of a similar concept.8 It is used for God as well as Christ for the same reason. In Arabic, however, *rabb* has a much wider and different application. Even in its general modern use, along with the sense of 'master,' the term has the sense of 'to raise, bring up (a child).'9 In the Quranic context, the term has even deeper and wider meanings. It springs from the three-letter root *RBB*, with the basic sense of 'to nourish,' i.e. to provide gradual developmental stages for someone/something so as to achieve completeness.10 An Arabic sentence is: *rabba waladahu wa rabbabahu wa tarabbabahu* (he nourished, cared and raised the child till it grew up). Some derivatives and other shades of meaning are: 1) to take care and improve, as in *ar-rabbu*; 2) to stay steadfast, as in *arabbatissahaabatu be haazihil balada* (the cloud lingered or showered over that city; and 3) to join things in a chain. Therefore, *ruboobiya* is 'continuous and constant nourishment and provision.' When the Quran says *al Hamdu lillaahe rabb el 'aalemeen* (1:1), it is referring to God as the Sustainer and Nourisher of all. Evidently, 'Lord' misses quite a bit of the original *rabb*.

In fact, in the case of the Quran, the problem is compounded by the traditional practice on the part of most translators to rely very heavily on the phenomenon of *asbaab an nazool* (Occasions of Revelation) rather than the language itself. This point can be illustrated with a couple of examples. Sura *An-Nisaa* (The Women), the fourth chapter of the Quran, deals mainly with matters of and about women. Verse 34 opens with a general policy statement: *Ar rijaalu qawwaamoona 'ala an nisaa. Ar rijaal* means 'men' (literally, *the* men), *'ala* is 'over/on, and *an nisaa* means 'women' (literally, *the* women). *Qawwaamoon* is generally translated as 'lords / overseers.' [11] In the Quranic context, however, the term has connotations very different from that conveyed by traditional translations or interpretations. The term springs from the three-letter root *QWM* with the basic meanings of 'to stand up, to be balanced, to be established, to stop and stay,' etc.[12] Some derivatives used in the Quran are: 1) *al-Qayyoom* (2:255, 20:111) – 'The Self-subsisting, Supporter of all,' meaning God; 2): *ad-Deen al-qayyam* (30:30, 43) – 'The upright religion,' meaning Islam; 3): *kutubun qayyama* (98:3) – 'Right and straight books (laws); 4) *laqad khalaqnal insaana fi ahsane taqweem* (95:4) – 'We have indeed created Man in the best of moulds;' 5) *al-qistaas al-mustaqeem* (17:35) – 'the straight balance;' 6): *wa kaana baiyna zaaleka qawaama* (25:67) – '..but hold a just (balance) between those (extremes). An Arabic expression is: *qaamar rajulul maraa wa qaama 'alaiha* – 'the man looked after and provided for the woman'; hence *qawwaam* (pl. *qawwamoon*) means 'provider and sustainer. Therefore, 4:34 does not refer to the superior status of males over females but to the social division of labour by which provision of sustenance is generally men's responsibility.

In contrast to this, traditional exegetes and translators have interpreted *qawwamoon* to mean 'masters / lords.' One of the well-known and respected Urdu translations from India translates it as *haakem* ('rulers').[13] The notion of men being superior to and lords over women comes from the Prophetic Tradition. One account of *sabab an nazool* (occasion of revelation) for 4:33 records that a woman complained to the Prophet that her husband had slapped her. The Messenger ordered retribution but then this verse was revealed. Another account reports Mohammed asking men to stop hitting their wives. 'Umar came to the Prophet and complained that that had resulted in the wives become unruly. Mohammed allowed husbands to beat their wives. That resulted in widespread beatings and several women came to the Prophet to complain. When Mohammed attempted to arrange retribution for men, the verse in question was revealed. Thus, the original regulation was retained by which husbands have the authority to beat their wives. Such Traditions formed the basis of early works of exegesis even in Arabic. For example, Zamakhshari, in his *Kishaaf*, translates *qawwamoon* as *musaitereen* (policemen) while the two Jalals, in their *Tafseer Jalaalain*, give *musalleteen* (controllers). Consequently, and understandably so, that led to *haakem* ('rulers / masters'). 15

Another aspect of the difficulties posed by translation is the idiom. The average educated English speaker cannot be unfamiliar with the problem, especially if one is bilingual. It does not take much explaining to show the ridiculous outcome if one was to literally translate into another language English expressions like 'to make one's blood boil' or 'hit the road' or 'chicken-hearted' and so on. Yet, many a translator of the Quran has tended to do just that i.e. translate the Quranic idiomatic expressions literally and come up against tremendous problems in explaining a particular passage. One case in point is the Arabic expression *kashf saaq* – literally, 'baring (one's) calf.' Verse 42, sura *Al-Qalam* ('The Pen') runs: *youma yukshafu 'an saaqen wa yud'awna ilassujoode fa laa yastatee'oon*. Translated literally, it reads: 'The day when calf will be bared, and (they) will be called upon to prostrate but they will not be able to.' The context of the passage is about Disbelievers and their plight on the Day of Judgement. Obviously, the literal translation makes no sense at all; it needs explanation and interpretation. Some conservative commentators have indeed given a literal background to it in the exegetical notes in their translations. It is said that on that fateful day, peoples of all religions will be called upon to recognise their God. All but the Disbelievers will be able to do it. At that juncture, God will bare His calf to show His person. All the Believers will come to know him but the Disbelievers will still be unable to prostrate before Him; they will feel humiliated and will cast their eyes down with acute embarrassment.16 Even the comparatively modern and liberal writers, while recognising the idiomatic nature of the expression *kashf saaq*, stick to literal explanation of events. Ashraf Ali Thaanewi, in his Urdu translation admits that the expression in question is idiomatic, but then reverts to the literal by saying

> '...Because the *kaafir*s (Disbelievers) had not accepted the Divine message during their earthly life, they will be ordered to prostrate but, they will develop stiff backs and thus will be unable to prostrate.' 17

Actually, *kashf saaq* was an idiomatic expression of the time used for an occasion of great difficulty and panic. Its origin lay in the practice of the Arabs to lift their long flowing robes up to their knees – so as to bare their calves – to run away from a precarious situation, especially in battle.18 Therefore, verse 68:42 does not refer to the Almighty pulling the heavenly garment up to bare His divine calf; it refers, using an idiomatic expression, to a time of turmoil in human life – an era of great difficulty for mankind, the time when human social fabric will be rewoven anew for a brighter dawn for all.

Let us consider one more example in this category of idiomatic use of language. Crimes and their punishments form an important part of any legal system. Conventional Islamic laws of capital punishment are widely regarded in the West as archaic at best and barbaric at worst. Amputation of a thief's hand is a very prominent example.[19] It is taken from the Quran:

> 'As to the thief, male or female, cut off his or her hands: a retribution for their deed and exemplary punishment.... But *if the thief repent after his crime, and amend his conduct, Allah turneth to him in forgiveness...*'[20] (my emphasis)

As far as translation is concerned, the expression *b'ad zulmehi* in 5:39 has been rendered as 'after his crime' by Abdullah Yousuf Ali (as given here) and as 'after his punishment' by A R Doi (see reference in note 20 for this chapter). As we can see, confusion is already creeping in. If one goes by Doi, repentance after the punishment becomes a spiritual matter, especially because writers like Doi do not specify what exactly is meant, in practical terms, by 'forgiveness of God'; furthermore, repenting *after* amputation has been carried out is futile. On the other hand, repentance after the crime would most probably render the punishment inapplicable – no thief, even with the slightest intelligence, will shy away from taking advantage of the facility and be saved from amputation.

Apart from these confusions, academics have been busy apologising to the West on behalf of Islam for this 'barbaric' punishment. The term *fa aqta'oo* ('then cut off') in 5:38 has always been taken in its literal meaning of 'severing.' It is ingrained so deeply in the minds of masses and elite alike that even jurists and legal experts of the highest level do not see it in any other way. In the 1960's, Mr. A R Cornelius headed the Supreme Court of Pakistan as Chief Justice. He was a Christian but very well-versed in Islam, particularly its law. On a visit to Australia to attend a conference on law, Mr. Cornelius, in an attempt to reduce the 'barbarity' of the punishment concerned, suggested temporarily paralysing a thief by reversible surgery using modern technological advances in medicine. Even then, it did not sit very well with the majority of the delegates. But more importantly, it is significant that Mr. Cornelius had taken *fa aqta'oo* in its literal sense.[21]

In my view, we do not have to and should not, as some modern writers have suggested, take it literally.[22] Linguistically, the term *fa aqta'oo* springs from the three-letter root *qaa, taa, ain* (QT') with the basic meaning of 'to cut, to sever' applied to *both* literal as well as figurative usage; for example, *qata' al-laham* is 'to cut/carve meat', while *qata' assabeel* is 'to block traffic on a path.' Some other idiomatic uses are: *qata' khasmahu bil hujja* (he silenced his opponent with arguments); *qata' rahema qatee'a* (he severed relations with his relatives); *qata' 'unq daabbatehi* (he sold his animal); *qute'at yadhu* (his hand was rendered useless). In the Quran, we find the following examples of non-literal use of the term: *qatu' ssabeel* for sodomy in 29:29; *qit'emin allail* (a part of night) in 11:81; *qaate'a tan amr* (final decision) in 27:32; and *tuqatta' aideehem wa arjuluhum min khilaafen* (normally taken literally as 'cut off their hands and legs on the opposite sides') may also be taken as 'bind and render useless their hand and feet.' Therefore, in 5:38, the Quran is not prescribing amputation but stopping and rendering useless the thief's hand. The strategies adopted for achieving that objective will vary according to time and society and shall depend upon the circumstances of the individual concerned; it may involve re-education, psychological assessment and due treatment, revision of personal circumstances such as physical welfare, sustenance and security. All measures taken, however, shall aim at stopping the thief from committing the crime in future.

Most probably, it was because of problems such as the above that made Guillaume remark;

> 'The Quran is one of the world's classics which *cannot be translated without grave loss*. [...]; indeed it may be affirmed that within the literature of the Arabs, wide and fecund as it is both in poetry and in elevated prose, there is nothing to compare with it.' [23] (pp. 73-74) (my emphasis)

2.3 INTERPRETATION / EXPOSITION

It follows from the above that a document like the Quran needs to be *interpreted* rather than *translated* if its meanings are to be transferred to another language. Also, in the light of our discussion so far, an interpretation / exposition of the Quran should be kept as independent as possible of *asbaab* (the traditional accounts of the occasions of revelation) if it is to be closest to the original. The conventional accounts of early Islamic history from Muslim sources should be used as academic precedence towards understanding the Quran. Modern exegetes and interpreters are not likely to get far in their work as long as they stand in awe of the classical ones. Knowledge does not advance if it does not work with an independent and free mind. Religion, like all other disciplines, must be approached and studied critically.

Any interpretation of the Quran should be attempted, if I may suggest, more or less on the lines of modern thinkers from the sub-continent such as Sir Syed Ahmed Khan, Inayatullah Khan Al-Mashriqi, Mohammed Iqbal, and Ghulam Ahmed Pervez. The approach basically rests on two fundamentals. We shall discuss them in turn as follows.

2.4. LANGUAGE AND CULTURE

As discussed earlier, a language in intricately interwoven with the culture it is embedded in; the various concepts, especially the abstract, have to be studied in their cultural context. So it is with the Quran. It was produced in a variety of the Arabic language which was current in Eastern Arabia during the early part of the last millennium. That variety of Arabic was very different from any currently in use today. Like all languages, Arabic too has undergone changes, structural as well as semantic, as a result of the influence of social and historical forces of more than a millennium and half; it is no longer the language Mohammed spoke and the Arabs of the 6th/7th century Hejaz understood. A considerable part of the poetry of the *jahilyya* (pre-Quran) days is fortunately still with us and provides a valuable reference point for the semantic concepts of the time as some writers have rightly noted.[24] Certain terms, such as *Allah, nabi, kafir* etc, had been in use in pre-Islamic Arabic.[25] The Quran often uses these terms in the same semantic concepts as those of *jahilyya*.[26] Therefore, a study of the *jahilyya* poetry can give a reliably accurate view of the socio-linguistic semantics of the day.

In addition to this external factor, an internal attribute of the Arabic language, namely, the semantic root system, can also help us to arrive at the particular linguistic concepts of the Quranic times. Each and every Arabic word stems from a basic root of letters with its own particular basic meaning. All grammatical derivatives of a given root retain its basic meaning in some shade or another. Lexicologists have even established the basic meanings of particular combinations of letters occurring in particular roots. For instance, the root of *al-burhaan* (evidential argument)[27] is BRh which has the basic meaning of being 'fair and bright'; Nawab Siddiq Hasan Khan reports that terms with B & R have the sense of 'to become apparent and exposed.' [28]

2.5 THE PRINCIPLE OF REPETITION (*TASREEF AL AAYAAT*) [29]

However, the Quran has given a vast number of terms its own semantic concepts, which can be derived by an overall study of the book to consider the various tools by which it establishes a particular concept–comparison, contrast, exemplification, definition. For example, the term *sebr* is usually translated as 'patience.' In English, as well as in Urdu, the term is normally used to denote the attribute of bearing and enduring hardship of some kind; it is evident in our usage of the term as 'be patient in adversity,' 'be patient and control your anger' etc as well as in the common expression for a person suffering from a medical problem or ailment. Consequently, the Quranic verse *inn Allah ma'as saabereen* (2:153) is normally taken to mean 'God is (pleased) with those (people) who suffer in dignity and take their misfortune in their stride.' But, the Quranic concept of *sebr* is quite different from the one above. It springs from the three-letter root SBR with the basic meaning of 'to constantly endeavour to achieve.' Some examples of its derivatives are: *assabeer* (a cloud which hangs at the same spot for the whole day; also, a mountain); *al asbera* (cattle that keep returning to their owner); *assibaara* (a piece of stationary metal/stone); *assaaboora* (a balancing weight for a vessel to stop it from rocking while sailing).[30] Since such persistent behaviour produces good results, *assubra* is a heap of grain (which is the product of perseverance and hard work). Because of the aspect of motionlessness, the term also came to be used in the meaning of 'imprisonment.'[31] In Sura *Al-Baqara*, we find '...*fa maa asbarahum 'alan naar*' – '...Ah! What boldness they show for fire,'[32] meaning that 'they have the ability to endure the fire,' but may also mean 'what is it that helps them endure the fiery punishment?' About Israelites, we find '*lun nasber 'ala ta'aamen waahed*' – '...we cannot remain on (the) one (same) food...' (2:61). Again in *Al-Baqara*, we see '...*rabbanaa afregh 'alainaa sabran wa thabbet aqdaamenaa..*'–'...Our Lord! Pour out constancy on us and make our steps firm...' (2:250) where 'firmness of steps' explains what *sebr* is in the Quranic context; it is 'steadfastness' and 'perseverance.' In Sura *Aal-e-'Imran*, we get the definition of *saabereen* (the steadfast): '...*fa maa wahanoo lemaa asaabahum fi sabeel Allah wa maa dza'ufoo wa maa ustakaanoo; wa Allah yuhibbus saabereen*' – 'but they never lost heart if they met with disaster in Allah's Way, nor did they weaken (in will) nor give in; and Allah loves those who are firm and steadfast (*assaabereen*). [33]

In view of the discussion thus far, I hope to have illustrated the point that the meanings of the Quran are best transferred to another language by the method of interpretation, which must be done on the basis of the Hejazi culture of the Arabic language of the Quranic times and the principle of repetition of expressions in the Quran. As Professor Izutsu has observed,

> 'But our basic rule must always be to try to elucidate as far as possible the semantic structure of words in question within the strict bounds of the Koranic contexts, *to let*, in brief, *the Koran interpret for us its own words.*' [34] (my emphasis)

Towards that end, for my readers who may be interested to dive a little deeper in the semantics and other linguistic aspects of the Quran, I have included a list of selected Quranic terms explained on the two principles discussed above. The subsequent chapters that follow the Glossary (Chapter 3) illustrate an attempt to interpret the Quran according to the methodology mentioned. However, before referring to the glossary, it may be desirable for many of my readers to get acquainted with the language of the Muslim holy book. I believe it is important for interested readers to have some basic information about the Arabic language if they are to fully appreciate the interpretation of the Quran that I have presented in the second part of the book.

2.6 A BRIEF INTRODUCTION TO ARABIC

Arabic is one of the world's major languages, used as primary tongue on two continents over an area stretching from Morocco in North Africa through the Arabian Peninsula right up to the borders of Turkey covering the entire Middle East. It is the language of Morocco, Algeria, Libya, Egypt, Sudan, Saudi Arabia, Lebanon, Jordan, Syria, Iraq, Kuwait, United Arab

Part One: Chapter Two

Emirates, Oman, Bahrain, Qatar, and North and South Yemen. In addition to that, Arabic speakers can be found in considerable numbers in southern Iran, Israel and the occupied territories. Also, there are sizable populations of Arabic speakers in the West, most notably in the United States and the United Kingdom. With a total world population of Arabic speakers in excess of 120 million[35], Arabic can safely claim to be among the top ten languages of the world. Apart from being important to us from the perspective of this book by virtue of being the language of the Quran, Arabic is also the language of a region immensely important internationally; its numerical, geographical, political, and cultural status was formally recognised by the United Nations in 1973 when it became its sixth official language (the others being English, French, Spanish, Russian, and Chinese).

Arabic belongs to the Semitic family of human languages of about thirty linguistic families in the world.[36] The term 'Arabic' may refer to one of three different forms of the language: colloquial (spoken), which is used in the daily lives of the Arab peoples; modern standard Arabic (also called modern literary Arabic), which is the language of the Arab media; and classical Arabic, which is the language of the Quran. The Muslim holy book has nearly always been a major grammatical and linguistic authority for Arabic. For more than twelve centuries, teachers, grammarians and linguists have referred to the Quran as the yardstick to measure the correctness of the Arabic language.

> '...the Moslem Arabic grammarians in the eighth and ninth centuries A.D. working at Basra attempted to purify Arabic to restore it to the perfection of the Koranic Arabic. [37]

2.7 SOME SALIENT FEATURES OF ARABIC

1. The Arabic alphabet consists of 29 letters (Appendix 1), of which 26 are consonants, and of the other three, *alif, waow, yaa* (which may stand for long vowels), the last two sometimes stand for consonants as well. Short vowels are not part of the alphabet and their sounds are normally denoted by diacritical marks above or below letters. Without the little hooks and dashes of the vowel marks written Arabic looks like speedwriting: it is as if the words 'classical Arabic' were written 'clsscl rbc'.

There are only three vowels in Arabic – *a, u,* and *i,* but each can be either long or short, making a total of six. Short *a* sounds like the English u in words like 'up' or 'but', whereas the long *a* is more like the a in 'car'. Short *u* is very much like the u in 'superior' while the long *u* sounds like the double o in words such as 'food' or 'root'. Short *i* has a sound similar to the initial i in words like 'incorrect' and long *i* sounds like the ee in English words such as 'feed' or 'eat.' In writing, the short vowels *a, u,* and *i* are not part of the main alphabet but are shown by short, slanted strokes of pen put above (for *a* as in but) or under (for *i* as in pin) the letter concerned; the

47

vowel *u* (as in p<u>u</u>t) is put above a letter and is shown by a short slash turned in at the top end. The long vowels are represented by letters *alif* (aa), *waow* (oo), and *yaa* (ee). Double letters are shown not by writing them twice as in English but by a diacritical mark shaped like a miniature w just above the letter which is to be pronounced double.

2. Arabic is written from *right* to *left* in cursive script, i.e. the letters are joined together, much like the English longhand. But, unlike English and other European languages, in Arabic, like many other scripts, most letters are joined with other letters in a 'broken' or abbreviated form.

3. Every noun in Arabic is either feminine or masculine; so are indicative pronouns. For example, *kursee* (chair) is masculine while *taawala* (table) is feminine. Therefore, in the sentences 'this is a chair' and 'this is a table', the pronoun 'this' has to agree with the gender of the noun it refers to; it will be *haaza kursee* and *haazehi taawala*, respectively.

4. Number in Arabic is represented by singular, dual and plural. The noun 'book' is *kitaab* (one book), *kitaabaan* (two books) and *kutub* (many books), respectively.

5. Adjectives must agree with the number and the gender of the noun they are describing. For instance, 'one beautiful chair' is *kursee jameel*, 'one beautiful table' is *taawala jameela*, 'two beautiful books' is *kitaabaan jameelaan*, 'two beautiful tables' is *tawalataan jameelataan*, and 'many beautiful pens' is *aqlaam jemeel*.

6. Order of words in an Arabic sentence is often quite different from that in English. Frequently, a sentence begins with a verb not a subject; for example, 'the president arrived this morning' can be written as 'arrived the president morning this' or sometimes even 'arrived morning this the president.' The second object is often placed at the end of a sentence, as in 'Gave John (to) James a book.'

7. A very important aspect of Arabic, which it shares with other Semitic languages, is a 'consonantal root system.' Almost every word in the language is a derivative of a 'root' (usually a verb) consisting mostly of three letters (consonants). The root represents a general, and often quite neutral, concept of an action or a state of being. The original root concept is refined and altered when various words are derived from it by applying a number of tools – prefixes, suffixes, change of vowel letters between consonants, addition of extra consonants in the middle, etc. Each of these changes produces a new word belonging to the same root-family displaying a new shade of meaning of, and a constant connection to, the original root. Also, the derivatives of a particular root carry the basic three (occasionally

four) letters in the *same* order of appearance. This may be better illustrated with an example.

The three-letter root '*ain, laam , meem* ('LM) has the basic meaning of 'to know, have knowledge, be informed,' etc, when pronounced '*alema* (with a guttural initial sound, which has no English equivalent) as an infinitive verb. With the first letter '*ain* carrying the vowel *i* (short) and the other two letters of the root vowel-less (pronounced '*ilm*), it becomes the noun for 'knowledge' (or, in its modern Arabic application, it means 'science' because scientific knowledge is one of the best and sure forms of information). Some derivatives are: '*aalim* (a knowledgeable, learned man); '*aalima* (a knowledgeable, learned woman); '*aleem* (more knowledgeable, very learned man); '*aleema* (more knowledgeable, very learned woman); '*ilmun* (theoretically - here, –*un* is a suffix turning the word into an adverb); '*ilmi* (scientific, erudite - here, the suffix *i* is the letter *yaa*, not a vowel, used as a suffix to create an adjective); *t'aleem* (education); *t'aleemi* (educational); *mu'allim* (teacher – male); *mu'allima* (teacher - female); *m'aloomaat / i'laam* (information); '*allaam / 'allaama* (a very highly learned person); *mut'allum* (learner, student – male); *mut'alluma* (learner, student – female). With another change in vowel sounds – *a* (short) for both '*ain* and *laam* – the same root (pronounced 'alama), giving another shade of meaning to the notion of knowing, becomes 'a sign, a token, mark, banner,' etc. Inserting the consonant A (*alif*) between '*ain* and *laam* (pronounced aalam) makes it 'world, universe, cosmos,'etc. 38

With a different order, the same three letters make a different root. '*ain, meem, laam* ('ML) – the infinitive verb being pronounced '*amala* – becomes 'to do, to act, to operate' with the basic meanings of 'action, work, deed' as noun. Some derivatives, with changes of vowels and other variations are: '*amali* (work-, of work, practical); '*amalan* (practically); '*umla / 'amaala* (wages, pay); '*ummaali* (worker, labourer); *m'amal* (factory, laboratory, place of work); '*aamil* (doer, practitioner, active); *ist'imaal* (use, application).

It is hoped that this brief introduction to Arabic will provide the linguistic background much needed to follow, understand and appreciate the Quranic language, doctrines and philosophy. It should be particularly helpful to readers who are not very familiar with Arabic. It would also be useful for readers to grasp the Quranic concepts given in the Glossary.

Chapter 3

A GLOSSARY OF SOME CONCEPTS AND DOCTRINES OF THE QURAN

Aadam – Adam – from root *alif, daa, meem* (AdM)
Udma (closeness, affinity, sociability): *adum Allah baiynahum b adim* – 'God created affinity between them; *al edaam* (all things agreeable); *al udma* (wheatish complexion); *idaam* (a typical member of a family); *aademi* (one related to *aadam,* man).

The 'story' of 'Adam's creation' in the Quran does not refer to a single individual but is the account of the origin of Man (mankind) and 'Adam' is the figurative representative of humanity.

However, one location in the Quran does give the impression of an individual named *Aadam,* who may have been a prophet (3:33)

Aakher (mas.), *aakhera* (fem.)–last, other–from root *alif, kha, ra* (AKhR)
Aakher is opposite of *awwal* (first) as in 57:3 – *huwa alawwal wa alaakher* [He (God) is the First and the Last]. Since there is nothing more after the 'last' one in a chain, the Quran terms life in the Hereafter (next life after death) as *khalqun jadeed* (17:49, 98; 32:10), i.e. life in the hereafter, though linked with life here, will be of a different kind and the first of a new chain of existence.

Ukhrun (step backward) is opposite of *qudumun* (step forward); *ta akhkhar* (backwardness) is opposite of *taqaddum* (forwardness) as *muta akhkher* is the opposite to *mutaqaddem;* the Quran uses *ma yastaakheroon* as opposed to *ma tasbeq* in 15:5 and also *mustaakhereen* (those who lag behind) opposite *mutaqaddameen* (those who go ahead) in 15:24.

Aakhar – another, other than; also, different as in 23:12
Therefore, Life assumed a new and different form in the shape of humanity; it will culminate in physical death and will be linked to the next, a very different, new form of life. In the Quran, *al hayaat ad-duniya* (life here, now) has been used opposite *qiyaama* and *aakhera* as in 2:85, 86; and *aakhera* is also used opposite *'aajela* (of now) as in 17:18, 19 and 75:20, 21), i.e. in the sense of 'future' and 'present', respectively; similarly, *ta'ajjal* is opposite of *ta akhkhar* as in 2:203; also, *aakhera* is opposite of *oola* [first (fem.)] in 79:25; in 26:84, *al aakhereen* means 'the future generations.'

So, the Quran's 'convinced' people (*momeneen* or 'believers' in ordinary English translations) are sure and aware of the importance of future as compared to the temporary, short-lived present.

Aaya – sign, symbol, verse – from root *alif, ya, ya* (AYh)
Aayaat (road/path markings); *aaya* is an outer, visible sign depicting something clearly to the onlooker.

Man's conceptual and perceptual capability is too finite to imagine and understand God's infinite person; He may be 'seen' and 'known' through countless signs scattered in the Universe; therefore, the Universe, and everything which exists in it, are God's *aaya*'s. By far the most important of these signs for Man is Revelation. A verse of the Quran is also an *aaya*; hence, a message (*risaala*) is also an *aaya*. Prophet Saleh's she-camel was also called an *aaya* (7:73) as was Noah's ark (29:15); perceptible facts of the physical universe are also called *aaya* (17:12). Also, commemorative structures (memorials) are *aaya*'s (26:128).

Al-Hajj – The Pilgrimage – from root *Haa, jeem, jeem* (HJJ)
Al hajju (to intend, to aim), as in *hajajtu fulaan* (I intended that); to some, it is 'to intend/aim a lot' or 'to aim for something noble and high,' hence, the pilgrimage to Mecca in 2:196 and 3:96); *al-hijja* (one year, with *hijaj* as plural, as in *thamaani hijaj*–eight years (28:27); *alhajju* also means 'to stop, to forbid,' as in 3:19 and 6:18, which gives *almuhaajja* (argumentation); an argument is *hujja* because it overcomes the opposition while it is also termed *bayyana* since it clarifies a statement as in *alhujjatu baalegha* – mature argument (6:150).

Therefore, Hajj is the global gathering of Islam, a super meeting held in order to resolve Muslim matters under the guidance of the Quran with the help of mature arguments. (Please see my treatment of Hajj in detail in the section on Islamic rituals).

Al-hubb, al-mahabba – Love – from root *Haa, baa, baa* (HBB)
The root has FIVE basic meanings: 1) whiteness and cleanness, as in *habab ul asnaan* (sparkle of teeth); 2) to emerge, as in *habaab ul maa* (bubble of water); 3) to stay firmly, as in *habb al-ba'eeru wa ahabb* (the camel sat down firmly); 4) to be pure essence, as in *habba tal qalb* (matter of the heart); and 5) to hold and protect, as in *hubb ul maa* (water pitcher/container/carrier). A couple of examples are: *habb ar rajul* (the man halted/stayed); *ahabb azzar'* (the crop grew grain, i.e. it showed growth).

Of course the Quran has used *hubb* (liking) in contrast to *kurh* (dislike, hate) as in 2:216 and 49:7, but 'love of God' is quite different in the Quranic context than the normal sense of 'love' (liking, adoration). In 2:165, for instance, "*wa min annaas man yattekhezu min doon Allah indaadan*.. (And there are men who take others besides Allah as equal)" defines 'love of gods' when it is followed by "*...yuhibboonahum* (they love them) *khubb Allah* (as they [should] love Allah)...", meaning thereby that 'loving' a god or God is following divine laws. This is further clarified and reinforced in 3:31,32 where it says: "*Qul in kuntum tuhibboon Allah fatabe'ooni*...(Say: 'If you do love Allah, follow me)...*"; and if one does that, Allah loves one back – "*...yuhbebkum Allah..*" which practically means "*...wa yaghfer lekum zunubekum..*(and will forgive your sins).*" Also in 5:54, we find "O ye who believe! If any from you reject (turn back on) their *deen* (system – Islam), soon will Allah produce a people who He will love (*yuhibbuhum*) and they will love Him (*yuhibboonahu*)."

Thus, in the Quranic context is not the ascetic practices of the *sufi* philosophy but practically following God' Law in all spheres of life.

Allah – God – from root *alif, laam, ha* (ALh)
Literally, 'the god'; originally, *al* (the) + *ilaah* (god); refers to the One Creator god of the Universe.
Aaleha ilaihe yaalahu – to seek refuge with him in distress,
Aaleha – to be wonderstruck,
Aalahu yyalahu – to provide refuge to someone,
Aaleha belmakaan – to take up residence in peace.

Therefore, *ilaah* is someone who is sought refuge and asylum with, and the one who commands awe. To some, it is a derivative of *laa hu yalaihu* – to be exalted and invisible.

To some others, *aalahu* means 'he became a slave' and *allahahu* means 'he made him a slave', therefore, *taaleehun* is synonymous to *t'abeedun* (subjugation). Therefore, *ilaah* is someone whose superiority and dominance is accepted, the one who is obeyed, as in 36:29, 25:23 and 43:84. Idols are also called *ilaah* by the same token in 7:138.

Allah is that high and mighty Being who is invisible to humans, who are awed and wonderstruck by His greatness; His control covers the entire Universe; He must be obeyed through His Law, which He gave to mankind through the process of Revelation and which is now enshrined in the Quran; therefore, in the Quran *ate'oo Allah* means 'obey (the Law of) God'; wherever in the Quran it says 'God does …' it means 'God's Law does..'; His Law is referred to as *sunnat Allah*, and His *sunna* is constant, permanent and unchanging. The Quran is a collection of God's attributes, laws, wisdom and instructions; God's obedience is the focal point of the Quranic teaching, i.e. He (*Allah*) is the One and Only Sovereign in the entire Universe.

We humans cannot comprehend God's person as we are finite and He is infinite; however, we can comprehend, within our intellectual limitations, His attributes - *al asmaa al husna* – recorded in the Quran; only that concept of God is correct which is based upon His Quranic attributes.

Amr- symbol, sign, order, advice… - from root *alif, meem, ra* (AMR)
Al amratu wa al tamoor (a sign made up of small stones to indicate a path in the desert); that gives it the sense of 'consultation' – *al eitemaar* (to cosult), as in 7:110, 26:35, 65:6); it may also mean 'to intend, decide, make mind up' (28:20); *mo'tamar* (site for conferring, conference room/hall); *ameer* (one who is consulted; also a guide for the blind); *amr* also means 'to become plentiful' (17:16), so *ameer* is 'prosperous.'

It also means 'order' (instruction) with *awaamer* as plural, and condition/affair/matter with *umoor* as plural; so, *al-ameer* is 'ruler' as in 'God orders you (2:67); in the sense of affair/matter, it appears in 22:62 – 'collective matter'; *al imra* or *amaara* (rule, government); *amrun 'adeem* (a great incident); a decisive moment/stage (16:33); some despicable matter (18:71);

al-ammaara (one who gives a lot of orders, also, one who causes a stir (12:53); *amr* is also used for 'opinion', 'will', 'desire' as in 18:82.

The Quran uses *amr* opposite *khalq* (7:52) in a significant sense. *Khalq* is creation from already existing components/elements, as humans do. But, the stage prior to this creation is the original creation (the Process of Becoming) and is the domain of *amr* (2:117). *Amr* is also Law of Nature (principles on which the Universe functions) as in 7:54 and 22:65. God's Law for Man's social environment is also *amr* (8:42) and is permanent (3:127) and eternal as that for the physical universe, and is revealed to Man through God's appointed prophets (45:17 and 65:5).

Angels – *malaaeka* – from root *alif, laam, ka* (MLK)
Alk (messaging); *almalaaka* (the messenger angel), from *alaka* (to chew) – a message is *al alooka* because it is chewed out of mouth;

To some, it comes from root *mlk* meaning 'power'; *malak* (executive angel) and *malek* (executive man) – that is why *malek* is 'king'; so, *malaaeka* are Nature's messengers, its executives, its workers – so they are in the Quran (22:75); but, that is only one aspect of them – in essence, they are called administrators who delegate work (79:5, 51:4).

The Universe operates several Divine schemes of work. The powerful agents manning these schemes are *malaaeka* (angels). They do not have freedom of choice so they carry out their designated tasks absolutely obediently (16:50). The laws under which they operate in the material universe can be discovered by Man; thus he can control and harness the forces of Nature; that is the concept behind the symbolic prostration of angels to Adam.

Malaaeka, in addition to Nature's forces in the material Universe, is also applied to forces operating within Man's inner (psychological) universe (41:30); the natural forces – be they external or internal – that cause fear and depression are known as *iblees* and *shaitaan*. These forces also affect men's physique (4:97, 16:28); they also 'keep record' of men's deeds, i.e. operate the Law of Retribution (10:21, 43:80); 'record-keeping' is also done by God (19:79) and one's record is displayed hanging in one's own neck (17:13, 14); it means that angels are Forces of Nature which *operating* under God's Law of Retribution, affect changes in an individual's personality accordingly.

Since *malaaeka* are invisible, we cannot see them (9:26, 40); as far as Revelation is concerned, it is beyond the bounds of human comprehension – it simply has to be accepted as an article of faith; however, the truth and wisdom of Revelation may be examined through knowledge. The Quran demands acceptance of angels as an article of faith, i.e. angels should be considered just what they are – they are Forces of Nature that can, and should be, harnessed and controlled by Man to be used for the universal benefit of all creatures.

Ard – Earth – from root *alif, ra, dawd* (ARd)
Ard (earth, ground) is everything which is low/down opposed to *samaa*, so, *ard anna'l* is the sole of a shoe; also, the part of a leg below the knee; Earth is *ard*

because it is under the feet; because the earth is the basic source of human sustenance, prosperity is *al araada; ardat al ard* (the earth became very suitable and fertile for farming yield; because *ard* is something low and down, *araada* means 'to be modest and obedient; in the Quran *ard* is used with *jibaal* in 18:47, where they carry figurative sense of 'lower' and 'higher' classes of society; *ard un wa samawaat* means the lows and highs of the Universe; socially, *samaa* is God's Law of Nature while *ard* is Man's economic environment.

To the Quran, the earth is 'source of sustenance' (7:10). If Economics is divorced from God's Law (now enshrined in the Quran), Man falls to an animalistic existence, where he enjoys quick but temporary benefits of the present but the higher aim of human life (the 'future') is lost (7:169) – it is a 'low' existence as compared to a 'higher' one (7:176); it is also a life of greed, selfishness and satisfaction of base desires and emotions (7:176). Monotheism is adopting God's Law of Nature as the basis of Man's economic system on Earth because He is the only god in *samaa* as well as *ard* (43:84); otherwise, human society develops grave problems (21:21, 22).

As the Earth is the source of sustenance for mankind, no piece of it may become private property – it is to benefit all creation (55:10), man and beast alike (80:32); not only the Earth but other elements of production of sustenance are also to be kept available to all the needy (56:74); any system which benefits a few instead of the wider human fraternity is anti-Quranic – that is why the Earth must remain accessible to the needy (51:10); means and sources of production – light, air, water, the earth, etc) – must remain under social control so that society can provide for all; this shift from private ownership of land to collective social control has been slow but sure in history (13:41); when the process is complete sometime in the future, the Earth will be "illuminated by the Light of its Sustainer" (39:69).

As-salaa – PRAYER – from root *saad, laam, wao / ya* (SLW/Y)
Commonly translated as *prayer*, the word has the basic meanings of 'to cling to something/someone.' Its derivatives include words like *as-sallaa* (the back, the hip where falls and touches an animal's tail), *al-musally* (the horse following another very close behind), *al-musalleen* (the followers), *sallu* (to praise and encourage – most probably by close support), and *as-salaa* (formal, ritual gathering of Muslims).

(See a detailed discussion on this important Quranic concept in the chapter RITUALS IN ISLAM).

'azaab – Chastisement – from root *ain, zaa, baa*
This root has three basic meanings: 1. sweetness and refreshment of water – *al'azb* (sweet and refreshing water as in 25:53); 2. agony, predicament – *'azab* (the layer of dirt and filth on the surface of water), *'azaba* (a plant lethal for camels), *'azaab* (punishment, chastisement, also hunger, thirst and discomfort; and 3. hindrance, prevention, stoppage – *'azoob* or *'aazeb* (a man, camel or

horse too thirsty to eat; also, one who goes to bed on an empty stomach, or one who is shelter less).

In the Quran, *'azaab* has been used for all the suffering of the Israelites under the Egyptians (20:47); in 2:7, it is used for deprivation pf good life; in the sense of legal sentence, see 4:25 and 24:2; God is *mu'azzib* (7:164) because breaking His Law brings suffering and pain for men, who are called *mu'azzab* (26:213); various forms of *'azaab* in the Quran are: degradation and decline in this world (20:134), hunger and fear (16:112), depravation of bounties (7:96), sectarianism and schism (6:56), intra-group divisions (3:104). Therefore, *'azaab*, in the Quranic context, is for not only in the hereafter but also in earthly life.

Baatel – untruth, falsehood – from root *ba, Ta, laam* (BtL)
Batal ashshaiy ([for something] to go waste); *baatel* (that which is not true to measure, sub-standard); *ibtaal* (to damage/destroy); to some, *baatel* is applied to whatever does not truly and fully serve its original purpose and function and are just a semblance of the real.

In the Quran *baatel* has been used opposite *haq* (true, right, correct, useful, functional), so any thing or action that is not *haq* is *baatel*, i.e. it does not produce the required results and goes waste, e.g. lifeless rituals. Since *baatel* does not deliver whereas *haq* does, the Quran has also used it opposite *ne'ma* (bounty) in 29:67 and 16:72. *Baatel* is also that which does not last because it is not true; only *haq* remains (17:81).

Baraka – plentitude – from root *ba, ra, ka* (BRK)
Barak al-ba'eer (the camel firmly sat); *al birka* (camel's chest, goat which lactates plentifully, a pond full of water); *mubaarak* or *fihi baraka* (congratulations for firm and lasting prosperity); pl. *barakaat*.

Since *baraka* is applied to plenty and prosperity with firmness and longevity, 'the Earth and Skies' are *barakaat* which Muslims stand to get (7:96); the Earth contains *baraka* (41:10) as is rain water (50:9); the Quran is *kitaab un mubaarak* (38:29) as well the night in which it was revealed (44:2) and Mecca is *al-Bak al-mubaarak* (3:95) being the location where the Quran was received; God is the source of all *baraka* (7:54).

Therefore, a Quranic social system should also be a source of stable and lasting plentitude for all mankind.

Bashar – man, human being – from root *ba, sheen, ra* (BShR)
Bashara (outer layer of human skin); *al-bashru* (to peel skin, to shave); *bishara* (news, good or bad, which causes a change in one's facial complexion); *bashshar* (to give [such] news) as in 3:20 and 16:58; *al-bashaara* also means beauty; *basheer* (harbinger of good news); *at-tabaasheer* (good news, early morning sun rays when dawn breaks); *al-mubashsheraat* (cloud-bearing winds that foretell rain).

Prophets in the Quran declare *ana basharun mithlekum* – 'I am but human like yourselves' (e.g. 24:33). Generally, *insaan* and *bashar* have been used synonymously as in 15:26 ans 15:28. *Baasharhaa* (2:187) means 'to have sexual intercourse with her' though sometimes it is used just for cuddling and kissing.

B'ath – rejuvenate, revive, release – from root *ba, 'ain, tha* (B'aTh)
B'ath an-naaqa (he released the bonds of the she-camel to roam); to some, it has the basic meaning of 'to revitalize' as in 83:4-5 [in this sura the Quran presents a great basic principle of economy. The commercial mentality of Capitalism believes in the extortionist practice of snatching more than it gives; it always pays less than what is fair. God's Law *wants* everyone to be treated fairly and justly. At the moment, capitalists think that things will never change but the Quran declares otherwise in the verse mentioned – 'they are free (*mab'uthoon*) only until *youmen 'adzeem* - the Big Day (the era when mankind, having had enough of extortion and exploitation, will rise to establish a universal just socio-economic system (83:6).

Al-b'athu (to dispatch someone) as in 10:75; also, to 'wake someone up' as in 6:60; *al-b'aethu* (one who keeps waking at night).

Baa'eth also means 'cause' or 'motive' because it removes impediments in one's way as in 2:56 and 2:259, where it refers allegorically to the life and death of nations.

Another usage is to send a prophet (2:149) as well as to appoint someone (4:35); also *b'athna 'alaikum* (17:5) means 'were given domination over you.'

Burhaan – proof, evidence, argument – from root *ba, ra, ha* (BRh)
Al-bara (white complexioned plump body); *al-barharha* (young fair-coloured maiden with fresh shiny skin); *al-barha tu wa al-burha* (a long period of time); *bara* (to cut); so, *al-burhan* is clear and shining evidence, a 'cutting' (decisive) argument.

The Quran calls itself *burhaan min rabbekum* – 'a clear evidence/argument from your Sustainer' (4:175) because it says what it says on the basis of clear evidence. That is why the Quran requires clear arguments from its opponents in support of their stance (2:111).

Deen – 'religion' – from root *daa, yaa, noon* (dYN)
deen (system), *medina* (city), *diyaana* (behaviour, specifically in religious matters), *mudun* (cities), *dain* (loan), etc. The Quran has used the word *Deen* to denote the set of values and principles, which form the basis of this divine message, called *Islam*, contained in the book known as the Quran (2:131, 132). This *Al-Deen,* previously given to all messengers, is the only system recognized as true, authentic , legitimate and the best for mankind. It has been called *Al-Islam* (3:19); also <u>*Deen-e-Qayyem*</u> (Right and straight system)- (98:5); practicalities of *ad-deen* are given in 90:11-18. In conventional western 'religion' (*mazhab*), God is worshipped and praised verbally through rituals. In *al-Deen* God's Law is practically followed. Putting their CONVICTION into PRACTICE (doing good deeds) is more important than rituals. In fact, rituals alone are futile (47:2, 3:142, 9:19.20, 2:177, 16:97).

Du'aa – Prayer (Supplication) – from root *daa-'ain-wao* (d'W)

Linguistically, the Arabic word for supplication is *du'aa*, with the basic meaning of 'to call or beckon.' Hence, the word *ad-da'aa'a* is used for the finger which is used to call somebody; *ad-daa'eea* is the clamour of horses during battle; also, it means the small amount of milk left in cattle so that it makes subsequent milking easy: *huwa minni d'awa tar rajul* means 'he is a call away from me.' *Ad-Daa'ee* is the one who calls or beckons – it is commonly used for Mohammed, the Messenger of God because he called / beckoned people to the Divine message; *Idde'aa* (*yaddda'oon*) means 'to wish'; *daa'en* is not only the one who calls or beckons but also the one who takes/escorts someone to someone – *da'aau ilaal ameer* means 'he escorted him to the chief.' In the Quran, we find: '... This is what ye were calling for.' (*tadda'oon*)-67:27; '... and call your witnesses or helpers (if there are any) besides Allah ...'(*wa ud'oo*) 2:23; 'On the Day He will say, "Call (*naadoo*) on those whom ye thought to be My partners." And they will call on them (*da'oohum*)...'-18:52; 'If ye call them (*tad'oohum*) to guidance, they will not obey. For you it is the same whether ye call them (*da'avtumuhum*) or you keep silent (*saametoon*).' 7:193; 'And remember ye said: "O Moses! We cannot endure one kind of food (always); so beseech (call) thy Lord for us...' (*fa ad'oo lenaa rabbaka*)-2:61.

Eemaan – conviction – from root *alif, meem, noon* (AMN)

Commonly translated as 'faith'; *amn* (fearlessness, peace – 2:240, 6:82); *aamana* (to provide peace and security) – that is why God is *al-Mo'min* (23:59); *aitemaan* (to trust and rely); *naaqa tun amoon* (a reliable she-camel); *mo'min* (one who provides and guarantees *amn*, i.e. peace and security); *amaana* (an article for safekeeping); *ameen* (secure, honest, peaceful); *balad un ameen* - a secure, peaceful city (95:3); *maqaam un ameen* - a secure place (44:52); also, in the sense of 'protection and prosperity' in 16:112, and 'reliance and trust' in 2:283, 12:11, 17, 64; followed by preposition *le, amn* means 'to agree and comply with', (2:55) while with preposition *be,* it means to 'believe in' (2:285).

In Quranic context therefore, to have *eemaan* (to become 'faithful') is to:

    a)   accept, to agree,
    b)   certify truthfulness
    c)   trust and rely, and
    d)   comply, obey

The Quran requires one to have *eemaan* in regards to FIVE basic realities (2:177) – God, the Last Day, the Angels, the Book, and the prophets; to deny any one of them is a folly (4:136). It means one has to be convinced of, trust, rely on and accept:

a) God's existence and His laws,
b) the continuation of life after death,
c) the Forces of Nature running the Universe, and that they can be harnessed,
d) Man's dependence on Revelation for guidance to the Truth through chosen men (prophets) and that Mohammed was the last and final of them,
e) divine guidance given in scriptures, of which the Quran is the final and true record of God's Word.

Everyone, including people believing in previous scriptures must now accept the Quran. Anybody, who has *eemaan* in the Quranic sense will be duly rewarded by peace, security and fearlessness (2:64, 4:136, 137). People who believe in the existence of God and His law operating in the physical Universe but do not accept His laws for human society are not *mo'min* ['faithful' (convinced)] – 23:84-90. Also, *eemaan* must be of free will and choice with understanding and sincerity (49:14). *Eemaan* is not just 'belief' or 'conviction'; it also means practically following God's Law (30:53).

Halaal – allowed – from root *Haa, laam, laam* (HLL)
It has the basic meaning: 'to open a knot ; to untie'. In Sura *Tahaa* (Chapter 20, Moses prays to God: *'wa ahlul uqda min lisaani'* - "*..*and remove the impediments from my speech" (20:27). In simpler words, Moses was asking God to *open the knot in his tongue.* Similarly, when something is melted, it is termed *hallun* – that its knot was opened (was untied). *Hall al ahmaal* means to untie (unpack) luggage, which led to its application as *hall al makaan* – to arrive at a place and stay. From this comes the expression *haleel* (husband) and *haleela* (wife) as they stay together at the same place. Hence, the figurative meaning of *halaal / helaal, al-hellu / al-haleel* as permissible / allowed.

Haraam – forbidden – from root *Haa, raa, meem* (HRM)
It has the basic meaning of 'to forbid ; to stop.' *Al-haraam*–all that has been forbidden. This is the opposite of *al-halaal* (to allow; to permit). *Ahram al-haaj* means 'the pilgrim reached a stage where several restrictions were imposed'. This is the status of *ahraam* , the symbolic ritual garb of Muslim pilgrims. *Ash-hurul haramu* were the four months (*Moharram, Rajab, Dhulqa'da, Dhulhijja*) during which armed conflict was forbidden. *Al-Mahroom* is the one whose needs are no longer met. *Al-Haram* is a common reference to the enclosed area of the Grand Central Mosque in Mecca (*Al-Masjid al-haraam)*, which contains the Ka'ba. The Messenger's Mosque in Medina is referred to as *Al-haram an-Nabavi ash-shareef.*

[For a detailed discussion of *halaal* and *haraam* please see Chapter 11; The Permissible and the Forbidden].

Hoor – Houri (paradisiacal maiden) – from root *Haa, waow, raa* (HWR) *Haar, yahoor, hawraa* (to return, to come back, to change from one condition to another, to decrease after increase [84:14]); *al-muhaavratu wat tahaavur* (conversation) as in 18:34 and 58:1); *al-mehver* (pivot); *al-hawr* (amazement, also white wood); *al-havariyyaat* (urban women because they are fair and clean); *al-huvvaari* (wheat flour); Christ's Companions are *al-havariyyun* (61:14) because they were washer men, or they lived hygienically clean, or they were sincere, or they were cream (the chosen few) of society;

hoor – plural of *ahvar* (m) or *hawraa* (f); *al-havar* (the white and black of the eye being very pronounced, to have fair skin, or the black of the eye being prominent) – such men and women are *hoor*.

In the Quran we find '...*wa zavvajnaahum be hoorin 'eenen*' (44:54, 52:20). *'Een* – plural of *a'ain* (m) or *'ainaa* (f) – means people with prominent eyes; *zowj* is 'companion'. Thus, in the verses above *hoor* means 'sincere companions, both male and female.' In 55:72 and 56:22, however, it refers to pure and clean women.

As Edward Lane has reported in his *Lexicon* that, *ahvar* (pl. *hoor*) means 'pure or clean intellect.' Therefore, in the paradisiacal (ideal) society proposed by the Quran, *hoor* will be friends, companions and partners (husbands and wives) who will be intelligent as well as sincere of heart.

'ibaada – Worship or Obedience? – from root *'ain, baa, daa* ('Bd)
'abd is a fragrant plant that is attractive and nourishing for camels; it makes them very thirsty at first but quite healthy later and induces heavy lactation; because of these original meanings (discomfort to be followed by betterment), *safeena mu'abbada* is a boat pasted ugly with layers of fat or charcoal in order to make it withstand water; therefore, *'ibaada* is an attractive activity which may be a little uncomfortable initially but bears pleasant results (2:286). In the Quran, we find 'Remind (the people) God's Law, because it will be beneficial for them' (51:55); 'I have created *ins* (urban men) and *jinn* (rural men) for My *'ibaada* (51:56); but remember, God does not require you to do it for any of His benefit: 'No sustenance do I require of them, nor do I require that they should feed Me' (51:57). *Ta'beed* is 'braking or harnessing a horse or camel'; thus, '..*a'budoo* - serve and obey, i.e. do *'ibaada - Allah wa ajtanebu at-taaghoot* -eschew Evil' (16:36); '*laa ta'budu asshaitaan* – do not obey rebellious elements' (19:44). The Quran has used *'ibaada* synonymously with *Hukooma* (government) – 18:110 to 18:26 to 12:40; Moses said to the Pharaoh, '..you have enslaved (under control) the Children of Israel' (26:22). According to the Quranic philosophy, 'people who do not establish a system according to God's Law are Rejecters – *kaaferoon;* God wants the Convinced – *mo'meneen* – to inherit power in the land so that they can 'do His *'ibaada* alone (24:55). *'abd* (pl. *'abeed* or *'ibaad*) is 'a slave' for its obvious applied connotation; therefore, we find the term used in that sense as well as its extension, 'worship' as in 23:47, 26:22, 2:178 and 26:71.

Iblees – Devil, satan – from root *ba, laam, seen* (BLS)
Ablas (he gave up hope) as in 23:77, also 'to be shockingly surprised'; *ablees* (to lose confidence in God's bounty and be permanently dejected). The Quran presents *Iblees* as representative of arrogance and rebellion (2:34) when he refused to bow before Man. In contrast there are the angels who are programmed to obey – 'all of the angels prostrated together' (38:73). Man is the only creature with the gift of 'freedom of choice' in the matter of God's Law. He transgresses, disobeys and defies Nature's Law only when he is overwhelmed by his own emotions of arrogance triggered by greed and selfishness. Such crafty and fiery human sentiments are called *iblees* 'made from fire' (7:12). Because human emotions are invisible, *iblees* is a 'jinn' ('concealed') – 18:50. Since these human sentiments remain with one till the last day, *iblees* is at work till Man dies (15:36) Rejecting the Quranic law results in the loss of all its natural and logical bounty and fruits. Accepting it alleviates all fears, anxieties and depression (2:38) and *iblees* is rendered helpless (15:42). *Iblees* (frustration) and *Shaitaan* – Devil (aggressiveness) are two sides of the same coin – in Paradise, Man was led astray by *Shaitaan* (2:36, 7:11-20, 20:116-120). These human sentiments are impediments in the way of the development of his personality. Overcoming these psychological obstacles help toward that goal much in the way that stones and rocks in a river help to guide and usher the water on its course in a smoother and better flow. Thus human life is a constant struggle to overcome these negative traits and is an ongoing battle between Man and Devil. Men who do not lose confidence in God's Law (39:53) succeed in keeping *iblees/shaitaan* at bay.

Insaan – Man, Human Being – from root *alif, noon seen* (ANS)
Uns (to be familiar); *al-humr al-insiyya* (domestic donkeys); *himaar* (wild donkey); *istaanas al-wahshy* (the animal was domesticated; *insun fulaan* (close friend of that person); *ins* (Man, sing. *insiy*); *al-anas* (the settled tribe – opposite to *ins*, the roving nomad tribes were *jinnun*); plurals of *ins* are *anaas* or *anaasy*, or *an-naas* meaning 'mankind' (25:49, 50); *unaas* – 'tribe' as in 2:60; it is also the root for *insaan* (man/human) with synonym *basher* (15:26-28); *aanas* (to see and feel as in 27:7 and 20:9; *eenaas* (to know something with certainty); *musttanes* – one who is freely familiar (33:53); *istaanas* (to seek permission as in 24:27).

The God of Quran is *Rabb an naas, Mullik an naas,* and *Ilaah an naas* – Sustainer, Sovereign and God of mankind; the Quran itself is *basaaer an naas* (guide to Man).

Jahannam – Hell
To some it mean 'deep' with Arabic origins as in *rakiyyatun jahannam* (a deep well) while some others take it as Arabization of the Hebrew 'Gahannaam.' It is considered to have been formed of two Hebrew words 'Gi' (valley) and 'Hannoom' (personal name of a man). The 'Valley of Hannoom' lay in the south of ancient Jerusalem where men were burnt and sacrificed as offering to

Moloch, the Ammonite god. So, *Jahannam* may be translated as 'the altar of mankind.'

The Quran aims at establishing a paradisiacal society (*janna*) so that human potentialities could develop fruitfully. Contrarily, a social order where mankind is 'slaughtered' and is 'reduced to ashes' is hellish (*jahannam*); the Arabic expression for that state is *jaheem* meaning 'to stop, to cease' as in "...*wa ja'lnaa jahannama lilkaafereena haseeraa* - ...and We have made Hell a prison for those who reject" (17:8). The Hell after death is beyond human comprehension but earthly hell is a natural consequence of men's deeds, individually as well as collectively, and is their own handiwork. That is why it says "...*wa inna jahannama la muheetum belkaafereen* - ...and, of a surety, Hell encompasses the rejecters" (29:54); it is a fire which consumes human efforts to ashes and reduces men to psychological wrecks because "*Naar uAllahel muqada* – the Fire of Allah, kindled (to a blaze), *allati tattle'u 'ala al-afeda* – That which mounts to the hearts"! (104:6,7).

Jihaad – 'Holy war' (?) – from root *jeem, haa, daa* (Jhd)
Al-jahdu (to achieve with utmost diligence); *juhd* (strength and extent); to some both *jahd* and *juhd* are used for 'strength and extent' while *jahd* is only for painstaking hard work, but the Quran has used *jahd* for the latter in 9:79. *Jihaad* thus means 'to employ one's extreme efforts to the fullest towards achieving a goal.' *Jahaada* is 'a grassless barren piece of land'; *al-ijtehaad* means 'to spend all disposable energy with backbreaking effort to do something'; *al-jaahed* (one who does not sleep).

In the Quran, we find *mujaahedeen* (those who work with their full capacity) in contrast to *qaaedeen* (those who just sit idly). Therefore, *jihaad* is 'constant perseverance in the work of God to establish and maintain the Quranic social order, even at the cost of one's life.'

(For a detailed discussion please see Chapter 10; Terrorism or Jehaad?).

Jinn – genie – from root *jeem, noon, noon* (JNN)
Jannun has the basic meaning of 'to conceal, to hide'; *jananun* (a grave); *janeen* (fetus); *junna / mijanna* (a shield); *laa jinna be haazal amr* ('there is nothing secretive in this'); *jinna* (madness); *majnoon* [m]/*majnoona* [f] (insane); *junoon* (insanity); *janna* (a garden with its ground covered [concealed] with grass; *junnat al ard* (grass spread well and looked nice); *nakhlatun majnoona* (a very tall date tree).

In the Quran, we find:

"*fa lammaa janna 'alaihe raaea kawkaban...* – When the night covered him over, he saw a star..." (6:77);

"*attakhazoo aimaanahum junna...* - They have made their oaths a screen..." (58:16);

"*in huwa illa rajalum behe jinna...*- He is only a man possessed... (23:25).

In Quranic times, the Arabs termed all invisible forces of Nature *jinn*, which included both good forces *malaaeka* (angels) as well as bad ones (*shayaateen*) as in 37:158. There exists a notion of an extinct pre-human species on Earth – during its early stages of development - which could survive in the intensely hot environment of the time:

"*wa aljaanna khalaqaahu min qablu min annaar essamoom* – And the concealed ones we had created before, from the fire of a scorching wind." (15:27). Incidentally, *Iblees* (the Devil) is also said to have been a *jinn* because of its being rebellious and invisible.

The Quran quite often mentions *jinn* together with *ins* (see above). *Al-ins* were groups inhabiting permanent settlements while *jinn* were nomadic tribes, known as *baddoo* (Bedouin) or *a'raab* (desert Arabs), 'invisible' to the town folks. Messengers of God were men sent to humans (7:35) – the Quran has mentioned no *jinn* (non-human) prophet; therefore, in 6:131, *yaa m'asher al-jinne wa al-ins* refers to (town and desert dweller) humans. Also, suras *Jinn* and *Ahqaaf* (72:1 and 46:29, respectively) narrate about 'a group of *jinns*' coming to the Prophet to listen to the Quran. They were nothing but Bedouin men. Similarly, *jinn* in the following verses mean 'the desert people': 6:113,129; 7:179; 27:17; 21:82; 34:13; 38:37, 38; 41:29.

From the same root we have *janna* (Paradise), used by the Quran for both a blissful existence in the Hereafter as well as a prosperous paradisiacal society in this earthly life. Such quality and standard of life has been eloquently summarized in 2:35: '…and eat of the bountiful things therein as (where and when) you will, but approach not this tree…', meaning thereby that in a paradisiacal society all basic needs are met satisfactorily and provisions are aplenty (20: 118, 119), but can be retained and sustained for ever only if that society follows God's Law – it will stay green for ever (2:25, 13:35).

The nature of Paradise after death is incomprehensible for men while they are in this life (32:17); that is why the accounts of *janna* (Paradise) are but a simile (13:35).

Kaafir – Disbeliever – from root *kaa, faa, raa* (KFR)
Kufr is 'to conceal, to cover, to hide', and is synonymous with *akhfa, satara* and *ajanna*. Thus, *kaafir* is 'a soldier laden with weapons', 'night' (because it covers everything in darkness), 'a dark cloud', 'a river/ocean' (because they conceal so much) and 'a farmer' (because he conceals seed in soil); also, 'a grave' is *alkafr*. Therefore, *kaafir*, in the theological sense, is 'someone who hides the truth behind falsehood.' In the Quranic context, *kufr* is not merely rejecting God's Word verbally, but more importantly, practically working against it. That is why it has been used in contrast to *eemaan* (2:4, etc) as well as *shukr* (14:7) – please see 3:114.

Khowf – Fear – from root *khaa, waow, faa* (KhWF)
Khowf (to apprehend a possible danger/loss) just as *tama'* is to look forward to a gain as in 7:56. Comparatively, *huzn* is 'grief', which is the depressing feeling *after* a loss (while *khowf* is an anxious feeling *before* it) as in verse 4:128 we see; '*wa in imraatun khaafat min ba'lehaa nashooz* – if a woman fears mistreat-

ment by the husband……..';

al-kheefa (state of fear); verse 16:50 says: '*yakhaafoona rebbehem min fowqehem wa yaf'aloona ma yumaroon* – they fear the control of their Sustainer and do whatever they are ordered' [they abide totally by God's Law because they know breaking it will bring negative consequence]; therefore 'fear of God' is not what one feels under an unpredictable, whimsical tyrant but is the conscious awareness of undesirable outcome of an action just as we don't touch a naked flame for 'fear' of getting burnt; that is why *al-khaafa* is the protective cover of bee farmers).

Maghfera – (God's) Forgiveness? – from root *ghain, faa, raa* (GhFR)
Ghafr (to cover protectively, such as a dustcover); therefore, it also means 'to hide, to conceal'; *al-mighfar wa al-ghifaara* (metallic net worn under a battle helmet to protect neck and shoulders); *al-ghifaara* (a fabric band to protect female headwear from hair oil); *al-jammaa ulghafeer* (a large battle helmet). Thus, in the Quran, *maghfera* is not divine clemency/forgiveness but Nature's protection from damage, as in 2:221 and 2:285; *ghaafer* (7:155), *ghafoor* (7:153) *and ghaffaar* (20:82) mean 'protector'; *istaghfaar* means 'to seek protection.' So, the Quranic concept of divine clemency does not comprise of verbally (in prayer) asking for God's forgiveness, but constitutes actions according to His Laws in order to be safe from dire natural consequences of one's own doing.

Mashiya – God's Will – from root *sheen, yaa, alif* (ShYA)
Shaa, yashaa, shaiaa and *mashiya* is 'to intend; *ash shai* (thing, physical or ideal).
In the Quran, *shai* in 2:20 and 2:48 means 'thing, object or matter'; *yahdi man yashaa* means 'whoever wishes/intends to be guided by Allah' or 'whoever can get guidance according to God's Law; *wa Allah yutee mulkahu man yashaa* – 'God grants power in the land according to His laws' (2:247); *wa maa tashaaoon illa unyashaa Allah* – 'and do not desire what Allah does not want (you to want)' (76:30), i.e. 'keep yourselves aligned with the Divine guidance and laws.'

Qitaal – armed combat – from root *qaa, taa, laam* (QtL)
Al-qatl (strike of a weapon; to kill with a stone or poison; to take life); *qaatalahu* (fought with him; one tried to kill the other; also, 'to degrade and subdue' as in 80:17, 51:10 as well as 9:31) – therefore, in 17:31 and 6:152 *laa taqtuloo awlaadakum* is not (literally) 'killing off your children' but (figurative) 'degrading and depriving them'; *Uqtuloo fulaan* (he was rendered ineffective); *qatal ashraab* (to dilute a drink).

Qatal ashayia khubra (he obtained complete information about); *innahu laqtilu sharr* (he knows evil very well); therefore, *wa maa qataloohu yaqeenan* (about Jesus) in 4:157 means 'they do not know the factual truth'; *al-muqattal* is someone 'very knowledgeable and experienced'; also, *istaqtal* (to apply oneself as a matter of life and death).

Part One: Chapter Three

In the Quran, we find various shades of meaning of this term:
2:61 – 'They used to murder / degrade their prophets'
2:54 – 'so subdue (submit) yourselves to God's Law'
4:29 – 'Do not destroy yourselves'
2:216 –'armed combat'
3:153 –'fighting had been made obligatory for them'.

Rabb – 'Lord' (Sustainer) – from root *raa, baa, baa* (RBB)
Rabbun is 'to sustain and nourish to help gradual growth' just as Mother Nature develops a drop of rain into a pearl; *rabba waldahu rabba wa rabbaba wa trabbaba* is 'he sustained the child so that it matured' (For details, please refer to Chapter 4, *Problems of Language...* of this work).

Rahma – Mercy (?) –from root *raa, Haa, meem* (RHM)
Rehm , rahem or *ruhm* – uterus; *rahma* – a free gift given at the time it is needed and which satisfies the need(s); it is Nature's free gifts to Man for his developmental needs (30:36-37); to provide means of growth to someone (17:24); agricultural crops are also *rahma* (30:46, 42:28); bounties of life (*na'maa*) which one gets free (11:9-10); in the story of Moses, protection of treasure for two orphans is also termed *rahma* (18:82); also, *rahma* is 'to cover, shield and protect from damage (10:21, 30:33) or wrong deeds or mistakes (30:36) or destruction (67:28); Divine Revelation (*wahy*) is also *rahma* (2:105, 43:32); since God is *rabb ul 'aalemeen* (Sustainer of all worlds), He has made it incumbent upon Himself to provide *rahma* (6:54) not only to mankind but also to the entire Universe (40:7) – God is not only *ar-Raheem* (progressive provider) but also *ar-Rahmaan* (emergent provider).

Because *rehm* is uterus (plural *arhaam*, as in 3:5), it is also applied to relations and relatives (60:3, 4:1, 8:75). Again, because of the natural environment of uterus, *rahma* is also used for 'compassion' (48:29).

The Quran does not agree with the Christian notion of the Original Sin (which makes Man dependent upon God's 'mercy' for salvation). Therefore, the term *rahma* does not give the Quranic meaning if it is translated as 'mercy.'

Ribaa – Usury / Interest – from root *raa, baa, waow* (RBW)
Raba, yarbu – 'to increase, to grow' as in *le yarbu fi amwaalennaas* – '…so that people's wealth grows' (30:39); *rabat wa anbatat* - growth of vegetation (22:5); *raba assaveeq* (he added water to barley to make it swell); *zabadan raabiaa* – 'foam that mounts up to the surface (13:17); *akhza raabia* - extra-strong grip (69:10); *rabva* – raised ground, plateau (23:50); *rabbaituhu* – I fed and raised him (17:24); *arribaa* – extra, on top of the capital, interest (on loans, etc).

Sura *Aal-e-'Imraan*: '…*laa taakuloo arribaa az'aafan muzaa'afa...* - …Devour not usury, doble and multiplied… (3:129).

The Quran is at war with those who practice usury (2:278-279).

Rasool – Messenger (*Nabi* – Prophet) – from root *raa, seen, laam* (RSL)
Rislun really means for something to get all impediments to be able to move on; *naaqatun raslatun* (smooth-walking she-camel); *iblun maraaseel* (smoothly moving camels); hence, *rasool* is 'one who sets off'; *ar rasalu* (a group/herd); *ja'atel khail arsaala* (horses came in groups); *alirsaal* (sending); *ar rasool* (one who is sent to mankind by God, *mursal*, and also, the message, *risaala*, he brings).

The Quran calls messengers of God *rusul* (plural of *rasool*) as well as *ambiyaa* (plural of *nabi*); these are two facets of the same person – he is *nabi* because he receives the divine message and he is *rasool* because he relays it to people; every *nabi* had a Book (2:213), so did every *rasool* (57:25). Messengers of God were all human beings (18:110) and male (16:43, 12:109, 21:7). A messenger would be the very first convert [convinced of the truth of the Message] (2:285) and would be the first to enlist in the group organized to establish a Divine social system (40:66); he would follow and obey the Revelation (10:109, 6:50) and see that others, too, followed it (4:64); he would never demand obedience for his own person (3:78-79), only God's – therefore, obeying him was obeying God (4:80); a Messenger had no power to benefit or hurt even his own person (10:49); he expected no reward for his work (10:72); Messengers were family men (13:38) and appeared in important central towns (28:59); their brief was to convey the Message and not to force men to accept it (28:56); all Messengers died (3:143); one must accept the authenticity of *all* Messengers (4:150).

The phenomenon of Revelation ended with Mohammed (33:41); therefore, after his death the right path can only be found in the teachings of the Quran (7:158).

Rizq – Subsistence – from root *raa, zaa, qaa* (RZQ)
Rizq (everything beneficial or natural subsistence for sustaining life, such as rain; also, a steady income); *murtazeqa* (people who receive stipends); *razqa* (a soldier's ration); originally, it meant to give something at the appointed moment but later it came to mean any gift. In the Quran, *rizq ullah* is 'all food' (2:60), synonymous with *m'aaesh* (15:20); also, *rizq* is subsistence for the growth of human personality after death (22:58); therefore, *rizq* is everything that Man needs for sustenance in the earthly life as well as in the hereafter. It must be accessible to all universally (2:3). Since it is done by the Quranic society under Divine laws, God attributes it to Himself (6:152, 11:6, 17:31). The sources of *rizq* are available equally to all the needy (41:10); no one is allowed to monopolize them because Man only puts in labour to produce *rizq* – the raw material is already provided by Nature free (56:64-73). The Quranic society controls all produce under a system of fair distribution on the basis of need (2:219).

Rooh – Soul – from root *raa, waow, Haa* (RWH)
Raha (feeling and motion of air, a breeze); *ar rooh* (happiness, enjoyment,

bliss, expanse); *makaan roohaani* (nice and clean house); *ar reeh* (air); *ar reeha* (a part of air – plural *reeaah*); idiomatically, *ar reeh* is victory, domination, power, revolution and turns as in 8:46; *tarveeha* (rest and relaxation); *traaveeh* (special Ramadan prayers because of intervals for rest); *ar raveeha* (comfort following hard times); *raaha* (cattle coming back at dusk); *ar ravaah* (sundown to night); in 34:12, we find *ravaah* (evening travel) opposite *ghuduw* (morning travel).

Ar rooh - human soul/spirit, Divine Revelation (16:2, 17:85) and the Quran (42:52); *rooh al qudus* – 'The Holy Spirit' in the story of Jesus was the Biblical revelation he had received (2:87); or the Archangel Gabriel – *rooh al amen* (26:193, 16:102). In the creation of Man, God 'breathed into him of His spirit', which gave him self/personality/ego by providing him with 'ears, eyes and a mind' (32:9). This Divine Energy we get in an undeveloped form. The purpose of human existence is to develop that energy enough for it to survive into the next phase of life after death. The practical way to achieve that aim is to establish a socially just society under the guidance of Quranic principles, which are designed to inculcate in humans attributes of God (divine energy) albeit within human limitations. In general, human body develops by 'taking' while human soul develops by 'giving.' The aim of developing human soul for the hereafter is not to be achieved at the expense of the body in this life. However, in case of a tie between a material/physical (body) and a spiritual value, the latter is to be upheld.

Sabr – Perseverance – from root *saad, baa, raa* (SBR)
Sabr (commonly, but not exactly translated as 'patience') basically means 'to persevere, to work consistently to achieve; *assabeer* (cloud which hangs at the same spot all day; also, a mountain); *al asbera* (cattle which regularly return to their owner); *as sibaara* (a piece of metal or stone which stays put); *as saaboora* (a weight of clay/earth put on a boat in order to steady it); since such perseverance and hard work yields very good results, a heap of grain is *as subra*; therefore, *sabr* is on-going perseverance with steadfastness. Because of the aspect of motionlessness, the term also came to be used in the meaning of 'imprisonment.'

In the Quran, we find '...*fa maa asbarahum 'alan naar–*...Ah! What boldness they show for fire,' (2:175), meaning that 'they have the ability to endure the fire,' but may also mean 'what is it that helps them endure the fiery punishment?'; about Israelites, we find '*lun nasber 'ala ta'aamen waahed–*...we cannot remain on (the) one (same) food...' (2:61); '...*rabbanaa afregh 'alainaa sabran wa thabbet aqdaamenaa..–*...Our Lord! Pour out constancy on us and make our steps firm...' (2:250), where 'firmness of steps' explains what *sebr* is in the Quranic context; it is 'steadfastness' and 'perseverance.' In 3:145 we get the definition of *saabereen* (the steadfast): '...*fa maa wahanoo lemaa asaabahum fi sabeel Allah wa maa dza'ufoo wa maa ustakaanoo; wa Allah yuhibbus saabereen*' – 'but they never lost heart if they met with disaster in Allah's Way, nor did they weaken (in will) nor give in; and Allah loves those who are firm and steadfast (*assaabereen*). *Sebr* has also been used in the sense of 'waiting and being patient' in 18:68 and 49:5; Muslims are asked to 'seek (improvement) with perseverance and *salaa* -the divine code of life- as God is with *saabereen* (2:153).

Saleeb – The Cross – from the root *saad, laam, baa* (SLB)
As-sulb, as-saleeb (strong and sturdy) as in *huwa sulbun fi deenehi* (he adheres strongly to his ideology; *sallab* (he made it hard and strong); *as-sulb* (the backbone, the spine,- with plural *aslaab*, because it is strong); *as-salbu* (to crucify) because it involves the convict's back being put against the cross. The Quran clearly and categorically disagrees with the notion of Christ's crucifixion: *wa maa qataloohu wa maa salaboohu wa laaken shibbeha lahum* – They did not kill him nor did they crucify him; it was confused to them (4:157).

Shaitaan – Satan – from root *sheen, taa, noon* (ShTN)
Shatan (a well-woven rope); *bear shatoon* (a very deep well); anything far away is *shateen* or *shaaten*; *shatana* (he went far away); *shatan saahebhu* (he opposed his friend, went the opposite way); therefore *shaitaan* is 'one who is far away from God's bounties and a rebel who has digressed. To some it may have come from *shait* (to get burnt away); thus *shaitaan* is 'one who has a rebellious nature with a fiery temper.'
In the Quran, we find '..Satan is a rebel against (Allah) the Most Gracious' (19:44); when an angry Moses unintentionally killed a Copt, he said, 'This is a work of Satan..' (28:15); therefore, acting under blinding emotions is Satanism (12:5). Brute tribes of fiery and rebellious temperament are called *shayaateen* (21:82, 38:37).
Shaitaan also means 'a snake' or 'intense thirst' as in 38:41, 8:11 and 37:65).

Shirk – Polytheism – from root *sheen, raa, kaa* (ShRK)
Ashshirk has the basic meaning of 'joining together closely'; *shaaraktu fulaanan* (I joined him/her); *ishtarak al amr* (the matter got confused); *mushaaraka* (to become a partner); *fulaanun shareeku fulaan* (he/she is his/her partner in work, or become part of a family through marriage – pl. *shurakaa*).
Shirk, a special term in the Quran, means 'to accept the non-divine as equal partners of God, to accept man-made laws as equal to God-made laws. The Quran holds that the Universe is assailable by men, who are all equal. Only God is superior to Man; therefore, for Man to accept anyone except God superior to him is degrading to him; that is *shirk* (associating partners with God) – it does not affect God, only Man loses his dignity; hence it is the gravest crime (31:13) to be a *mushrik* (active noun with *mushrekoon* and *mushrekeen* as plurals); sectarianism is also *shirk* (30:31-32); a *muslim* and a *mushrik* are opposite poles (3:63).

Shukr – Gratitude – from root *sheen, kaa raa* (ShKR)
Ashshukr has the basic meanings of 'to be filled' and 'to express'; also, 'full

Part One: Chapter Three

and plenty; *shakerat annaaqa* the she-camel's udders filled with milk; *al-mishkaar* (an animal low on feed but high on milk yield); *shakerat ish shajara* (branches appeared on the tree); *ishtakeratis samaa* (it rained heavily); *shakara fulaan* (he was extremely generous); *shukr* on the part of Man is 'obedience of, and expression of gratitude to, God' whereas *shukr* on the part of God is 'to reward justly or excessively.'

In the Quran, '..*fa inn Allah shaakerun 'aleem* is 'God is that who knows all and rewards justly' (2:158); in 39:65-66, *shukr* is used opposite to *al-khaasereen* (the losers) whose efforts are rendered futile; in 14:5, *shakoor* (exaggerated form of shaker) is 'one whose efforts come to full fruition; *shukr* (to express and expose) has been used opposite *kufr* (to conceal, to suppress) in 14:7 – therefore, '..*washkurooli wa laa takfuroon*' in 2:152 means 'keep My bounties open (for all) and do not suppress them'; Muslims were told to 'keep exposed Allah's bounty if you obey Him alone' (16:114) because previous peoples suffered dire consequences like fear and hunger after they had started 'to conceal God's bounties' (16:112); *shukr* and *kufr* are used as opposites also in 76:3.

Siraat – Bridge? – from root *saad, raa, taa* (SRT)
Sarata – 'to swallow whole (without chewing), to gulp'; thus *siraat* is a long and sharp sword (because it 'swallows' what it strikes); also, 'a long, straight and clear path' (probably because wayfarers 'gulp' it, or vice versa.

To consider the Quranic expression of *as-siraat al-mustaqeem* (1:5) to mean 'a straight, narrow, sharp and precarious bridge spanning between this world and Paradise with Hell underneath' is erroneous. *Siraat* is 'a path' as it has been clearly used synonymously with *tareeq* (path) in 49:30.

Siyyaam – Fasting - from root *saad, waow, meem* (SWM)
It basically means to abstain, to stop or to hold oneself. Some of the derivatives are: *sawm* (fast), *saama* (he fasted), *siyaam* (fasts), *sayyaam* (one who fasts a lot), *saaem* (a male who fasts), *saaema* (a female who fasts), *masaam* (place to stop), etc. Some common uses of the expression are: *saam al maa* (the water stopped), *saama 'an en nikaah* (he did not marry), *saama an al kelaam* (he abstained from speaking), etc. Incidentally, in English the word used for this activity (fasting) is taken not for its meaning of *speed* but for another application of the word, i.e. *to be strong and resilient* as in acid-*fast* or stead*fast*.

(See a detailed discussion on this important Quranic concept in the chapter RITUALS IN ISLAM).

Tahaara – Cleanliness – from root *taa, haa, raa* (ThR)
At-tahaara is basically 'to clean, to remove dirt'; *taharahu* may be substituted with *taHarahu*, meaning 'to take away, to remove.' In the Quran, God said to Jesus, '..*wa mutahirruka min allazeena kafaroo* - ..I will clear thee (of the falsehoods) of those who blaspheme..' or '..I will take you away from those who reject (you)..' (3:55); *taaher* (clean and purified) with *mutahhra* its

69

exaggerated form; *tahoor* is something which is clean and cleanses others, e.g. rainwater is *maa un tahoora* (25:48). *Tahaara* is not only physical cleanliness but also mental and spiritual (5:41) and also 56:79. *Rajlun taaher uththiyaab* (a man with a clean and pure heart); therefore, *wa thiyaabaka fatahirr* (74:4) means 'keep your person free of all base notions and ideas.'

Talaaq – Divorce – from root *taa, laa, qaa* (TLQ)
Talaq ('he became free'); *talaqtil maraa min zowjehaa* ('the woman got free of her husband'); *atlaq al-aseer* ('the captive was freed'); *naaqatun taalequn* – an unbridled she-camel; *at-taaleqa* – a free-roaming she-camel; *at-talq* – deer/gazelle or she-camel (which is free in the wild); *lisaanun tulqun* – a sharp tongue; *mutlaq* – boundless, as opposed to *muqayyad* (limited).

In the Quran, we find *fan talaqaa* – they both set off (18:71); *wa antalaq al-malaa* – the chiefs spoke (rapidly); Moses said to God, *laa yantaliq lisaani* –'my tongue will not be fluently' (26:13).

(See a detailed discussion on this important Quranic concept in the chapter WOMEN, SEX and MARRIAGE).

Taqdeer – Destiny? – from root *qaa, daa, raa* (QdR)
Qadartush shai means 'I measured the thing'; *qadarash shai bish shai* is 'he measured the thing against the (other) thing': *qadartu 'alaihe s sowb* ('he made clothes according to his measurements); *qaddartu alaihesh shai* means 'I made measured changes to the thing'. Therefore, *taqdeer* basically means 'to make something according to a measure / standard.' Some examples of its derivatives are: *miqdaar* (a model, pattern, or a standard); *qadrun* (measurement such as volume, size, weight, etc); *haaza qadrun haaza* ('this is exactly like this'); *jaa' 'ala qadrin* ('he arrived according to the estimate'); *jaawaza qadrahu* ('he transgressed his limits'); *aqdar* (a horse which trots in a way that its hind hoofs exactly follow the spots made by the front hoofs); *al muqtadar* (the middle part of something –most probably because that is the most 'balanced' part). Since to make something exactly according to a set standard and specific measurements, one needs the ability, prowess and control, *qadrun* also means 'to have power and be in control', e.g. *qadartu 'alash shai* ('I had the power needed to change the thing according to my standard'); *maa lee 'alaika maqdura / maqdara / qudra* ('I don't have any control over you'); *qaader* (one who has power and control); *qadeer* (one who shapes things according to set standards); *qadr* (value; standard; guiding proportion; also: to assess and respect). When something is given with no consideration of measure, it carries a sense of plenitude. On the other hand, if it is done with careful measuring, it has an implication of shortage, e.g. *qadrun* (shortage); also, *qadr* (cauldron-a huge cooking pot) as in *qudooren r raasiyaat* ("cauldrons fixed") as in 34 : 13.

In the Quran, we find the following examples:

1 *fa qaddara hu taqdeera* - ordered them in due proportions (25:2)

2 *be qadrehaa* - according to its measure (13:17)

3 *wa kullu shaien'endohu bemiqdaar* - every single thing is with Him in (due) proportion (13:8)

Part One: Chapter Three

4 *zaaleka taqdeer ul 'Azeez al 'Aleem* - such is the judgement and ordering of (Him), the Exalted in Power, the Omniscient (6:96)
5 *qad j'al Allahhu le kulle shaien qadraa* - Verily, for all things has Allah appointed a due proportion (65:3)
6 *qaddarnaa bainakum al maut* -We have decreed death– ordered / apportioned) to be your common lot (56:60)
7 *innahu 'ala kulle shaien qadeer* - For he has power over all things (He has the control of ordering proportions for all things (41:39)
8 *be qadrem m'aloom* - in due and ascertainable measures (15:21)
9 *un taqderoo 'alaihem* - before you gain (control and) Power over them (5:34)
10 *yabsutu* - does provide (sustenance) in abundance, and *yaqdiru* - He straiten it (17:30)
11 *thumma je'at 'ala qadaren yaa Moosa* - Then didst thou come hither as ordained, O Moses (20:40)
12 *qaddara fa hadaa* - hath measured and granted guidance (87:3).

Qiaama – Judgment Day? – from root *qaa, waow, meem* (QWM)
Qaama, qiyaaman (to stand, to be balanced, to be established, to be persistent); *aqaama* (to balance and make upright). *Qawwaam* (provider of sustenance: 'Men are *qawwamoon* for women (4:34). The word *qiyaama* therefore means 'to stand up (suddenly) in a balanced way'. According to the Quran, this expression has been used for mankind to be resurrected in the Hereafter as well as a global uprising for a balanced life. (Also see the entry for *Aakher*, above).

Tasbeeh – Rosary or Endeavour? –from root *seen, baa, Haa* (SBH)
Sabhun (to swim); *sabaha binnahr wa finnahr sabhan wa sabaaha* (he swam in the stream); *as saabehaat* (boats); *as swaabeh* (horses, because they resemble swimmers in their movement); *assabbaah* (good swimmer); also, *sabhun* is 'to work hard a lot to make a living,' whereas *as sabhu* is 'to roam and tour the land'; therefore, *sabhun* means 'to strive diligently to the best of one's ability' just as 'to go rapidly through air or water' – idiomatically, for the motion of astral bodies through space; *subhaan Allah* is 'to obey God eagerly and earnestly,' so is *tasbeeh*; later on, *tasbeeh* came to be generally applied to worship, specifically to a string of rosary beads.

In the Quran, heavenly bodies are said to be 'floating speedily in their orbits' (36:40); Mohammed is told, 'You have a long day full of struggle' (73:7); 'all birds, aware of their routes, fly on [as if they were swimming]' (24:41); 'every creation in the Universe is earnestly busy in following God's Law' (57:1), e.g. angels (2:31) and thunder of clouds (13:13); Muslims are required to 'diligently keep busy in God's work day and night' (30:17, 33:42, 56:96).

Tauba – Repentance – from root *taa, waow, baa* (TWB)
Taaba, tauban, tauba, mataabaa (to return, to come back); if one takes a wrong

turn on a trip one has to return to the point and resume the journey on the original correct path; such a person is *taaeb*. Therefore, *tauba* is a concept involving taking practical steps to undo a wrong action and rectify a mistake. In the Quranic context, one must adhere practically to God's Law all the time. In case of transgression, one must *do* something to erase the ill effects of the wrong action and then resume following the Law. In that situation, God's Law cooperates with the *taaeb*. That is the sense of '*innal hasanaate yuzhibn assiyyaat* (11:114) – 'Verily, good deeds push the bad ones away.' Thus, people are *tawwabeen* (2:222) and God is also *tawwaab* (110:3).

Thawaab – Reward – from root *Thaa, waow, baa* (ThWB)
Thaaba, yathoobu, thowbaa – to return, to come back; *thaaba jismohu thowbaanan wa athaaba* (his body returned to its original condition after having been ill); *thaab alma* (the water returned to its original level); *bierun thayyeb* (a well which fills with water again); *thaaba bethowb* (to come back); *kullu raaj' thaaeb* ('all returners are thaaeb); *al-mathaaba* (the place for congregation, the meeting point); *thaab annaas* ('people gathered'); *atthowb* (fabric-pl. *thiyaab*, probably because the thread keeps returning during weaving); *thawwaab* (a fabric dealer); *thiyaab* is also taken to mean 'the personality' of the wearer – thus *fulaan danis athiyaab* means 'he has an awfully bad temperament'; *thaaba* is 'to gather' because it was an Arab practice to wave a piece of cloth to gather people; *tathweeb* is 'to gather people by calling out', therefore it is also used for the call *assalaatu khairun min annowm* in the dawn prayer.

In the Quran *thawaab al-aakhera* (3:144) is 'the return one gets in future or the Hereafter'; *thawaab adduniya* (3:147) is 'the return one gets in this earthly life'; this will be, among other things, in the form of distinctive symbols indicative of prominence such as gold bracelets, silken garments and raised thrones, etc. Therefore, *thawaab* of good deeds in this life is inheritance of power in the land (24:55) and of bad deeds bring bad results such as humiliation (83:36 and 3:152). Thus, *thawaab* is the natural outcome of actions both individual and collective. It follows that in *wa thiyaabaka fatahirr* (74:4), the Prophet was not told to 'keep your clothes clean' but was asked to 'maintain an exemplary elevated personality and temperament (see 11:5 and 71:7) and also to keep his movement free of bad elements and people.

Zabah – Slaughter – from root *zaa, baa, Haa* (ZBH)
Zabah or *yazbah* is 'to cut throat at front at joint of head and neck, to rent asunder'; *zabahathu al'abra* is 'tears choked him'; *attazbeeh* – deep slaughter; *azzibh* – the slaughtered.

The Quran has used *yuzabbhoon* synonymously with *yuqatteloon* as in 7:141. *Qatl* is not only 'kill' or 'murder' but also 'to degrade, to humiliate' (please see entry under QtL). Therefore, in 2:49 and others, when it is reported about the Pharaoh's practice of killing off the male Israelite babies and sparing the females – '*yuzabbhoon abnaakum wa yastahyuoon nisaakum* – it does not

Part One: Chapter Three

mean that all new-born Israelite boys were actually physically murdered by slaughtering – had that happened even for one generation, the Israelites would have been wiped out as a group in Egypt (we know there were thousands of Israelite males who emigrated with Moses in Exodus; Moses' own brother Aaron stands testimony to the fact that all male children were not literally killed off) – it means that state policies were such that Israelite males were rendered docile and servile enough not to be able to make any trouble for the government.

In Sura *Assaaffaat*, when Abraham's son is saved by God from being slaughtered by him, we find that the boy 'was saved for a great sacrifice – *wa fadainaahu be zibhin 'azdeem'* (37:107). Here, *zibh* is 'slaughter' or 'sacrifice' in an idiomatic sense meaning 'extremely hard times.' It refers to the harsh conditions Ishmael had to face when he left the fertile and scenic Palestine for the barren wilderness of Arabia for the noble mission of spreading the message of Monotheism.

(Zil)Qarnain – (of) Two Horns – from root *qaa, raa, noon* (QRN)
Al-Qarn - horn of an animal, the part of head where a horn is, the top of head; *al-qarn al-qowm* – chief of group; it has two basic meanings: 1) something that emerges forcefully, and 2) to join/combine together, as in 14:49; *al-qarn* – a period of time (generally, a century, but also a part thereof) – from this sense we have *al-qirn* (contemporary, as in 6:6), with *quroon* as plural; from 2) above we have *qurrenat al-usaara fil hibaal* ('the captives were bound together in ropes') as in *muqarraneen fil asfaad* (14:49) – 'shackled together in chains'; *qarn ush Shaitaan* (Satan's group/power); *aqrana lil amr* ('he had the ability to do/control over') as in *muqreneen* in 43:13; *al-qareen* (comrade, colleague) as in 4:38; *al-qareena* – wife.

Zil Qarnain (18:83), mentioned in Sura *Al-Kahaf* –'The Cave', is almost invariably taken by Western, as well as Oriental, authors to refer to Alexander the Great of Macedonia. Modern research, however, has suggested that it really refers to Cyrus the Great, the ancient Persian emperor and the two horns represent Media and Persia, the two vast empires he ruled over; in ancient Persia 'a horn' meant 'an empire'. About 150 years ago, archeologist discoveries in the area yielded a statue of Cyrus with two horns on its head like a ram (see *A History of Persia,* vol. 1, by Sir Percy Sykes). Cyrus was responsible for liberating the Israelites from their agonizing bondage of Babylon. From his base in Persia, he first marched towards the west conquering the lands up to Lydia in Asia Minor and reached the ocean where the Sun appears to be going down in the water (18:86). Then he marched eastward to Bactria (18:90). His third campaign was to the Caucasian mountains, where he constructed a barrier in the pass to protect the people from the barbarian hordes from the north (18:94). Cyrus was a follower of the great sage Zoroaster.

Part 2

The Quranic Islam

Chapter 4

MAN, GOD AND THE SUPERNATURAL

What is Man? Where has he come from? What is he doing here? What is his destiny? Is he alone in the Universe? What is the purpose of his life? Questions such as these have plagued mankind ever since *homo sapiens* saw the dawn of civilization. We are still trying to find satisfactory answers to these age-old queries and feel bewildered much like Ulysses of the Greek mythology. Of course, there have been several theories attempting to unravel the mysteries of human existence, creation of life and the force(s) operative behind all of it. Roughly, such theories may be classed, according to the Western mind, in two groups – religion and science. Most religions claim the process of creation to have been spontaneous with a pre-planned scheme as well as a future purpose. Scientists, on the other hand, believe in a gradual creation over long periods of time. For Science, it is difficult to see a conscious purpose and a planned end to creation. The universe and life itself are preferred to be explained in terms of Darwinian notions of evolution and natural selection through survival of the fittest.

4.1. IS THERE A GOD OR NOT?

The question of the existence of God is central to the topic of this chapter. The concept of God has been under debate for as long as human intelligence has lived. Whether to recognize and accept the existence of (a) God or reject and refute it has always been a daunting problem for humans; it is unresolved to the present day.[1] Philosophically, the question of God has been linked to Man's personality and his alienation from his very self.

> Thus the 'problem of God' is posed today as a feature of a more basic problem of human alienation and authenticity. The debate revolves around the following kind of questions – 'Is the presence of God constitutive of man's historical existence or destructive of it? In order that a man may exist, "stand forth" as a man in freedom and in human action, what is required – that he recognize and acknowledge the presence of God, as the Old and New Testaments say, or that he ignore and refuse God's presence, as the Revolution and the Theatre say? In order that people may exist, organized for action in history as a force to achieve historical destiny, what is required – that they disown God or own themselves to be his people? What is it that alienates man from himself – the confession of god's presence in history and in man's consciousness or the suppression of him from history and the repression of him from consciousness?'[2]

Historically, most men have believed in the existence of powerful beings ruling over and controlling their lives as is evident from earliest records of history, for example the god-kings of Babylon and Egypt. As human consciousness developed, the existence of God increasingly came under scrutiny resulting in its extreme form, the total denial. The rival and opposing notions of existence and non-existence of God have been in intense competition for acceptance by human intellect, at times quite fiercely. In modern times, non-believers have displayed subtle rejoice over 'the death of God.'[3] Psychologists have suggested that Revelation was nothing but voices inside a human brain.[4] Atheists have considered 'God' to be merely a projection of Man's mind.[5] Modern day socialist philosophers consider the idea of God and religion an emotional refuge and psychological sedation of the downtrodden:

> Religion is the sigh of the oppressed creature, the feelings of a heartless world, just as it is the spirit of unspiritual conditions. It is the opium of the people. [6]

Still others have come up with cosmic theories of gods really being extra-terrestrial intelligent life-forms from outer space. In the 1960's, a German writer by the name of Eric Von Daniken produced his thrilling work *Chariots of the Gods* in which he presented scientific data from historical accounts and archaeological finds to support his theory of 'gods' – really, intelligent beings, from outer space. Lately, there has been a renewed interest in this theory and some writers have dealt with it in greater detail and stronger conviction. It has been suggested that our solar system has a tenth planet by the name of Nabiru with an orbit of more than 3000 years. Inhabitants of that planet, far more advanced technologically than humans, descended on Earth about 2-3 orbits ago and genetically engineered the production of first human beings. They also oversaw the construction of giant atomic reactors for fission of water into hydrogen and oxygen – we know them as Egyptian pyramids. Currently the human race is passing through a hands-off phase till the gods from Nabiru visit us again, which may be when the planet next passes from close to Earth about 1,500 years from now.[7]

Arguments and counter-arguments have been presented from both sides. Ontologically, it has been said, 'if you understand what God is, you understand that he must exist.'[8] On the basis of this argument St. Anselm (c. 1033-1109), Abbot of Bec and later Archbishop of Canterbury defined God in his *Prologion* as 'something than which nothing greater can be conceived.'[9] But, St. Thomas Aquinas (1224/5-1274), in his *Summa Theologica*, rejected this argument thus: 'The existence of truth is in general self-evident, but the existence of a Primal Truth is not self-evident to us.'[10] Cosmologically, the theory of Cause & Effect states 'the Universe must have a cause as everything has a cause'. [11] In Muslim philosophy, prominent proponents of this argument have been men like Al-Kindi (9th century) and Al-Ghazali (11th century). But, this argument can be extended beyond God who must have had a cause. Teleologically, it has been said that 'there is an end or purpose in the world, so there is a designer – God.'[12] The secular counter-argument to this has asked if we know for certain of a purpose and end to the world; evolutionists have pointed out that, as it appears, life does not need an external designer. David Hume also objected and asked, 'How do we know what it was like to 'design' a world?'[13]

4.2. ATTRIBUTES OF GOD

In the domain of Religion, however, it appears that the real question is: What kind of a god is He? In other words, what attributes He possesses. As is evident from the dominant beliefs and practices of monotheistic systems (Judaism, Christianity and Islam) as well as polytheistic systems (such as Hinduism), the Supreme Being is intelligent, compassionate and a 'hands-on' God, i.e. He is constantly watching each and every human action, individual or collective, making spontaneous decisions depending upon the conduct of humans and affected by the intention and behaviour (worship and good deeds) of the humans concerned; He has a Grand Design for the Universe and an individual design for each and every one of us, which we, in our finite and limited capacity often do not understand – everything that happens is essentially good, even suffering. A Jewish religious leader, Rabbi Dan Cohn Sherbok, was reported in *The Daily Telegraph* (22.7.'95) to have commented on the Holocaust: 'We cannot fathom the working of God's plans.' Irenaeus, Bishop of Lyons (c.130-202) said,

> God chose to allow suffering and evil to exist in order to bring about a greater good – human freedom and the ability to have a relationship with God.[15]

Incidentally, the traditional Islamic philosophy takes a similar view. Allah, it is said, 'tests' (*yubla*) men with adversity:

> 'But sure We shall test you with something of fear and hunger, some loss in goods, lives and the fruits (of your toil), but give glad tidings to those who patiently persevere, - who say, when afflicted with calamity: "To Allah we belong and to Him is our return. They are those on whom (descend) blessings from their Lord, and Mercy, and they are the ones that receive guidance."'[16]

This view of Traditional Islam is not compatible with the Scripture. Hunger and fear are God's punishments for violating the Divine law (16:112). Why would God send punishment (hunger and fear) *before* a crime is committed? And secondly, why does God need to 'test' men? According to the Scripture and popular belief, He is All-Knowing; he already knows the capacity and capability of each one of His creation. This creates a logical as well as theological problem.

This problem stems from translating the terms *balaa* and *ibtelaa* as 'test.' Lexically, the two terms spring from the three-letter root *baa, laam, waow* (BLW) with the basic meaning of a) to find out, and b) to expose reality. In God's case, one cannot apply a) for reasons of his being All-Knowing. It is b) which is applicable here. *Balia* or *yablaa* means, for example, for fabric 'to become worn-out' so as to reveal its original condition.

Therefore, *balaa* means for a man's character and temperament to 'reveal its real colour', which may be bad like a worn-out fabric or good (as the original state of something is not necessarily bad). So, in the Quranic sense, adversity serves to bring out the best in men just as polishing an old metallic object restores it to its former glory rather than being an exercise to measure one's performance.

Human suffering has been traditionally glamorised by religion in general and monotheistic systems in particular. Buddhism simply accepts suffering and evil as facts of life and recommends that we realistically face them and try to minimize the effect with moral actions. In Hinduism, human suffering attains new theological heights in the form of Reincarnation, where an individual returns after death to earthly life in a lower form (a cat or a dog, for instance) if sins have been committed in the previous life. We are quite familiar with the pride of place suffering occupies in Christian philosophy where Jesus himself becomes the role-model by getting sacrificed for the sins of Man. One wonders if Christ's suffering was part of a grand Divine Plan. If it was, and Christ knew it, why did he have to utter his famous complaining line of *Ely, Ely, lemaaza sabaqtany* ('God, God, why have thou forsaken me?') on the Cross? Some may say that this last utterance shows the human side of Jesus. But, the orthodox dogma holds that He was not human, only God in human form. Also, this show of weakness is not a very good example for Christ's followers. Furthermore, the intriguing question remains: did God accept Jesus' sacrifice? Obviously not, because if He did, why do we still have so much misery and suffering around the globe?

The Quran's God is essentially a compassionately caring god (1:2); this notion is verbally repeated round the clock all over the Muslim world in the form of the very well-known utterance *b ism Allah, ar-Rahmaan, ar-Raheem* – 'With the name of Allah, the most Compassionate, the most Caring and Merciful' as a good-luck charm at the start of an action. Allah is a Being whose composition is beyond human comprehension as He is unique (42:11); there is nothing like Him – he is incomparable (112:1-4); He is the sole master of the Universe (12:39-40, 18:26), the All-Knowing (36:79), the Originator and the Creator of all things (2:117, 36:82), the Sustainer and Provider of all things (6:165), and of the entire Universe (1:1), and of mankind (114:1).

As we shall see later, He created Man and bestowed him with freedom of choice. But, since He does not want Man to hurt himself, Allah provided a system of Divine Guidance to be sent to mankind to follow if they so choose.

The Quran's God, far from being the deity given to bursts of anger and acts of vengeance in the form of severe punishment, is a legal god; He operates the Universe under permanent laws (33:27) – He even follows His laws strictly (6:12, 35:43) and consistently (33:62), and is tolerant (3:155, 42:25); He is everywhere [*huwa ma'kum aina maa kuntum* – 'He is wherever you are' (57:4); He is closer to man than his jugular vein (50:16) – yet, no vision can grasp Him (6:104).

In a nutshell, the Quran's God, by dint of being the cause, the originator, the sustainer, the provider, the law-giver, the maintainer, and the overseer of the Universe, is Nature itself.

4.3. CREATION OF MAN

Next to the existence and attributes of God is the issue of the origins of mankind. Adherents to Charles Darwin's Theory of Evolution hold that after life had started on Earth millions of years ago, it went through various evolutionary changes till the human species appeared around 200,000 years ago as a result of the twin principles of Natural Selection and Survival of the Fittest. Religion, in contrast, maintains the scenario of spontaneous, planned and deliberate creation of Man by God overseeing the work of His angels. Once Man had been born, naturalists believe, he learned by trial and error, slowly, gradually and painfully discovering the functioning of the universe around him and adapting to it. The religionists, on the other hand, hold that the Creator very compassionately decided to send down His guidance to mankind through his chosen agents, the prophets. Both the Bible (The Old Testament, Book of Genesis) and the Quran tell in very similar ways the story of Man's creation, his abode in Paradise and eventual Fall resulting in expulsion and the subsequent line of prophet-messengers. Some modern Muslim writers from the sub-continent – Syed Ahmed Khan, Inayatullah Khan Al-Mashriqi, and Ghulam Ahmed Pervez – have attempted to show that the Quranic account, when viewed in the light of the linguistic points discussed in (chapter 2, Part 1) of this work, show a marked departure from that of the Bible and is almost identical to the modern scientific evolutionary view of life and creation. Before discussing that a little later, I first wish to present the Quran's concept of the Universe and the Creator.

4.4. THE QURAN'S WORLD-VIEW

The Quran gives no specific time, or time-scale for that matter, for the creation of the Universe. It does, however, report *how* and *why* it was created by describing various stages as well the purpose and end of it. The Universe was created out of nothing, i.e. it came into being from a state of non-being:

> 'The Originator of the heavens and the earth: when He decreeth a matter, he saith to it: "Be," and it is.'[17]

It was created in six stages complete with planets such as the Sun and the Moon (10:3-6). Creation is an on-going evolutionary process:

> '...It is He who beginneth the process of creation and repeateth it...'[18]

Other planets, multiple in number, were created and are revolving in their respective orbits:

> 'And We have made, above you, seven tracts, and We are never unmindful of Our Creation.'[19]

In the beginning, the Universe was one gaseous mass from which various astral bodies were created:

> 'Do not the Unbelievers see that the heavens and the earth were joined together before we clove them asunder...?'[20] (and) '...the sky had been smoke...'[21]

The Universe is terminal and has a fixed period of existence:

> 'Seest thou not that Allah merges Night into Day and He merges Day into night; that He has subjected the Sun and the Moon (to His Law), each running its course for *a term appointed*...?[22]
> (my emphasis)

Life originated in water:

> '...We made from water every living thing...'[23]

Later, various life-forms and species were gradually developed:

> 'There is not an animal on the earth, nor a being that flies on its wings, but forms communities like you. Nothing have We omitted from the Book...'[24]

Man originated from non-living matter:

> 'Among His Signs is that He created you from dust; and then ye are men scattered.'[25]

Man was created from a unitary cell:

> 'O mankind! Fear your Guardian Lord, who created you from a single Person, created out of it his mate, and from them twain scattered countless men and women...'[26]

Thereon began Man's evolutionary journey which will take him beyond this earthly existence:

> 'It is He who produced you from a single soul; then there is a resting place and a repository...'[27]

Thereafter, Man travelled through evolution by sexual reproduction instead of asexual:

> 'And of everything We have created pairs...'[28]

Human existence does not end with the physical life on the earth; the trail of evolution does not dry up here; it goes on:

> 'You shall surely travel from stage to stage.'[29]
> 'They say: "What! When we are reduced to bones and dust, should we really be raised up *a new creation*?'[30] (my emphasis)

That means there will be life *after* death:

> 'The Day that We roll up the heavens like a scroll rolled up for books; - even as We produced the first Creation, so shall We produce a new one...'[31]

Now, to the creation of Man:

4.5. THE STORY OF 'ADAM'

Both in the Judeo-Christian and Islamic philosophy there is a widespread belief that 'Adam' refers to a single person, in fact the very first human individual ever created. Muslims also firmly hold the notion that Adam was also the first messenger of God to humanity. The accounts of the creation of the first man, both in *The Old Testament* (Book of Genesis) and the extra-Quranic authentic literature of early Islam, endorse this view.

In the Quran, however, we get a different picture. Throughout the Muslim holy book, there is only one location which gives the impression that there was a prophet by the name of Adam (3:33). Save for this solitary location, the Quran appears to have used the term 'Adam' synonymously with 'mankind.' As such, it should be written with the first letter in the lower case – adam – meaning 'man.' This view is supported by the fact that, at most places, the Quran has employed the *plural* form of verbs in connection with Adam. It will hopefully be made clearer by the time we finish the story of the creation of 'Adam' from the Quranic perspective.[32]

In the Quran, as has been claimed by some modern writers on Islam, the emergence of Man on the evolutionary stage has been narrated allegorically in the form of a parable. It appears in 2:30-39, 7:19-25 and 20:120-121 among other locations. Following is the conventional translation by A Yousuf Ali with its possible interpretation from the Quranic perspective.

> 'Behold, thy Lord said to the angels: "I will create a vicegerent on earth." They said: "Will thou place therein one who will make mischief therein and shed blood? – whilst we do celebrate Thy praises and glorify Thy holy (name)?" He said: "I know what ye know not." (2:30)

Almost universal among writers – Muslims and non-Muslims alike – is the assertion that Man is *God*'s vicegerent on Earth. For instance, Watt thinks that in verse 2:30, God'…made Adam *his* khalifa on earth.' [33] This appears to be erroneous. God does not need a vicegerent on earth because He is omnipresent and omnipotent; His power and rule are never suspended. The term *khaleefa* literally means 'successor' (one who follows, or comes after, or replaces); Man is the successor of species *previous* to him on the trail of organic evolution. Furthermore, the verse in question does not say *khaleefaty* ('My successor') or *khaleefatenaa* ('Our successor') or *khaleefat Allah* ('God's successor'). A successor to (one who comes after and thus replaces) God is inconceivable.

As we have seen above, life on earth, travelling on the evolutionary path, came to the point when it was time for the next species – the humans – to appear. All previous creation (which included 'angels')[34] had been following Nature's commands instinctively and had no ability to go against natural laws (3:82, 13:15, 16:48-50) but this new species was to be given the attribute of 'freedom of choice' and 'free will' (76:3) by giving him tools to acquire knowledge and think (90:8-10) and express himself through speech (55:3-4) and writing (96:4-5).[35] The most probable outcome of this change would have been a clash of Nature and Man's novel faculty, resulting in mischief and bloodshed. In 15:29, we find the source of this human faculty of free will when God 'breathes' into Man 'of My Spirit'; this Divine energy bestowed Man with his attributes and faculties exclusive of all other creatures on Earth. That is why the Quran claims that Man has been moulded in the 'best of mould' (40:64, 64:3, 95:4) and is 'the best of *most* of the created' (17:70).

> 'And He taught Adam the names of all things; then he placed them before the angels, and said: "Tell Me the names of these if ye are right." (2:31)
> They said: "Glory to Thee: of knowledge we have none, save what Thou hast taught us: in truth it is Thou who art perfect in knowledge and wisdom." (2:32)
> He said: "O Adam! Tell them their names." When he had told them their names, Allah said: "Did I not tell you that I know the secrets of heaven and earth, and I know what ye reveal and what ye conceal?" (2:33)

God (Nature) provided Man (Adam) with the ability to learn *asmaa* (names) [35], i.e. the capacity to obtain knowledge. This faculty again is unique to Man in the animal world as well as Nature (even 'angels' do not possess it; 'they' know only what Nature lets them know and they do whatever they have been programmed to do [66:6]; they never defy Nature [16:49]).

> 'And behold, We said to the angels: "Bow down to Adam." And they bowed down; not so *Iblees* 36; he refused and was haughty: he was of those who reject.' (2:34)

By dint of the unique faculty of gaining knowledge, Man can learn how Nature and its forces ('angels') work; consequently, he can harness the forces of Nature and subjugate them to his service. But, there is one natural force which does not automatically fall under Man's control – he must learn to do it and work harder at it – and that is the negative and rebellious side of his own self. 37

Iblees is symbolic of Man's fiery defiant make-up in more ways than one. The Quranic parable tells us that, upon his refusal to bow down to Man, God asked, '… "What prevented thee from prostrating when I commanded thee?" He said: "I am better than he: Thou didst create me from fire, and him from clay" (7:12). Here, using his faculty of free will, Satan defies Nature with an air of arrogance based upon a false notion of superiority by origin. At that, he was deprived of life's bounties: "(Allah) said: "Then get thee from here, for thou art rejected, accursed" (15:34). "And the Curse shall be on thee till the Day of Judgment" (15:35). In other words, Man's negative attitude towards God's Law causes him to be deprived of good in life.

Now, the fiery Satan displays depression and disappointment by shifting responsibility from his free will to his natural disposition and blames God for his defiance – "*Rabbe aghwaytani* – Lord! Thou hast put me in the wrong…" (15:39). 38

The Devil asked for respite till 'the day they (men) are raised up (7:14) and was given it (7:15) 39. He left with a challenge to Man's ability to control his own unbridled emotions and base animalistic sentiments as long as Man lives:

> "…I will lie in wait for them on Thy Straight Way: then will I assault them from before them and behind them, from their right and their left: nor will Thou find, in most of them, gratitude (for Thy mercies)" (7:16-17).

God accepted the arrangement knowing fully *how* Man's devilish and satanic side was going to lead him astray from the Divine way:

> '(Allah) said: "Go thy away; if any of them follow thee, verily Hell will be the recompense of you (all) – an ample recompense. And arouse those whom thou canst among them with thy (seductive) voice, make assaults on them with thy cavalry and infantry; mutually share with them wealth and children; and make promises to them." But Satan promises them nothing but deceit.' (17:63-64)

However, men who follow God's law would not fall prey to the Devil:

> '"As for my servants, no authority shalt thou have over them;" Enough is thy Lord for a Disposer of affairs.' (17:65)

Thus began mankind's tenure on Earth.

> 'And We said: "O Adam! Dwell thou and thy wife in the garden; and eat of the bountiful things therein as (where and when) ye will; but approach not this tree, or ye run into harm and transgression.' (2:35)

At the dawn of human social life on Earth population was scant and land vast and fertile; therefore there was no scarcity of subsistence. Since private ownership of land did not exist, people could obtain food from anywhere and wherever possible and whenever they required. Hoarding of food was unknown because subsistence meant to meet one's needs not deprive others through private ownership and hoarding. That early life on Earth was Man's paradise:

> "There is therein (enough provision) for thee not to go hungry nor to go naked; nor to suffer from thirst, nor from the Sun's heat" (20:118, 119).

But, Man/Adam was warned at the outset about the Devil (Man's own negative attributes, such as greed and selfishness) who had vowed to distract mankind from the Straight Path:

> 'Then We said: "O Adam! Verily, this is an enemy to thee and thy wife: so let him not get you both out of the Garden, so that thou art landed in misery" (20:117).

The biggest devilish pitfall to be avoided was to destroy the unity of mankind – men originally *were*, and are meant to be, but one nation: 'Mankind was but one nation, but differed (later)...' (10:19) – and branch off into groups in the manner of a tree which has branches with a common original base.[40]

> 'Then began Satan to whisper suggestions to them, in order to reveal to them their shame that was hidden from them (before): he said: "Your Lord only forbade you this tree lest ye should become angels or such beings as live for ever."'
> 'And he swore to them both that he was their sincere adviser.'
> 'So by deceit he brought about their fall:...' (7:20-22)

The human satanic characteristics of greed and selfishness soon made men lose their original blissful state of existence; it was the natural and logical consequence of *mushaajera* (meaning intra-group clashes, rivalries and tussles – the Arabic word is a derivative of *sha jar a* [a tree]). Men's own ulterior motives had them wrongly believe that their permanent welfare and real power actually lay in disunity. Their myopic vision showed them that they could live 'for ever' through their individual progeny, which would otherwise be lost in the sea of humanity if men continued to live as one global family.[41]

> '...when they tasted of the tree, their shameful parts became manifest to them, and they began to sew together the leaves of the Garden over their bodies. And their Lord called unto them: "Did I not forbid you that tree, and tell you that Satan was an avowed enemy unto you?"' (7:22)

Thus, when Man realized his folly (because the consequences of his greed and unwise attitude were manifested), he was embarrassed and attempted clumsily to 'cover up' his actions with flimsy excuses and justifications.

> 'They said: "Our Lord! We have wronged our own souls: If Thou forgive us not and bestow not upon us Thy Mercy, we shall certainly be lost."' (7:23)

However, noteworthy is Man's response to God's rebuking rhetorical question ("Did I not ...") in 7:22. In contrast to the Devil's arrogance, Man accepted responsibility for his actions and sought ways of rectifying his mistakes. But, the damage had been done.

> 'Then did Satan make them[42] slip from the (Garden), and get them out of the state (of felicity) in which they had been. And We said: "Get ye down[43], all (ye people), with enmity between yourselves; on Earth shall be your dwelling place and your means of livelihood – for a time."' (2:36)

There is an interesting academic point worthy of our notice in 2:36. The Arabic text for 'then they (were made to) slip' uses the pronoun *humaa* ('both') as suffix to *azalla* ('misled'), meaning thereby that *both* Adam and his (female) partner were guilty of the slip.

This stands in contrast to the Biblical account according to which the Devil misled Eve who in turn misled Adam into sinning. Because of this 'misbaviour', and also because of the Biblical account of the creation of Eve (Genesis, *The Old Testament*), traditional Christianity has looked down upon woman. St. Paul advised unmarried women to follow his example and stay single, saying: 'Man has not come out of woman; woman has come out of man. He has not been created for her, she has for him. Woman should attend church in silence; they are not permitted to speak. According to law, they are inferior to men. If they need to know something, they should ask their husbands when they are back in their homes. It is degrading for a woman to speak inside a church.' Women may not enter Paradise because, according to St. Hivonymus, 'Woman is the Devil's door, path of vices and scorpion's sting.' [From *Woman in Antiquity* by Charles Seltman, as in the Urdu work *Mataaleb ul Furqaan* by G A Pervez (1976), Idara Tolu-e-Islam, Lahore, Pakistan].

It is only fair to put on record that the situation is not very different in traditional Islam. A Tradition, on the authority of Ibn Abbas, has been quoted in the classical work of exegesis (*tafseer*) by Ibn Kathir:

Part Two: Chapter Four

After Iblees had been reproached by showing him how knowledgeable Adam was, he (Adam) was put to slumber and Eve was created from his left rib. Waking up, Adam felt attracted to her because she was his own flesh and blood. Then she was wedded to him and they were told to take up residence in Paradise.

Another Tradition by Ibn Masud and Ibn Abbas and others says:

After Iblees' expulsion, Adam started abode in Paradise but was lonely. Therefore, while he slept, Eve was created out of his rib. Waking, he asked her, "Who are you and why have you been created?" Eve said, "I am a woman and have been created to keep you company and give you pleasure."

Still another authentic Tradition reports:

Woman has been created out of a rib. The top-most rib is the most crooked; therefore, if you try to straighten it, you will break it; if you wish to have some benefit from it, you can do it with the crookedness still there.
[From *Mataaleb ul Furqaan* by G A Pervez].

Thus mankind was deprived of the original blissful existence, realized the error in judgement due to succumbing to temptation, accepted responsibility for the fateful action and started efforts to rectify the blunder. But Man knew very little so he started to learn to live with the new situation.

'Then learnt Adam from his Lord certain words and his Lord turned towards him; for He is Oft-Returning, Most Merciful.' (2:37)

In this way began mankind's journey on Earth towards their end. During this earthly physical existence, men have to constantly battle against satanic and devilish forces of greed and selfishness on the part of their fellow men in the quest to regain the lost Paradise. The entire recorded history seems to be nothing more than the story of this eternal quest. The Lord's 'words' (*kalemaat*–singular, *kalema*) is the divine guidance which God promised and duly sent to mankind through his chosen messengers (7:158, 6:116, 10:64, 18:27). Man was told:

'We said: "Get ye down all from here; and if, as is sure, there comes to you Guidance from Me, whosoever follows My Guidance, on them shall be no fear,[44] nor shall they grieve.
'But those who reject and belie Our Signs, they shall be Companions of the Fire; they shall abide therein.' (2:38-39)

It is significant that in this verse, and several others, fear (*khowf*) has been said to be a negative situation which can be avoided by following God's Law, but traditionally the image of Allah (the Quran's God) has been of a fearsome deity. True that in some Quranic verses Muslims have been asked to 'fear God,' but generally, Allah is not to be feared. Fear is a negative feeling and is to be avoided. One of the main features of Paradise is absence of fear. This popular notion of 'Allah's fear' comes from several verses in which the term *taqwa* has been translated as 'fear' (for instance, see Yousuf Ali's rendering of verse 5:2). Most Western writers have been simply following the trend. Professor H A R Gibb, for example, in his *Islam* (1975, Butler and Tanner, London) presents a fearsome picture of the Quranic God:

> "(He) 'misleads whom He will and guides whom He will' (lxxiv, v. 34). Man must live in constant fear and awe of Him, and always be on his guard against Him (such is the idiomatic meaning of the term for 'fearing God' which runs through the Koran from cover to cover), yet he is bidden to adore Him, to magnify and praise Him, and even to commemorate His Name."-
> (p. 38; Chapter 4, Doctrine and Ritual in the Koran)

This misconception (slight confusion and bewilderment on Gibb's part), results from taking *taqwa* as 'fear.' Lexically, the term springs from the three-letter root *waow, qaa, yaa* (WQY) with the basic meaning of 'to safeguard, to protect.' *Waqa al fars min al hafaa* – 'the horse treads carefully to protect its hoofs'; *sarjun waaqen* is 'a saddle which is just right and safe for the horse.' In the Quran, it has been used in the same sense, i.e. 'to protect oneself against damage, to safeguard', and the way to do that is to align oneself with the Law of God (3:101, 13:37, 38:28, etc).

4.6. HUMAN NATURE

Before we leave the subject of the origins of mankind, and move on to what happens next, it seems desirable to consider one important point – human nature (man's instinctive behaviour). It is a popularly held belief and commonly accepted dogma that there is a set pattern of human behaviour in certain situations, which can be applied universally to the whole of mankind as a species. In other words, there are some situations to which, under similar conditions, every human being is most likely to respond in more or less the same way.

However, a closer examination of the human behaviour does not entirely endorse this view. A universal human response pattern does seem to exist as far as the physical body is concerned, but socially people, individuals as well as groups, have been known to respond differently, at times contrastingly, to the same situation. Even the same individual/group may, and does, react differently to the same situation at different times; our recorded history stands testimony to that fact. Nearly all human social behaviour is learnt. That is why we see a variety of moral standards and codes of ethics being adhered to throughout history around the globe. One man's conscience differs from that of his neighbour – even his brother or sister – as does one group's from that of another. Let us see the Quran's verdict on this important issue.

In Arabic, the term 'Nature' (the superhuman forces which control the Universe) is translated as *fitra*.[45] The linguistic root of this term is *faa, taa, raa* (FTR) with the basic meaning of 'to rent, to tear, to force open for the first time.' It is reported by Ibn Abbas that he overheard two Bedouin Arabs quarrelling over a water-well, claiming control by asserting '*anaa fatartuhaa* – I started digging it up first.' Also, a quotation by Ibn al A'raabi reports that '*anaa awwalu man fatara haaza*' means 'I am the one (who) initiated this.'[46] It is in this sense of initiation and pioneering that the Quran calls God *faater essamaawaate wal ard* (the Beginner of heavens and earth) in, for instance, 6:14. Another expression for the same is *badee' ussamaawaate wal ard* (9:102); the sense of producing/doing for the very first time is very clear in '*fatarakum awwal marra* – created you (all) for the first time' (17:51). Therefore, *fitra* is 'Nature's original law of creation.'[47] Thus *fitra* is also the source of mankind and all the human characteristics and attributes (instinctive behaviour) at the animalistic level. At that most basic level, the most important, and by far the only, natural instinct Man possesses is preservation of life. Beyond that, almost all human behaviour is learned and acquired. That is the reason we find such an incredibly broad spectrum of social conduct by men across history, ranging from brute barbarism to saintly selflessness. The Quran holds the view that Man is not capable of finding the Truth easily without the help of Divine Guidance, in the absence of which the baser (satanic/devilish) elements of human personality take over.[48] Obviously, God cannot be conceived as having such undesirable attributes. Thus the general misconception about human nature, which is popularly based upon verse 30:30, can be cleared in the light of our discussion above:

> 'So set thou thy face being upright, the nature in which Allah has made mankind: no change (there is) in the work (wrought) by Allah: that is the true Religion: but most among mankind know not.'

The verse refers to God's original law of creation of the universe, which served as a model for the creation of Man in terms of its originality and permanence; so, Muslims are asked to follow only God's law. Its practical aspects are elaborated in the verse that follows:

> 'Turn ye in repentance to Him, and fear Him, establish regular prayers, and be not ye among those who join gods with Allah.' (30:31) [49]

4.7. WITHER MAN?

As we have seen, according to the Quran, man is composed of two component parts – body and (conscious) self. He was created a long, long time ago. In the beginning, he lived a peaceful and happy life. Then, his own negative characteristics took the better of him and mankind splintered into quarrelling rival groups. This state of affairs continues to this day. In this earthly life, Man is constantly trying to re-create the original paradisiacal society. All this while, he is also seeking, and getting, assistance from the forces of Nature which run this Universe (angels); he can harness them and get them to serve him. But, according to the Quran, creating a utopia is not an end in itself; it is a means to an end. It is to develop the human self [the divine energy breathed into him to the exclusion of all other life-forms – also called personality, ego or consciousness – the Quran calls it *nafs* (91:7)] enough so that it is able to transfer itself to the next stage of existence on the evolutionary ladder. Life does not end with death; it goes on (23:16) because life is going through continuing evolution (84:19) and, that is why, life on this Earth is a temporary stay for mankind (6:98). Man's *self* has endowed him with the characteristic of FREE WILL (76:3). The 'self' or *an-nafs* is capable of going into the next evolutionary stage of life, where there will be no more (physical) death (37:58.59), if it is developed during this earthly life through *anfaaq* (64:16).50 At the end of this transitory life, Man crosses the threshold of *death* to cross over to the next phase of existence.

4.8. DEATH AND THE HEREAFTER

Everyone has to face death; no one escapes it (3:184). The Quran mentions *two* lives and *two* deaths for man (2:28).51 No one comes back to this life (23:99, 100).52 The living cannot communicate with the dead (27:81). Once the body dies, it starts to decompose. That is why it is disposed of in various ways such as burial and cremation. The burial place – grave – is *qabr* in Arabic. Since it was the traditional way of burial among the Arabs at the time, it has been mentioned in the Quran.53 There is no preferred or recommended way of disposal of a dead body mentioned in the Quran. Therefore, it can be inferred that any method deemed fit by the Quranic government will be the Islamic way. It is a widespread belief in the Muslim world that, once buried, a corpse is visited by angels, brought back to life and interviewed. Depending upon the result of the interview, the dead person starts receiving reward or punishment, which continues till the Day of Judgement (Resurrection). This view is erroneous and has no basis in the Quran. Reward or punishment in the grave is not possible because, according to the Quran, the dead will be raised on the Day of Judgement:

> 'After that, at length ye will die.
> Again, on the Day of Judgement, will ye be raised up.' 54

Furthermore, why should those *not* buried in graves (cremated or drowned) escape this Divine procedure?

The physical body decomposes and disintegrates but the *self* goes on into the next phase of life (stage of evolution) if, as we have said above, it had been developed enough in this life according to the laws of the Quran, such as *anfaaq* (39:42, 64:16). A *developed* self will go to Paradise and will have no more death. It will 'live' forever: '"Is it (the case) that we shall not die, except our first death....?" [55] An *undeveloped* self will be banished to Hell, where it too will stay forever: 'But those who reject (Allah) – for them will be The Fire of Hell: No term shall be determined for them, so they should die.......' [56]

An important point to note here is that, from the Quranic perspective, we, in our present state of existence *cannot* conceive what life is like in the Hereafter: 'Now no person knows what delight of the eye are kept hidden (in reserve) for them ...' [57]

Therefore, the accounts of Paradise and Hell given in the Quran are *examples* of them in a figurative sense. Furthermore, Man 'enters' *janna* (Paradise) or *jahannum* (Hell), as a consequence of his deeds right here in this physical, 'earthly' life. This happens when Man creates a good society according to the Quran (*janna*) or a bad society by rejecting it (*jahannum*): [58]

> '....and for a Garden whose width is that (of the whole) of the heavens, and the *earth*......'[59]   (my emphasis)

The followers of God's Law – *'Ibaad Allah* – create the fountains of *janna:*

> 'A fountain where the Devotees of Allah do drink, making it flow in unstinted abundance.' [60]

And above all,

> 'The parable of the Garden which the Righteous are promised! Beneath it flow rivers: perpetual is the fruit thereof and the shade therein: such is the End of the Righteous; and the End of Unbelievers (Rejecters) is the Fire.' [61]

It is the same with HELL: '.....they are themselves but fuel for the Fire.' [62]

Its fire engulfs human feelings:

> '(It is) the Fire of Allah kindled (to a blaze), which doth mount (right) to the Hearts.' [63]

Also, such will be the feeling of anxiety, misery and depression that:

> 'Who will enter the Great Fire, in which he will then neither die nor live.' [64]

And worse:

> '....Death will come to him from every quarter, yet will he not die...' [65]

4.8. THE DAY OF JUDGMENT

The belief is that, at some point in the future, there will be a precise moment of time when God will roll up the heavens and earth – in fact, the entire Universe -, and bring back to life *all* mankind ever created and hold court to punish and reward men according to their deeds committed during life on earth; it is the Day of Judgment. In Islamic eschatology, it is popularly known as *al-qayaama*, [66] among other names, such as *al-haaqa* (69:1), *al-qaare'a* (101:1) and *as-saa'a* (22:57). Traditional Islamic literature abounds, with great details, in Prophetic sayings and other reports about that momentous occasion. From the Quranic perspective, however, we have seen that Man will not retain his current physical form after death. How different the post-death existence will be from the earthly form is not comprehensible for mortal men during their pre-death life (32:17) and all the accounts of Hell and Paradise in the Quran are simply metaphorical (13:35); so, it appears, are the accounts of the Day of Judgment. What is certain, however, is that mankind can create hellish or paradisiacal societies for themselves entirely out of their choice and resultant of their deeds (please refer to the Glossary for the etymology of *janna* and *jahannum*). It appears that the Quranic term *al-qayaama* refers to a universal uprising of man for the abolition of age-old exploitative institutions and establishing a just system of universal social welfare. It will be the era of the great showdown when the downtrodden and the meek will reach the end of their tether and stand up to defy the oppressive minority of the powerful ruling class. It will be the colossal clash of the have-nots to reclaim their due rights from the haves. Man will overturn the old selfish systems based upon wrong man-made principles and put in place the just and right programmes of providence and justice for all based upon God-given values. In the process, mankind will undergo a time of great upheaval because it is hard work uprooting millennia-old established systems:

> 'On the Day We shall remove the mountains and thou will see the earth as a level stretch, and We shall gather them, all together, nor shall We leave out any of them (18:47);
>
> '...a Day whereon men will be like moths scattered about.'(101:4);
>
> 'On that Day will men proceed in groups sorted out, to be shown the deeds that they (had done)' (99:6);
>
> '...That Day there will be for you no place of refuge nor will there be for you any room for denial (of your sins)!' (42:47);

Just and fair social and judicial systems will be established:

> 'The balance that Day will be true (to a nicety)...' (7:8);
>
> 'That Day will every soul be required for what it earned; no injustice will there be that Day...' (40:17);

Everything will take on a new form in a different light:

> 'One day the Earth will be changed to a different Earth, and so will be the Heavens..' (14:48)

That era will usher in a new dawn:

> '...the Day when hearts and eyes will be turned about...' (24:37);

In short,

> '...the Earth will shine with the light of its Lord...' (39:69).67

4.9. PRE-DESTINY

Last, but by no means the least important of supernatural issues, are the questions: Is Man's destiny pre-determined? Or, he is the master of his own destiny? Is he a mere pawn on Nature's chessboard, or he possesses the faculty of decision-making for himself? Are events – physical as well as social – predictable? Is everything that happens in this world pre-determined? Did God, at the dawn of Creation, decide what was going to happen in the human social world? Has He a definitely irrevocable plan for each and every individual? If it *is* pre-decided, can we change our destiny? Are we inescapably bound to our fate? Can we know what lies in store for us? How does prior knowledge of our destiny affect us? Questions such as these have nagged Man ever since he began conscious logical thinking. Let us try to find some answers from the Quran's viewpoint, but first allow me to briefly present the popular concept of pre-destiny.

The overwhelming majority of religious-minded people in general, and that of Muslims in particular, holds the following view. At the moment of Creation, God laid down the rules which were to govern the operation of the Universe. He also decided the chronology, the timing and the manner of each and every event that was to take place till eternity (the end of the Universe). He also decided the actions and behaviour of each and every individual product of His creation – non-living matter, the living beings and, of course, Man. A very popular statement in Urdu says: 'Not even a leaf stirs without His permission.' Many hold the belief that God alone has the authority to allocate *rizq* (sustenance): that is why we see so much disparity in the distribution of wealth.68

Some believe that one's pre-destiny can be changed through extensive prayers,69 good deeds 70 and exalted intermediaries like saints. 71 It is all a matter of pleasing God either by individual action/pleas or influencing His decisions through someone.

Many also believe that only the major events in one's life are pre-determined (such as marriage 72 and education) but not the minor steps leading to a particular major event. That, they say, is the demarcating line between Man's freedom of choice and his pre-decided destiny. It is believed that each and every individual is subtly taken through life being driven willy-nilly to one's destiny by the invisible hand of Fate. This view raises a number of intriguing questions.

The afore-mentioned view obviously clashes with the concept of a universally just and fair God. It does not adequately explain why God lets innocent and helpless beings like children suffer in poverty and disease. Why is the West fabulously prosperous while much of Africa, Asia and South America are dirt poor? What infinite Divine wisdom decreed the Jewish nation to be downtrodden and homeless for two thousand years? Why is the world's wealthiest nation (the US) next door to one of the poorest (Mexico)? Why has Kashmir been denied liberty so far while East Timor has been granted the same? Why are the Palestinians still stateless while Israel is a well-established state? Why do we see 'good' people suffer and 'bad' thrive? Why were Muslims a superpower a millennium and a half ago but not now? Why are some individuals born deformed and diseased? If one's destiny is unchangeable, why do we at all try to get it changed? Why do we pray and beseech God when we are in the doldrums? Above all, if we are mere instruments in the grand machinery of Fate, why should God punish or reward us for our actions? After all, we are only following God's intended programme, are we not?

Let us try to see if the Quran can answer questions like these.

There are a number of words in Arabic to express 'fate' or 'destiny', but the most common is *taqdeer*. Readers will do well to refer to the Glossary for a detailed etymology of the term and other derivatives of the three-letter linguistic root QdR; I have also supplied examples of its usage in the Quran. It should become obvious that *taqdeer*, according to the Quran, is not pre-deciding what actions an individual or a group will take in future simply because the notion clashes with the idea of the human faculty of free will as we have discussed earlier in this chapter. It is Nature's pre-determination of its laws and their outcome. God has ordained certain standards and measures for the functioning of the Universe. For instance, it is pre-determined for water to solidify at 0° C and vaporise at 100° C; for fire to burn and scorch and for the Earth to exert gravitational pull, and so on so forth. In the physical world of living matter (plants, animals and humans), Nature has similarly ordained their *taqdeer* – some animals are herbivores, some are carnivores while Man is omnivore. The Sun, the Moon and all the other astral bodies are likewise bound to their respective *taqdeer* – their natural life spans and their properties. But, as has been mentioned before, Man is different from the rest of Creation in having the freedom of choice:

> 'Say, "The Truth is from your Sustainer; let him who will, be convinced, and let him, who will, reject.' (18:29)

Nonetheless, it is to be noted that men are free to choose an action but they must bear the naturally ordained and pre-determined consequence of that action. If one touches fire, one must suffer burns (because that is the *taqdeer* of that action). After that, one must turn to another action with a different *taqdeer* – like applying an ointment on the burn.

Similarly, in the human social world, Man is free to choose his actions but must bear the natural consequences of them. The laws governing the physical as well as the human social universe are unchanging and constant (6:34; 10:64, 17:77, 33:62, etc.). Whoever does anything shall get its consequence– individual or collective (99:7-8). Therefore, one must act - individually or collectively - to get results in this universe. To get the desired results, the *taqdeer* of the Universe (i.e. the related Laws of Nature) must be discovered and kept in view at all times. The Natural laws, as we have seen, are the standards and measures of things set by God. In other words, they are the *aqdaar* – the 'permanent values' which run the entire Universe. The Quran maintains that these *aqdaar* were given to mankind in one of the darkest hours of its intellectual existence. That is why it has been called *laila tal qadr* – the 'Night of Values.' [73] Historically, the time of the descent of these Permanent Values – which are available in the Quran – was the Arab month of Ramadan.[74] That is why that month has been reserved for Fasting – a refresher course of learning self-control through studying the natural values given by God through Mohammed in the form of the book we know as the Quran.

Having seen the theological basis of the Quranic teachings, let us now look at the practical aspects of that philosophy in various domains of man's social life on Earth during his pre-death existence (the first life).

* * * * * *

Chapter 5

THE QURANIC POLITICAL SYSTEM

5.1. INTRODUCTION

The importance and place of politics in our lives cannot be overemphasised. It is the umbrella under which we all live. In fact, all the various spheres of life – education, economics, health, social issues, private concerns, law, etc – are controlled by politicians, even when they are not obviously qualified to do that.[1] Indeed, politics is about the only field of work for which one does not require any formal qualifications or training.[2] Still, these untrained and unqualified individuals control and run various social, technical and professional institutions of society. Not infrequently, we come across a minister of science or education who has had no training in those disciplines. Such apparently amusing, but really tragic, issues require one to look seriously and academically at the world of politics. In this chapter, I propose to do precisely that from the perspective of the Quran, i.e. I propose to illustrate the well-known Muslim declaration *la illah illAllah* – 'There is no god but Allah.' That I shall do in two parts. First, I shall trace various human efforts at devising and developing a suitable political system. I shall also present the viewpoint of the Quran regarding those efforts (*la illah*). In the second part, I shall present the political system proposed by the Quran (*illAllah*).

Linguistically, the term 'politics' is thought to be a derivative of either the Greek *politicos* or the Latin *politicus* meaning 'pertaining to citizens or the state.'[3] In English, too, it is used in the same sense. The Arabic term for 'politics', *siaasa* will be dealt with later in this chapter. Anthropological studies show that when Man came out of caves and jungles to start a social, human life, there appeared clash of conflicts in those early settlements. Men tried to grapple with those issues. That was the beginning of politics, i.e. a system which tries to resolve disputes and diffuse clashes and conflicts. Since then there have been a number of attempts to formulate principles and devise rules of politics in order to create peaceful societies living a life of harmony and social justice. Let us look at some of the prominent human endeavours in the field of politics.

5.2. SECTION ONE: *LA ILAAH* – THE HUMAN ENDEAVOUR

At the dawn of human civilization, when the Earth was sparsely populated, means of transport and communication were rudimentary and brainpower was yet to make its full impact on human affairs, brute physical might was the deciding factor in individual and social disputes. That made the male the dominant variety of the human species and gave birth to patriarchal society. The most physically powerful male of a tribe would become its chief. The physical supremacy also made him the wealthiest. That was the beginning of FEUDALISM. This system eventually developed into hereditary MONARCHY. Men have felt the need to have a powerful figure having the last word in case of a dispute (sovereign) since ancient times. As early as the third century BC, Chanakiyya (Kawtalliya), the famous Hindu politician and Chandragupt Mawria's prime minister, observed:

> 'Without king, in a state of nature, the strong devour the weak.' [4]

By this time in human history, physical might had been relatively sidelined as a result of the advent of religion, knowledge and general awakening of human conscience. It was no longer possible to blatantly assert supremacy on the basis of pure muscular strength; it required to be justified by some sort of philosophical basis. The result was the notion of 'the *divine* rights of the king.' Kings claimed to derive their right to rule from God. The pharaohs of ancient Egypt, the mighty kings of Babylon, the Hindu *maharaja*s, the medieval kings of Europe, all made that claim. Even traditional Muslim rulers, especially the Mughals of India, thrived under the title of *dhil Allah 'al alard* (God's shadow on Earth)! Chanakiyya also acknowledged the divine rights of royalty.[4] Confucius, the ancient Chinese philosopher, medieval Western thinkers like Spinoza and St. Augustine and, above all, the famous Italian writer Machiavelli, favour a strong ruler. However, some proposed the notion that the rulers should work towards the welfare of the ruled.[5] As a consequence of the importance of religion, priests shared political power with kings as a matter of course but from behind the scene. As reported by Walter Ullman, St. Ambrose asserted in late 4th century AD:

> "The emperor is within the Church, not above it." (p. 40) [6]

Before that, Chanakiyya had already expressed similar views when he wrote:

> "The priest is not a part of the political system, but the king is not above religious law." [4]

As time passed, the clergy felt that they were left out and began to stake their own claim on political power. The justification was inherent in the notion of the divine rights of kings. Claiming to be closer to God than any other social group, the religious leaders pushed their right to political power as but natural and logical. This was the beginning of THEOCRACY – rule by the religious establishment. In modern times, the most illustrative example of theocratic government is the one established in Iran in 1979 as a result of the revolution, which overturned the rule of Shah Mohammed Reza Pahlavi, a hereditary monarch.[7] An example of political power shared by temporal and religious rulers is modern Saudi Arabia, where the royal family and the religious leadership are interdependent on each other and rule by collusion. This is nothing new; it has been happening since the rise of religion and is based upon a philosophy reflected in the Biblical:

> "Render unto Caesar, the things that are Caesar's; and unto God the things that are God's." [8]

In such a political set up, the clergy provide justification and credence to the rulers, who in return protect and assure the welfare of the priests. Some writers have rightly noted this convenient collaboration between two powerful and greedy groups:

> "The former (the state) pays a shadowy deference to religion; the latter (the church) do not meddle with the external fabric of the political and social system, which is the concern of the former." [9]

This notion of DUALISM appears to be based upon the ancient Zoroastrian philosophy from Persia, according to which, the Universe is operated by two parallel, equally powerful gods – Yazdaan (for 'Light' or 'Good') and Ahraman (for 'Darkness' or 'Evil'). This has given birth to a number of notions of dualism – good & evil, virtue & sin, ruler & ruled, master & slave, *Rahmaan* (God) & *Shaitaan* (Devil), and *Deen* (Religion, or the spiritual) & *Duniya* (the mundane), etc.[10] This philosophy is believed to have made its way from Persia to Greece via India to become the basis of Aristotelian and Platonic thought.[11] One of the better-known disciples/followers of Zoroaster was a figure called Mazdak, who fared prominently in propagating Zoroastrian philosophy. Mazdak is generally believed to have lived not long before Mohammed, the founder of Islam.[12] He will make his appearance again a little later when we discuss Socialism. For the moment, it is notable that the clergy and the temporal rulers have been co-ruling the masses by dividing life up into religion and state, resulting in public and private lives and laws.

This arrangement worked satisfactorily as long as a given society was religiously homogenous. But, with the passage of time, social compositions underwent change to give rise to societies comprising of a number of groups adhering to different religious ideologies. The resulting religiously heterogeneous societies necessarily developed a political philosophy known as SECULARISM, operative in most countries today, especially the West. Under this system, a country is not run on a permanent philosophy or ideology. The politics changes according to circumstances, and consequently, laws change.

Everything is subject to change according to changing needs and circumstances. Only the material and financial interests of the country remain permanent.

Whatever the political system, there is the crucial question of SOVEREIGNTY to be considered, i.e. who has the last word in a dispute? Under the systems discussed so far, sovereignty belongs either to one person (king or queen in a monarchy, the priest in a theocracy, or both the king and the priest in dualism) or to a group of people (as in secularism's democratic systems). This brings us to the hitherto most celebrated political system of all – DEMOCRACY. But, let us first see what the Quran has to say about the discussion so far.

5.3. WHAT THE QURAN SAYS

As to the question of sovereignty, the Quran maintains that it belongs to God's Word alone. In Sura *Al-Kahaf* (The Cave), it says:

> "..nor does He share His Command with anyone whatsoever!" (18:26).

To make it clear that this does not refer to 'worship' of other gods in any spiritual sense and is meant for human social systems, it states in Sura *Aal-e-'Imraan* (The Progeny of Imraan):

> "It is not that a man, to whom is given the Book, and Wisdom, and the Prophetic Office, should say to people: 'Be ye my servants rather than Allah's'. On the contrary: 'Be ye *rabbaaneen* – (servants of Allah alone!)..." (3:79).

Secondly, political power and responsibility are not to be obtained on the basis of inheritance as we find in Sura *Al-Baqara* (The Cow):

> "And remember that Abraham went through testing times following his Lord's Commands, which he fulfilled: He said, 'I will make thee an *imaam* [leader] to the people.' Abraham asked, 'and from my offspring?' He answered, 'My promise is not within the reach of wrong-doers!'" (2:124).

Thirdly, religious leaders (priests) are not desirable even to exist in a society, let alone be delegated political power as laid down in Sura *Younus* (Jonah):

> "Say: 'See ye what things Allah has sent down to you for sustenance? Yet ye hold forbidden some things thereof and (some) lawful." Say: 'Hath Allah indeed permitted you, or do ye forge (things) to attribute to Allah?'" (10:59).

Most of them are parasites according to Sura *At-Tauba* (Repentance):

> "O, ye the Convinced! There are indeed many among the priests and anchorites, who in falsehood devour the wealth of men and hinder (them) from the Way of Allah.."(9:34).

And, as to the dual rule under the dichotomy of religion and state, the Quran stands in clear negation of it all. As we find in Sura *Al-An'aam* (The Cattle) that God is one and it is He who has created both Light as well as Darkness:

> "Praise be to Allah, who created the heavens and the earth, and made the Darkness and the Light. Yet those who reject (the Deen) hold (others) as equal with their Lord!" (6:1) [13]

Decisions must be based upon God's Law alone. We see in Sura *Al-Maaeda* (The Table Spread):

> "...If any do fail to judge by what Allah hath revealed, they are the Rejecters!" (5:45) [14]

Coming back to our discussion after this short digression, we note that the problems associated with, and created by, political systems such as monarchy and theocracy gave rise to the idea of DEMOCRACY, where sovereignty is said to lie with the majority of citizens. The idea was not new. As early as ancient Greece, men had begun to think on these lines and had formulated consultative assemblies of free citizens. Plato and Aristotle believed that men were born either slaves (the majority) or masters (the minority). Their rights were not equal; neither was the minority answerable to the majority. But, Plato himself had noticed the faults of this philosophy. He observed that the minority of rulers exploits the majority of the ruled.[15] His disciple Aristotle reached a similar conclusion when he remarked that it was essential for men to keep within the law. [16]

After this early period, medieval and modern thinkers such as St. Thomas Aquinas[17] and priest John of Salisbury[18] promoted the notion of democracy. The English philosopher John Locke's idea of democracy was the closest to what we know of it today.[19] His philosophy concentrated on the general welfare and protection and safety of the citizens' lives and property; it was the government's responsibility, to be fulfilled through a contract between the citizen and the state. Freedom of expression and belief (religion) was to be granted and legislation was to be achieved through consultative bodies. A very important question was to decide upon the criteria of right and wrong to formulate laws. Because of the unpleasant experience of Christianity, the dominant majority of the West did not want religion to have any part in it. Thus, the notion of 'the Will of the People' appeared, manifested in formulae like 'Government of the people, for the people, by the people.' [20] The idea of 'the general will of the people' was promoted, among others, by the French thinker Rousseau around 1762-63.

5.4. A CRITIQUE OF DEMOCRACY

Currently, the idea of Western Democracy is operative in most countries around the world. It is claimed that this political philosophy is the result of Man's intellectual efforts over the last two millennia or more and is the best prescription for our social ills. Democracy also claims to be the true reflection of the popular will of the majority.

But, is it really so?

Firstly, the popular will of the majority is not always necessarily right. The term 'right' should be applied to whatever is *really* true and simply not because the majority takes it to be so. Man is fallible and prone to making mistakes. There is no guarantee that the majority always makes a decision for the common good rising above their own individual and selfish desires. Furthermore, as we have seen above, there is no guarantee that the people's representatives in the legislature are intellectually better than the voters. Mistakes can be - and are - always made. As admitted by UNESCO in a report in 1947,

> "It is wrong to think that the majority's decision is always right. It can be wrong. Therefore, a minority has the right to agitate against a majority decision to get it changed.' [21]

Secondly, some thinkers have clearly stated that Democracy is an illusion:

> 'When politics is viewed practically, not theoretically, one has to admit that to consider the ruler and the ruled the same and equal is practically impossible. Practically, the government comprises of one group of people and the governed are another group. In post-tribal societies they can never be one and the same. To consider them as such creates the worst state of power in a state.' [22]

That is why it has been said:

> 'If Rousseau had not written his book before the practical experience of democracy in modern times, he would not have been under any false hopes.' [23]

That the majority's decision can be wrong is also the position of the Quran. The *kuffaar* (Rejecters) were told in Sura *Al-Anfaal* (The Spoils of War):

> "...Not the least good will your forces be to you even if they are multiplied (*wa lau kathurat*): For verily Allah is with the Convinced!" (8:19)

The Israelites with Moses were in the right despite being in the minority. Thus, we find in Sura *Ash-Shu'raa* (The Poets):

> "Then Pharaoh sent heralds to (all) the cities, (Saying): 'These (Israelites) are but a small band. And they have surely enraged us. And we are a multitude amply fore-warned.'" (26:53-56)

Also, in Sura *Al-Jinn* (The Jinn):

> "At length, when they see that which they are promised, then will they know who it is that is weakest in (his) helper and least important in point of numbers." (72:24).

And, as a matter of principle that majority or abundance does not necessarily mean right / good, the Quran says in Sura *Al-Maaeda*:

> "Say: 'Not equal are things that are bad and things that are good, even though the abundance of the bad may dazzle thee...'" (5:100)

Therefore, democracy does not deliver what it promises. It is the same old wine (of a tiny minority ruling and exploiting the vast majority) in a new bottle; only the label has been changed, not the contents.

5.5. MORALITY AND ETHICS

Significantly, in the political systems discussed so far morality and ethics have been conspicuous by their absence. In fact, modern notions of politics are completely devoid of a moral fibre. Influential writers have said that a ruler should possess the cunning of a fox along with the courage of a lion; the ruler must always be vigilant and should surprise enemies with sudden attack and totally destroy them; integrity and expansion of the state takes precedence over everything else – that is why the ruler is free to take any steps necessary towards those ends, and 'Princes don't need to keep a faith and are beyond morality.' [24]

It appears that the traditional religious morality of Christianity (turning the other cheek, etc) did not work for the West and consequently, morality and ethics found no role in modern politics. Some Western authors admit this. R H Tawney says:

> 'This new branch of political knowledge, reluctantly at first, but then confidently, says that no moral code supersedes the (state) law.' [25]

Indeed, as long as a political system is not based upon a permanent set of moral and other values, it will remain vulnerable to corruption and exploitation of the many by a few. Democracy is an attractive façade, acting as a distracter, for the oppressive rule of a tiny minority – the privileged class, mostly the clergy, landowners and business tycoons.

The United States is the biggest capitalist society today. How much influence does corporate America wields on the national and international policies of the country is more or less an open secret now. It has rightly been said:

> 'What is good for General Motors, is good enough for America.'

It has been reported that in a high level meeting of corporate representatives the then American president (late) Lyndon Johnson remarked:

> 'We (the Government) are doing what you have employed us for.' [26]

In fact, these kingmakers are the real rulers behind the scene. Greed and personal interests are paramount in their lives; morality means nothing to them. They constantly deceive the masses for their own selfish gains. They are experts at moulding public opinion in their favour through sophisticated propaganda and other ploys of mass psychology. As the French philosopher Rene Guenn remarks:

> 'The principle of the Public Will has been devised to deceive; it is (wrongly) taken to mean that laws are formulated according to popular consensus but the truth is that this consensus can be quite easily diverted or changed.' [27]

Therefore, Democracy's claim that the right to use a piece of paper (casting a vote) creates universal equality is nothing more than a sham, a deception.

5.6. SOCIALISM

Before we move on, it is desirable to dwell for a while on the idea of Socialism which is the adopted philosophy of nearly half of humanity today, even after the fall of the Soviet Russia, the biggest socialist state ever. Although Socialism is related more with economic systems, it is worth our while to examine this philosophy from a political angle. As we have seen, the notion of 'the Public Will' is quite ancient. It has been said that Mazdak, a disciple/follower of Zoroaster, was probably the first socialist thinker ever.[28] He promoted the notion of public welfare in his teachings based upon the Zoroastrian philosophy of Dualism of Light (Yazdaan) and Darkness (Ahramin). This philosophy was echoed in the Aristotelian and Platonic ideas in ancient Greece. In modern times, the German philosopher Hegel based his idea of 'a conflict of ideas' on the same philosophy; this clash of opposites takes place because of the 'Spirit of the Age', it was said. Later, the famous Karl Marx said something similar using 'economy' instead of 'idea' while his incentive was 'historical necessity.' According to Marx, the entire human history is the story of economic struggle and conflicts resulting from it. The

Part Two: Chapter Five

Chinese leader Mao Tse Tung had his own brand of the philosophy of opposites.29 It is to be noted that Marx was dissatisfied with the economic as well as political systems of his day:

> 'Political power is nothing but the ability of one section of society to subjugate another.'

He hoped that,

> 'When progress does away with social classes, and all production falls under general national control, the nature of the ruling class's political power will change.' 30

5.7. NATIONALISM

The idea of nationalism–belonging to a group of people on the basis of geographical entity–is a relatively modern one in human history. It still seems to be going strong with individuals carrying passports of a country (which is really a particular piece of land), calling it 'home' or 'motherland' or 'fatherland', and laying down their lives for it if need be. Today this idea is widely accepted as natural, but the Quran declares it to be unnatural and hence undesirable. It is declared in Sura *Younus*:

> "Mankind was but one nation, but differed (later)…" (10:19).

The system of divine messengers was to resolve those differences, according to Sura *Al-Baqara*:

> "Mankind was one single nation. And Allah sent Messengers with glad tidings and warnings; and with them He sent the Book in truth, to judge between people in matters wherein they differed…" (2:213)

Differences in colour and distribution in groups is merely for easy recognition. Distinction comes with personal character, behaviour and ideology. Sura *Al-Hujaraat* (The Inner Apartments) says:

> "O mankind! We created you from a single of male and female, and made you into groups and tribes, that ye may know each other. Verily, the most honoured of you in the sight of Allah is (he who is) the most righteous of you…" (49:13)

Some modern thinkers have indeed arrived at the same conclusion. Bertrand Russell, the last great British philosopher, wrote (translated from Urdu):

> Even more harmful than religious fanaticism is national fanaticism, i.e. an individual is responsible to his state alone. Undoubtedly, this belief is even against the most modern self-interest because patriotism pure

does not benefit even victorious nations. 31

We have already come across Nicolo Machiavelli's stand on morality in this regard. Another thinker, Romelin, writes (translated from Urdu):

> The basic duty of a state is to guard its interests and develop strength. It should care about the interests of other states only if it does not clash with its own. Stability of the state takes precedence over all moral codes and is worthy of all sacrifice. 32

That is why Walpole, the British politician, is reported to have said that virtuous men can never save an empire because (translated from Urdu):

> 'they cannot go to the extent which sometimes becomes necessary for it' because 'State matters are not subject to moral codes.' 33

Most politicians as well as patriots are two-faced. The Italian politician Govour summed it up (translated from Urdu):

> 'If we do for our own selves what we have done for the state, we will be labelled nasty devils.' 34

5.8. INTERNATIONALISM

During the 20th century the idea of nationalism contributed to devastating global wars as well as numerous minor conflicts. These unpleasant experiences led to the notion of peaceful co-existence for all nations of the world. Consequently, first the League of Nations and then the United Nations was established. It was hoped that that would solve mankind's problems. But, as we know well, the dream of all humanity living in peace and harmony is still as elusive as ever. It is hardly surprising. If a group of national representatives, driven by patriotic sentiments and guided by their own respective national interests, meet to discuss 'international' issues, it does not guarantee universal good on a global basis. The UN is an impotent organization when it comes to international politics and serves only a decorative purpose. That is why Bertrand Russell suggested one global government for all mankind. 35 That is exactly what the Quran says in Sura *Al-Baqara*:

> "Those who break Allah's Covenant after it is ratified, and who sunder what Allah has ordered to be joined, and do mischief on earth: these cause loss (only) to themselves." (2:27) 36

This can be achieved only by following a permanent set of values. This Quranic prescription for etenal and universal peace for mankind is reflected in what Professor Joud said in his *Guide to the Political Philosophy of Morals and*

Politics (translated from Urdu):

> Good life means to have permanent values. Therefore, I can say that the State has the duty to create conditions in which individuals are able to achieve permanent values. That alone is the criterion for social development and progress.' 37

Let us now see what political system the Quran suggests for Man.

....

5.9. SECTION TWO: *ILLALLAH* – THE QURANIC PRESCRIPTION

Linguistically, the Arabic term for 'politics' *siaasa* is derived from the three-letter root *seen, waow, seen* (SWS) with three basic meanings according to standard Arabic lexicon:

a. moth-eaten, as from *soos*, the silk worm;
b. to groom, as in *saayes,* the groom of horses;
c. to administer and govern 38

In addition to these, the root also has the basic meaning of 'nature' and 'origin.' Its derivatives include *siaas* – administrator / governor; *sayyaas* – one who administers / governs well; *taswees* – to appoint administrators / governors; and of course *siaasa* – administration of a country, i.e. politics.

Therefore, this eloquent Arabic expression means a system wherein is established a stable and just society in which life is groomed to the best. Following are the constitutional components of the Quranic political system.

(i) SOVEREIGNTY
The Quran states very clearly that all humans are absolutely equal in all respects and, as such, deserve equal respect and rights:
- '*wa laqad karramnaa beni aadam* – We have honoured the children of man...' (17:70)
- That is why no man has the right to rule over another. (3:79)
- Sovereignty belongs to God alone. (18:26; 17:111)
- Only he has the last word as He is the Highest Judge (*ahkam al haakemeen*). (95:8)
- Not only that, He is the Best Judge (*khair ul haakemeen*). (7:87)

(ii) UNIVERSALITY OF THE MESSAGE (THE QURAN)
- The Quran addresses the whole of mankind because they are but one group. (10:19)
- The aim of this Message is to resolve men's differences and make them one global community. (2:143, 213)

- It is desirable to merge them into one nation because only that (group or ideology) survives which works for universal welfare. (13:17)
- The best code of life and constitutional basis for law is the Quran. (5:48)
- The purpose and aim of the Quran, and the Messages before, is to convince people to follow God's Law. (21:25)

(iii) PRACTICALITY OF THE QURAN
- Only the Quran is to be followed. (6:155)
- No other code is to be followed. (7:3)
- That means no code is to be made according to people's desires (5:49); not even the Divine Messengers are allowed to do that (38:26), and
- neither is Mohammed! (39:14) [39]
- Those who do not follow the Quran are making a big mistake. (5:44, 45)

Therefore:

> "O ye who are convinced! Obey Allah, and obey the Messenger, and those charged with authority among you. If ye differ in anything among yourselves refer it to Allah and His Messenger..." (4:59)

[A Point Of Order]

An interesting point of order must be made here regarding Verse 4:59. Generally, it is taken to refer to three levels of obedience being binding on Muslims – God's, which means following the Quran; the Messenger's, which means following the Prophetic Tradition (Hadith); and of the rulers of the day, which means following the laws made and implemented by the government. This interpretation, devised for the benefit, and under the auspices of, the second (Muslim) century caliphs – who were, for all practical purposes, dictatorial monarchs – has been widely, but wrongly, accepted by Muslim scholars. A case in point is the great Sir Syed Ahmed Khan of Aligarh, India fame. He interprets *ool el amr minkum* – 'those charged with authority among you' to mean obeying the British colonizers of India. In one of his articles, he states:

> 'It is in the best interests of all inhabitants of India, especially Muslims, that they quietly live under the protection of the English Government. They should fully understand that this is also the guidance of the religion of Islam, i.e. we must be loyal to those whose subjects we are, enjoying the peace; we must not think ill of them nor collaborate with those who do; we should accept them (the British) as our worldly rulers and the Almighty as the King of kings and our real Lord.' [40]

When the British, during their time in India, were engaged in conflict with the Ottomans of Turkey, Syed Ahmed wrote:

> '..and even if the policy of the English Government is against the

> Turks, we cannot ignore our religious duty of loyalty and obedience to our rulers.' 41

This interpretation is against the teachings of the Quran for the following reasons.

God's Law (the Quran) was transmitted to men through the Messenger. He is to be obeyed because he is the honest guardian of the Divine Message (81:21). As we have already discussed, the Messenger asks Muslims to obey God alone through the Quran (5:48; 6:156; 7:3) *not* his own self (4:35; 39:14). That clearly means that obedience of the Messenger is but that of God. During the lifetime of the Messenger, he was the central authority for Muslims to obtain Quranic judgement on any given matter (4:59). Indeed, as it says in the Quran: "He who obeys the Messenger, obeys Allah…" (4:80). After his death, this responsibility passed on to his rightful and righteous successors. They too asked citizens to follow God's Law (the Quran). There was no question of obedience of the Messenger as different from that of God's because he had not left behind any collection of his sayings/instructions. 42 Every successor must have regarded the judgements of his predecessors, and those of the Messenger, but as precedence only because nothing can supersede God's Word. That is why Muslims are asked by the Quran to make decisions through consultation (42:38). Even the Messenger was asked to consult Muslims (3:159). In fact, according to the Quran, principles and values are more important than persons or personalities:

> "Mohammed is no more than a Messenger; many were the Messengers that passed away before him. If he died or were slain, will ye then turn back on your heels?…" (3:144)

That is exactly what Abu Bakr, the first caliph meant when he said to mourners at Mohammed's demise,

> 'If you worshipped (followed) Mohammed, be informed that he is dead; but if you worship (follow) Allah, be informed that He never dies!' 43

And that is why, on the same occasion, 'Umr bin Al-Khattab, the second caliph, made an historical utterance: '*husbunaa kitaab Allah*' – The Book of God suffices for us! 44

Therefore, in essence, obedience is only for God's Law (the Quran). Clearly, the rulers are to be obeyed only if they enact laws according to the Quran (10:35; 5:77, 25:52; 26:151). Even parents are not to be obeyed if they ask you to go against God's Law (29:8; 31:15). Obedience and loyalty is only to be for one who has the appropriate knowledge (10:89), and refer to God's Law for judgement (31:15).

That is why Abu Bakr, on appointment as the first successor to the Messenger, said in his inaugural address,

'Support me as long as I abide by God's Law; if I digress, remove me.' 45

(iv) HEAD OF STATE, OFFICIALS
The Quranic criterion for appointment to a responsible public office is that the candidate must have STRENGTH (the ability to do the job) and HONESTY (27:39; 28:26). Delegation of responsibility shall be according to suitability (4:58), performance (46:19), and personal character in line with the Quranic ideology (49:13). No position of authority shall be hereditary (2:124).46 Similarly, all the officials of the Quranic government shall be appointed on the same criteria of ability, knowledge, and character (2:247).

(v) LAWS, SUB-LAWS, RULES, REGULATIONS
The Quran gives the constitutional framework and legal boundaries, within which the State is to decide upon the relevant details according to the needs of the time.

> "O, ye the Convinced! Ask not questions about things which, if made plain to you, may cause you trouble…" (5:101) The details shall be arrived at through a process of consultation.

(vi) THE PRINCIPLE OF CONSULTATION
In line with its approach of generally giving principles and not their details, the Quran has left the details of the procedures (for example, to appoint officials or the composition and structure of government agencies) to the society of the day. But, it has suggested the basic principle of CONSULTATION (3:159; 42:38).

In addition to the regional organization of consultative bodies, there shall be an annual event for a universal consultative gathering of the representatives of the entire Muslim nation (*umma*) at Mecca, in the vicinity of the K'aba; it is called the Hajj (the annual pilgrimage).

(vii) POLITICAL PARTIES
Since the entire nation will be one party - *hizb Allah* (58:22) to follow and abide by the same one constitution (the Quran), there shall be no political parties in the Quranic Consultative Assembly.

(viii) FOREIGN (NON-MUSLIM) NATIONALS
In the Quranic society there shall be no independent sovereign Muslim nations. All the Muslims will be citizens of the only Muslim country in the world. So, the question of a Muslim foreigner shall not arise. Of course, there may be non-Muslims living in the Quranic country. They will be classed as foreigners. They shall have every basic human right – sanctity and protection of life, property, food, shelter, honour and respect, education, health, freedom of religion, etc – accorded to Muslim citizens. But, they will not have the right to take part in state affairs like consultation and official duties. They will be able

to send their representatives to Muslim parliament but shall not have a say in proceedings and official / state matters (3:118; 4:114; 8:72;).

(ix) WOMEN
- Women are absolute equals of men and worthy of respect as human beings (17:70).
- They deserve full reward of their deeds (3:195; 4:124).
- They possess potential and capabilities equal to that of men (33:35).
- Therefore, they can, and will, take equal part in establishing and running the Quranic society (9:71, 111, 112).

(x) RESPONSIBILITIES AND OBLIGATIONS OF GOVERNMENT
1. Protection of lives of all residing within the country, including establishing a legal system for dealing with loss of life (2:178; 5:32).
2. Protection of property (2:188; 4:29).
3. Guarantee of shelter (2:58).
4. Protection of honour and respect (24:2-4; 33:59).
5. Freedom of choice in marriage (4:3, 19).
6. No suppression of individuality (7:32).
7. Guarantee of law and order and safety (2:38).
8. Due reward to everyone according to law (17:20, 21).
9. No exploitation, i.e. fairness for all (39:7; 53:39).
10. Guarantee of justice (*'adl*) for all (16:90); even for enemies (4:135; 5:8).
11. Equality in the eyes of the law for all (10:15).
12. Well-being (*ehsaan*), beyond justice, for all (16:90).
13. Guarantee of sustenance (*rizq*) to all (6:151; 17:31), even animals (11:6).
14. Freedom of choice of religion (nationality) for all (2:256, 9:6, 10:99, 18:29).
15. Protection of religious centres / places of worship of all (22:40).

In a nutshell, the Muslim nation will make its concern the welfare and well-being of all humanity regardless of their religion (2:143, 3:110, 4:75, 22:41).

(xi) THE CONTRACT
All this will be done through a contract between the Quranic government and its citizens (Muslims) through which the State has jurisdiction over life and property to use them according to the Quran; in return, the State guarantees its citizens a paradisiacal existence – all needs met, comprehensive welfare provided, a peaceful life completely free of worry and anxiety guaranteed.

> "Allah hath purchased of the Convinced their person and their goods; for theirs (in return) is *al-janna* (the Garden of Paradise)..." (9:111)

Of course, foreigners (non-Muslims) living within the Quranic country shall not be subject to this contract. But, as mentioned earlier, they will be entitled to all rights and welfare with the difference that the State shall not have jurisdiction over their person and property.

(xii) INHERITING THE EARTH – *tamakkun fil ard*

In summary, the responsibility and obligation of the Quranic government is a colossal one. It requires access to and control over all resources. This huge task can only be done by an independent and sovereign nation. Therefore, an Islamic society requires its own country (*tamakkun fil ard*) so that it can fulfil its duty of establishing a system according ot the teachings of the Quran with guaranteed sustenance for all:

> "(They are) those who, if We establish them in the land, establish the Quranic System (*as-salaa*) and provide comprehensive growth (*az-zakaa*), enjoin the right and forbid the wrong, and (must) refer all matters to God ('s Law)." (22:41)

Incidentally, the inheritance of Earth is achieved by following God's Law:

> "Allah hath promised, to those among you who are convinced and work righteous deeds, that He will, of surety, grant them in the land inheritance (of power) as He granted it to those before them... with a specific purpose:

> "...that He will establish in authority their system (*deen*)..." [47] (24:55)

(xiii) FOREIGN POLICY, DEFENCE

1. Honour your agreements, commitments and keep your promises (17:34),
   individual as well as collective (5:1), even with the enemy (5:8).
2. If you breach of agreement by the enemy, announce the abrogation of the contract *before* taking action (8:58).
3. In case of an offer of truce, investigate it fully (4:94).
4. Fight the aggressors but do not transgress (2:190).
5. Have the means of battle (a standing army) ready (8:60).
6. Fight in the cause of Allah, i.e. struggle to establish God's Law (2:244).
7. Fight hypocrites and traitors (4:88).
8. In times of adversity, such as war, be extra mindful of God's Law (8:45).
9. Try peace before war; be respectful to enemy leaders (27:29).
10. The purpose of your fighting is to eliminate war (47:4).

* * * * * *

Chapter 6

THE ECONOMIC SYSTEM OF THE QURAN

Economy is perhaps the most important area of human civilization as it involves short-term as well as long-term management, production, distribution and consumption of articles necessary and essential for human existence and survival. It has always been an important issue throughout the history of mankind – even in the 'pre-money' days. But since the introduction of coins and notes as legal tender economics has assumed an even more important place in human life. The Quran has treated this subject at length with the seriousness it deserves. In fact, the entire structure of the Quranic society rests on its economic base. But, before we look at the system of economy proposed by the Quran, let me very briefly retrace the two dominant, prevalent, and rival economic systems operating in the world today.

6.1. CAPITALISM

It is the economic system currently in place in the majority of countries around the globe. [1] Capitalism rests on the fundamental principle of 'the sanctity of private ownership'. It means that the worker is the sole owner of whatever they may earn or make by way of money. [2] Also, the owner has the legal and sole right to dispose of their earnings in the way they see fit. They may spend all they have earned or save some of it. This extra which may be saved forms the second foundation stone of capitalism. Any savings may be invested to generate more money. The sum of money invested is known as 'capital' – hence the term 'capitalism', and the money it generates is called 'interest'. The capitalistic economic system is also referred to as 'free economy.' [3]

6.2. SOCIALISM

As opposed to capitalism, socialism bases itself on the idea of 'collective' or 'social' ownership. No citizen can own anything. Everything is owned collectively by society under state control of short-term as well as long-term management, production, distribution and consumption of wealth. [4] The system is based upon the Marxist principle of 'from everyone according to capacity and to everyone according to need'. Also known as 'controlled economy' [5] socialism is in force in several countries like China, Cuba and most notably, until recently, in the demised and dismembered USSR.

After this brief reminder of the two prevalent economic systems, let us turn to the Quran. But, before we get to it, let me dwell for a moment on the Arabic word commonly used for 'economy' or 'economic system'. It is *iqtesaad*. It springs from the three-letter root *Qaaf – Saad – Daa* (QSD), with the basic meaning of 'to intend, to prepare to do something, to get ready to do.' [6] *Al-qasdu fil amr* means 'to adopt a middle and balanced approach'. Therefore, *iqtesaad* means a balanced system of economy.

6.3. THE QURANIC ECONOMIC SYSTEM

Before I present the fundamentals of the Quranic economic system, allow me to introduce its basis and background. In my view, it is important to have this introduction if we are to fully appreciate the economic system of the Quran.

TWO IMPORTANT INTRODUCTORY POINTS

A: The Concept of Life
What is 'life'? What constitutes a 'human being'? Why are we here? Where are we going? Why was this universe created? Questions like these may be answered according to 'the materialistic concept of life': Man is a highly developed (social) animal, comprised of certain chemicals arranged in a certain proportion. These chemicals disintegrate when the body reaches the end of its natural life (death) and that is it. Dust is returned unto dust, in the Biblical expression. But the Quran offers 'the spiritualistic concept of life':

(i) Life is going through evolution and Man still has to undergo further evolutionary stages:

> 'It is He Who hath produced you from a single soul [7]; then there is a resting place and a repository .....' (6:98)

(ii) Evolution is the decided path of life:

> 'Ye shall surely travel from stage to stage.' (84:19)

(iii) Life does not end with death; it goes on:

> 'Again, on the Day of Judgement [8], will ye be raised up.' (23:16)

(iv) Man is made up of two components, a body and a personality which is called *an-nafs* 9 by the Quran:

> 'By the soul (ego or personality), and the proportion and order given to it.' (91:7) 10

(v) This ego / soul / personality has been given to Man as the Divine Energy called *rooh* and was breathed into Man at birth:

> 'But He fashioned him in due proportion, and breathed into him of His spirit .....'   (32:9)

(vi) In a nutshell, the Quran states its concept of life, death, and personality (consciousness) thus:

> 'It is Allah that takes the souls (of men) at death, and those that die not (He takes) during their sleep; those on whom He has passed the decree of death, He keeps back (from returning to life), but the rest He sends (to their bodies) for a term appointed.' (39:42)

(vii) The Divine Energy (*rooh*) gives Man his self / ego / personality, which has endowed him with the characteristic of FREE WILL. Man has the capacity and potential of choosing his own actions and shaping his own destiny:

> 'We showed him the Way: whether he be grateful or ungrateful.' (76:3)

(viii) By being grateful (choosing the right way, which is recorded in the Quran), Man can develop his soul so that his life can go on to the next stage of Evolution (the Hereafter), where there will be no death:

> '"Is it (the case) that we shall not die, except our first death....?"' 11 (37: 58, 59)

(ix) Real life is in the Hereafter:

> 'What is this life of this world but amusement and play? But verily the Home of the Hereafter,- that is Life indeed, if they but knew.' (29:64)

(x) Development of Self

Now we come to an important question. How does one develop one's soul / self / personality / ego so that one's life can continue after death?

The human instinct is to seek self-gratification. In the physical universe the body thrives on whatever it takes for itself. But in the spiritual world the soul/self gets developed by whatever is given to others. Greed and selfishness destroy the soul and any chances of its development:

> '...and entertain no desire in their hearts for things given to (others) but give them preference over themselves, even though poverty was their (own lot). And those saved from the covetousness (greed) of their own souls (selves), - they are the ones that achieve prosperity.' (59:9)

(xi) And how exactly is it done? Through *anfaaq*!

> 'So fear Allah as much as you can 12; listen and obey; and spend in charity for the benefit of your own souls. And those saved from the covetousness of their own souls, - they are the ones that achieve prosperity.' (64:16)

(xii) What is *anfaaq* ?

Nafaq is a tunnel (open at both ends) as opposed to *sarab,* which is a cave (open only at one end). *Munaafiq* (a hypocrite) is a person who enters a system through one opening and slips out through another. *Anfaaq fi sabeel Allah* is the practice of keeping open and available Allah's bounties for everyone:

> 'Say: "If ye had control of the Treasures of the Mercy (benevolence) of my Lord, behold, ye would keep them back, for fear of spending them: for man is (ever) niggardly!"' (18:100)

(xiii) *Anfaaq* is meant for Man's own benefit:

> ' ... Whatever of good ye give benefits your own souls (selves)....' (2: 272)

B: God's Law enforced by Man

The second important introductory point is that Nature's law takes effect automatically in the physical world (non-living as well as living matter). But in the human social world God's law has to be introduced, implemented and established by humans themselves. When Man establishes God's law in human society, he represents God Himself:

> 'It was not ye who slew them; it was Allah; when thou threwest (a handful of dust) 13, it was not thy act, but Allah's....' (8:17)

Man's hand becomes God's Hand:

> 'Verily those who plight their fealty to thee plight their fealty in truth to Allah: the Hand of Allah is over their hands: .....' (48:10)

Man has the duty to perform God's duty in human society:

> 'And why should ye not fight in the cause of Allah and of those who, being weak, are ill-treated (and oppressed)? – Men, women, and children, whose cry is: "Our Lord! Rescue us from this town, whose

Part Two: Chapter Six

people are oppressors; and raise for us from Thee one who will protect; and raise for us from Thee one who will help!" (4:75)

Bearing these two important introductory points in mind, let us turn to the topic proper, i.e. the economic system of the Quran.

When the Quranic social order is established in a human society, one of the basic responsibilities of the authorities is to provide *rizq* (universal sustenance) to everyone:

'....- We provide sustenance for you and for them (your children)...' (6:151; 17:31)

This monumental task of providing sustenance is not limited to humans and extends to include *all* living beings *all over* earth:

'There is no moving creature on earth but its sustenance dependeth on Allah:....' [15] (11:6)

This basic responsibility of the Quranic State was reportedly well-understood and adopted as official policy by early Muslim leaders. The Prophetic Tradition (*Hadith*) contains the following report.

Omr ibn Al-Khattaab, the second successor of the Messenger is reported to have said: "Even if a dog dies of starvation on the banks of Furaat, [16] Omr will have to be answerable for it on the Day of Judgement." [17]

This chief responsibility of providing universal sustenance is assumed under the over-all charter of the Quranic government:

'Allah has promised, to those among you who believe (are convinced) and work righteous deeds, that He will, of a surety, grant them in the land, inheritance (of power), as He granted it to those before them; that He will establish in authority their religion (system) – the one which He has chosen for them; and that He will change (their state), after the fear in which they (lived), to one of security and peace; they will worship (obey) me (alone) and not associate aught with Me. If any do reject Faith (the system) after this, they are rebellious and wicked. So, establish *As-Salaa* and *Az-Zakaa* and obey the Messenger; that ye may receive mercy.' (24: 55, 56)

And this is practically done through a contract between the state and the citizenry under which the state assumes the responsibility of providing guaranteed universal welfare and security to all individuals within its jurisdiction; in return, the citizens recognize and accept the state's right, access and discretion over them and all the wealth they produce.

'Allah hath purchased of the believers (convinced) their persons, and

their goods; for theirs (in return) is the Garden (of Paradise): ......'
(9: 111)

This Garden of Paradise (*Janna*) is bestowed upon the Convinced (*Momeneen*) by God in the Hereafter but in this earthly life it is established as a just, fair and comprehensive social order in which, among other things:

> '...and eat of the bountiful things therein as (where and when) ye will...' (2:35)

and,

> 'There is therein (enough provision) for thee not to go hungry nor to go naked, nor to suffer from thirst, nor from the sun's heat.' (20: 118, 119)

To discharge its monumental duties and responsibilities, the Quranic State shall work within the boundaries of the Quran's set of permanent values (the constitution).

6.4. THE CONSTITUTIONAL FRAMEWORK

(i) No Private Ownership

> '...His are all things in the heavens and on earth...' (2:255)

To properly carry out this huge universal task of comprehensive welfare of its people the Quranic Government needs to keep under its control all the sources and means of production of wealth. The ultimate source of all, or most, wealth is land (earth). Therefore, no one can own land as all land (the entire earth) belongs to God. Earth has been called *ardellah* -Allah's earth – in (7:73). Also:

> 'It is We Who will inherit the earth and all beings thereof....' (19:40)

The produce of earth is for ALL:

> 'And We have provided therein means of subsistence,-for you and for those for whose sustenance ye are not responsible. And there is not a thing but its (sources and) treasures (inexhaustible) are with Us; .....' (15: 20, 21)

Therefore, the earth and its produce must remain open and accessible to all. It is *sawaa a lis saaeleen* – alike for all for the asking! (41:10)

(ii) Wages of Labour

The second fundamental principle is that one is only entitled to any wages (money) earned through labour (work):

> 'That man can have nothing but what he strives for.' (53:39)

Why not? This important principle, which clashes with the very basis of capitalism and its philosophy of investment and notions like 'absent partner' in businesses, rests on the following argument by the Quran. When Man arrived on the scene, the Earth had already been provided by Nature with the means of subsistence such as water, air, vegetation, etc; Man had no contribution towards the creation of these resources at all. Even all the underlying physical laws under which the earth yields its resources were already in place; Man had nothing to do with them either. All Man does to produce wealth is work, and that is what he should be, in all fairness, entitled to a return for. The Quran elaborates this principle with the help of examples of how natural universe operates:

> 'See ye the seed that ye sow in the ground?
> Is it ye that cause it to grow, or are We the Cause?
> Were it Our Will, We could make it broken orts; and ye would be left in wonderment, (Saying), "We are indeed left with debts (for nothing): Indeed we are deprived."
> See ye the water which ye drink?
> Do you bring it down (in rain) from the Cloud or do We?
> Were it Our Will, We could make it salty (and unpalatable): then why do ye not give thanks?
> See ye the Fire which ye kindle?
> Is it ye who grow the tree which feeds the fire, or do We grow it?
> We have made it a reminder and an article of comfort and convenience for the denizens of deserts (the needy of the world).'
> (56: 63-73)

(iii) Interest

Interest / usury is absolutely forbidden and deserves Hell:

> 'O ye who believe (are the Convinced)! Devour not Usury, doubled and multiplied; but fear Allah; that ye may really prosper. And fear the fire, which is prepared for those who reject Faith (the system).' (3: 130, 131)

That is why there can be no 'investment', in the modern economic sense of the term, to make money as an absent partner:

> 'That which you give in usury (interest) for increase through the property (wealth) of (other) people, will have no increase with Allah....'
> (30:39)

Reports from *Hadith* support this view as follows.

> 1. It is reported in *Musnid Abu Daood* that the Messenger said, "Surely, earth is Allah's and the people are (also) Allah's".
> 2. That is why he declared as unlawful the practice of sharing the yield of land as an absent partner by saying: "Whoever has land must work on it himself or hand it over, free, to a (Muslim) brother of his." (Muslim; Abu Daood)

3. It is reported in *Nisaee* that the Messenger was asked, 'Is the owner of land entitled to take a little grain off the farmer?' He said, "No." He was then asked, "Not even hay?" He replied, "Absolutely not."

(iv) Surplus Wealth

The principles mentioned above spring from the basic rule that nobody needs more money than that required to meet their needs, as all their welfare will be taken care of by the State. Therefore, every able-bodied citizen is expected to work according to capacity and is entitled to only what his needs require. So, everyone is required to surrender to the State all the wealth they produce except what is necessary to meet their needs:

> 'They ask thee how much they are to spend (keep available for others);
> Say: "Whatever is beyond your needs." [18] (2: 219)

It is the responsibility of the Quranic Government to administer this system:

> 'Take (from them) what is surplus (of their needs); and command what is right;...' (7: 199) [19]

(v) Banks

The expression 'Islamic Banking' is a classic example of contradiction in terms. It is akin to 'Islamic Pub' or 'Halaal Swine.' Since there will be no surplus wealth with anyone, and interest being forbidden, there is absolutely no place for institutions like banks in the true ultimate Quranic order of things.

(vi) Easy Wealth

In the light of the principle of labour, easy money cannot be made in the Quranic society:

> 'They ask thee concerning wine (intoxicants) and gambling,[20]
> Say, "In them is great sin, and some profit for men; but the sin is greater than the profit." .....' (2: 219)

and,

> 'O ye who believe (are Convinced)! Intoxicants and gambling, sacrificing to stones, and (divination by) arrows, are an abomination,- of Satan's handiwork: eschew such (abomination) that ye may prosper.' (5: 90)

That, then, is a brief introduction of the economic system of the Quran which it expects men to establish in the ultimate fair and just human society.

*　　*　　*　　*　　*　　*

Chapter 7

WOMEN, SEX AND MARRIAGE

Marriage is one of the most important institutions of human civilization. It is the social state in which a man and a woman decide to live together to have a happy life in all respects including sex. From times immemorial, it has been the pivot around which living in most societies revolve and is the tool for propagating mankind. In its self-declared role and status of being a comprehensive guide for humans the Quran has duly dealt with the question of marriage and its related issues. This chapter intends to trace the Quranic guidelines in an attempt to answer some of the concerns raised. I shall seek to treat issues like choice of partner, the marriage ceremony, rights and responsibilities, divorce and the related rules and regulations as stipulated in the Quran. I do not see myself as justifying the Quranic viewpoint on human sexuality as compared to extra-Quranic ideologies. Rather, I wish to present the Quranic perspective in its pristine quality in comparison to the 'traditional' Muslim ideas. Wherever appropriate, I shall also refer to the confusion caused by popular beliefs based upon culture - largely derived from *Hadith* (the Messenger's Tradition) – which have little or no basis in the teaching of the Quran in the matter; in fact, for the most part, they are anti-Quranic.

7.1. MARRIAGE IN TODAY'S CONTEXT

Marriage and its related issues are a matter of serious concern for Muslims, especially those who have migrated to other cultures, specifically the West. It is important for both the first as well as the subsequent generations of immigrants for different reasons. The first generation – the parents – worry that their traditional values are being eroded because they are not able to discharge their parental obligation of getting their offspring married off to desirable partners at the right time (age). The younger generation are faced with cultural and religious confusion resulting from a clash between values learnt at home and those acquired from the host society. They have greater economic and personal freedom than their parents ever had. The national legal systems quite often are on their side in issues like multiple marriages and divorce. Consequently, there is increasing anxiety and confusion. Therefore, a serious academic study of the Quranic perspective in this regard is needed more than ever before; hence, this chapter.

7.2. WHAT *IS* MARRIAGE?

Let me approach the topic academically by raising this very simple and basic question, the answer to which may not be very obvious. This apparently simple question really asks 'why do we marry?' In other words, 'what is the aim and purpose of marriage?'

Some of the traditionally popular answers are: we marry because 'Allah has ordained marriage for all Muslims'; 'a human being simply cannot live without a partner of the opposite sex'; 'we have a duty to procreate and propagate the human race'; 'it is the legitimate channel of satisfying our basic needs and urges', etc.

> The Quran states its concept of the relationship of the sexes thus:
> "And among His signs is (this) that He created for you mates (*azwaaj*) from among yourselves, that ye may dwell in tranquillity (*le taskunoo*) with them, and He has put *mawadda* and *rahma* between you (r hearts): Verily in that are Signs for those who reflect." [1]   (30:21)

Further, the relationship between the two must be very close and intimate as this is the objective of conjugal union.

> "...They (your women) are your garments (*libaas*) and ye are theirs garments..." (2:187)

This union aims at intimacy and closeness not only in the physical and emotional sense but, more importantly, also in the ideological sense.

> "Do not marry unbelieving women (*al mushrekaat*) until they become Convinced: a slave woman who is Convinced is better than an unbelieving woman, even though she allures you. Nor marry unbelieving men (*al mushrekeen*) until they become Convinced: a slave man who is Convinced is better than an unbelieving man, even though he allures you ..."

A shared basis of ideology is desirable because otherwise life becomes miserable:

> "...Unbelievers do beckon you to the Fire..."

On the other hand, sharing the Quranic ideology will provide a blissful life:

"... but Allah beckons by His Grace to the Garden (*al Janna*) and protection (*al maghfera*)..." (2:221)

Therefore, the objective of marriage is to have a union with a partner of one's own choice, based upon a shared ideology, to lead a life of closeness, happiness and complementary existence under the guidance of the Quran.

7.3. THE LOGISTICS

This union is to take place through a firm CONTRACT (*meesaaqan ghaleezaa*).2 It has been so eloquently called *an-nikaah* in 4:6.3

Obviously, there are two essential requisites for any contract. One, the parties involved be of mature age and sound mind, and two, they have complete freedom of independent choice on the basis of equality. That is why the Quran links marriage with maturity:

"...until they reach the age (*balaghoo*) of marriage (*an-nikaah*)..." (4:6),

which is the time known as the prime of youth:

"...until he attains the age of full strength (*hatta yablugha asshudda*)..." (6:152)

As to the freedom of independent choice, it says:

"...marry women of your choice / liking (*maa taaba lakum min annisaa*)..." (4:3)

and,

"...ye are forbidden to inherit women against their will (*karhan*)..." (4:19)

It is clear that the Quran is against a *forced* marriage, i.e. marrying under duress due to parental / social pressure (emotional blackmail). But that is not the case with an *arranged* marriage, where arrangements may be made on behalf of the woman (or the man, for that matter, considering the Quranic standpoint of equality of sexes):

"And if ye divorce them before consummation, but after the fixation of a dower for them, then the half of the dower (is due to them), unless they remit it or is remitted by him in whose hand is the marriage tie (*be yadehee 'uqda tun nikaah*)..." (2:237)

The Quran has not even mentioned, let alone recommend, an officiating priest for the marriage ceremony. However, as it is a contract (4:21), it must be recorded, witnessed and made public. 4

It is a pity that 'traditional' Islam approves of marriage without witnesses. Maulana Abul Ala Maudoodi, the founder of Jamaat-e-Islami, a much celebrated scholar of modern times, sanctions it. Using a hypothetical situation where a couple are the only survivors marooned on a remote island after a shipwreck, he permits *temporary* marriage. Please refer to his *Zabt e Wilaadat*, and his monumental work *Tafheem al Quran*, more specifically to *Tarjumaan al Quran*, August 1955, Lahore, Pakistan .

How can one forget/overlook the fact that the Quran calls it *meesaqan ghaleeza* (a firm covenant/contract)?

7.4. DOWRY / GIFTS

The tradition of dowry (gifts given to the newly-weds by the bride's parents) has not been mentioned in the Quran. However, the husband is obligated to present the wife with some gift(s).5 The Quran uses the terms *sadaqa* and *ajr* for such gifts. It is not a transactional payment – just a gift:

> "And give the women their dower (*sadaqaatehinna*) as a gift (*nehla*)..." (4:4)

7.5. RIGHTS AND RESPONSIBILITIES

As a matter of principle, the Quran stands for equality of sexes. To start with, both were created from the same original source.

> "O people! Abide by your Sustainer's law, Who created you from ONE being ; and from that created its partner and from them made males and females in abundance.' 6 (4:1)

Both command respect simply because of being human:

> '...and we have (bestowed) respect upon children of Man.' (17:70)

They were both deceived by the Devil:

> '... then they were both misled by the *Shaitaan*...' (2:36)

Both stand equally to receive the outcome of their respective deeds:

> 'And whoever does of good deeds – be it male or female – and has conviction, they will enter Paradise....' (4:124 and 3:195)

They enjoy equal rights (and responsibilities):

> '...and for them (females), just like to them (by males) according to the equitable...' (2:228)

The Quran could not have been any clearer than this on the equality of sexes. But, sadly, the traditional Islam reduces the woman to a position completely and absolutely subservient to the man, especially within marriage. The Messenger is reported to have said,

> *Any woman who dies while her husband is pleased with her enters Heaven.* (Abu Daood, al-Tirmadhi, Ibn Majah, etc.)

> *A woman's prayers or good deeds will not be accepted [by God] as long as her husband is upset with her.* (Ibn Hajar al-'Asqalani in *Fath al Bari*)

> *If a wife would truly acknowledge the rights of husband over her, she would remain standing [in his service] as he eats his lunch or supper until he finishes.* (Al-Hindi in *Kanz al-'Ummal*)

And to top it all,

> *If I were to command anyone to prostate to another, I would have ordered a woman to prostate to her husband because of the enormity of his rights over her.* (Abu Daood in *Sunan*) 7

Both have equal right and access to whatever they respectively earn :

> '...to men is allotted what they earn and to women is allotted what they earn...'(4:32)

Both have equal responsibility in the eyes of social as well as legal law:

> 'The fornicator-male as well as female–, so flog each of them with a hundred lashes....... and let a group of the Convinced witness their punishment.' (24:2)
> 'Say to the Convinced men to lower their gaze and guard their chastity...' (24:30)
> 'And say to the Convinced women to lower their gaze and guard their chastity...' (24:31)

Both have equal potential:

> 'Verily, (for) the Muslim men and women, the convinced men and women, the devoted men and women, the true men and women, the steadfast men and women, the submissive (to the will of God) men and women, the truthful men and women, the self-controlling men and women, the guarding men and women of their chastity, and those men and women who remember God in abundance, Allah has prepared great reward and protection.' (33:35)

Therefore, both partners have equal rights and responsibilities within a marriage contract. That is why, in case of a marital discord, they have equal rights to break up the partnership. More of that (divorce) comes later; first, some issues within marriage.

7.6. RIGHTS AND RESPONSIBILITIES WITHIN MARRIAGE

Once married, a couple are faced with certain social issues: setting up home as a nuclear family or within an extended one; behaviour towards and relations with the in-laws; work, jobs and career; when to have children and how many and how to raise them, etc.

These are what they are – social issues. The Quran has not dealt with them specifically or in detail because social norms are subject to change with the passage of time. It provides basic guidelines from which specifics may be derived or inferred.

To be a nuclear family or be a part of an extended one is purely a matter of choice and depends upon the particular social environment a couple finds itself in. According to the Quran, when they have reached the age of maturity (4:6), they are responsible for their own decisions. In general, however, they must behave respectfully, if not lovingly, to their parents: "...; Be good to (your) parents..." (6:151).

This is because old age brings frailty and feebleness of faculties, such as nerves and memory (36:68; 16:70; 22:5) and also because they (parents) cared for them (children) when they were little. Therefore, one must be polite to one's parents:

> "Thy Lord hath decreed that ye follow none but Him, and that ye be kind to parents whether one or both of them attain old age in thy life, say not a word of contempt (*fa laa taqul lahumaa uf'fin*), nor repel them, but address them in terms of honour (*wa qul lahumaa qaulan kareema*). And out of kindness, lower the wing of humility, and say, 'My Lord! bestow on them thy mercy just as they cherished me in childhood.'" (17:23, 24)

The same holds good for one's in-laws:

> "It is He Who created man from water; then has He established relationships of lineage (*nasaban*) and marriage (*sehran*)..." (25:54)

They are both (wife as well as husband) free to work (to be gainfully employed) and pursue careers as is clear from 4:32 quoted earlier.

As far as planning a family (deciding when to have a child) is concerned, it needs special attention. It is dependant upon our understanding of the Quran's viewpoint on human sexuality. In view of its importance I shall deal with it later.

7.7. DIVORCE – *ONE OR THREE?*

Contrary to the popular impression, divorce is *not* a private affair of a couple. Neither is it the exclusive privilege of the husband, left to his whim in an angry moment or due to some other ulterior motive (58: 2, 3, 4).8 The situation has to be dealt with calmly and rationally. If the situation of discord (*shiqaaq*) persists, divorce can take place through a court of law but only after efforts at reconciliation have been made.

> "If ye fear a breach (*shiqaaq*) between them twain, appoint (two) arbiters, one from his family, and the other from hers; if they seek to set things right, Allah will cause their reconciliation...." 9 (4:32)

Again, for the wife, it says:

> "If a wife fears cruelty (*nushooze*) or desertion (*ae'raaz*) on her husband's part, there is no blame on (either of) them if they arrange an amicable settlement between themselves–and such settlement is best–even though (men's) souls are swayed by greed. But if ye do good and practise self- restraint, Allah is well-acquainted with all that ye do." (4:128)

But, if and when all reconciliatory efforts have failed, the case goes before a court of law of the Quranic government:

> "O Prophet! When ye do divorce women, divorce them at their prescribed periods...." (65:1).

Thus separated, this shall be counted as the *first* divorce of a maximum of three a couple are allowed in their entire married life. After this first separation, the man is free to marry another woman but the wife has to wait (*'idda*) for a period of three menstruations if she wishes to marry a man other than the husband she has divorced. (This is only to see if she is pregnant). But if she decides to remarry the same husband, she does not have to wait.10 Also, women no longer menstruating due to age or medical reasons have no waiting period. There is no *'idda* for a wife whose marriage has not been consummated.

In case a couple remarry one another after this first divorce, they have one more chance of separation / divorce (with the permission to remarry) in their married life if things unfortunately come to a head once again. The procedure mentioned before shall be repeated and they will be registered as having availed the *second* chance in the history of this marriage.

If things between them come to the same sad end the third time, they shall be allowed to divorce the *third* time which will be the FINAL separation of the two. If they ever wish to remarry one another, the only situation shall be if the woman has married another man and has been divorced through afore-mentioned proper procedure.

7.8. DIVORCE IN TRADITIONAL ISLAM

It is tragic how traditional Islam, based upon *Hadith* and *fiqh* (jurisprudence) formulated during the late Umayyad and early Abbasid periods of autocratic, monarchical (and hence, non-Quranic) rule, deals with divorce and related issues.

First, the right of divorce rests exclusively with the husband who can exercise his right arbitrarily at will or whim without having to give reasons for his decision. He can do it simply by uttering the word *talaaq* three times (*talaaq thalaatha / baaen*) in the privacy of their home. On the contrary, the wife has to go to a court of law (*khul'*) if she wishes to 'be divorced'. Once divorced thus, the couple can remarry only if the wife is temporarily married to another man for one night, the marriage is duly consummated, and she is divorced the next day!! This is termed *halaala*, derived from the verb *tehellu* in 2:230. [11]

Such rules and regulations are clearly demeaning to women and are certainly against the Quranic spirit. They owe their origin to the basically flawed notion of the female inferiority, sadly derived from *Hadith*.

> 'Conservative Muslim thinkers have even revived discredited anthropological theories purporting to show that the cranial capacity of women is far smaller than that of a man. "Women have less reason and faith," goes one famous hadith'. (p. 301) [12]

Based upon the Biblical version of the creation of Man (Adam and Eve), the *Hadith* maintains that the woman was created for the sole purpose of serving and pleasing the man. Abu Hurayrah reported that the Prophet said,

> 'Take good care of women, for they have been created from a crooked rib, and the most crooked part of a rib is its upper part. If you try to straighten out a rib, you will break it and if you leave it [alone] it will remain crooked. So, take good care of women.' [13]

No wonder that traditional Islam considers women as a necessary evil, which may be quite easily discarded. Abdel Aziz bin Abdullab ibn Baz, the Grand *Mufti* (juror) of *Masjid el Haraam* (the Grand Mosque – Ka'aba – in Mecca, Saudi Arabia) states in his *Majmu' Fataawa* (A Collection of Decrees) that "some women are bad omens, and therefore, divorcing them is justifiable." This he bases upon, and cites, a Prophetic tradition saying,

> "If bad omens exist in anything, they exist in [some] houses, women and mounts."

That should explain why Muslim men in general, and conservative men in particular, have been behaving so arrogantly towards women for centuries. Their display of male chauvinism is at its worst when they are husbands. They give themselves the right of divorcing wives unilaterally and arbitrarily on the flimsiest of excuses – setting foot out of their house without prior permission of the husband, answering him back when he is reproaching her, not minding the house to his liking, mere suspicion of lewdness, not being respectful and subservient to her in-laws, and being unable to produce a male child or being barren. This background should also provide a backdrop for some other issues which are discussed later in this chapter [for example,

> 'Men are lords over women..' from *An-Nisaa* (The Women) – 4:34].

That should explain the Quranic statement "Divorce is only permissible twice…" (2:229) 15

7.9. SOME CONFUSING POINTS CLARIFIED

(i). 'Men are *Qawwamoon* over women ' (4:34)
This verse is frequently quoted by traditionalists to establish male supremacy over women, specifically in the realm of marriage. The misconception has occurred due to translating *Qawwamoon* as 'overlords' or 'masters'. In fact, the term springs from the root *qa-waow-meem* (QWM), which basically means 'to be balanced and established'. Some other derivatives from the same root are : *qaama* (to rise, to stand up), *aqama* (to straighten, to regularize), *qawwaam* (provider of sustenance), *qeema* (price), *isteqaam* (balance), *musteqeem* (balanced), *taqweem* (to maintain balance, hence calendar), *qiwaam* (preservant), *qiyaama* (the Day of Uprising), *qayyum / qeyyaam* (provider – Allah – of balanced sustenance), etc.

The particular biological and physical constitutions of men and women make them suitable for certain areas of society as far as division of labour is concerned. Men have superior muscular strength while women go temporarily out of action due to menstruation, pregnancy and childbirth. Consequently, the Quran recommends that men take the general overall responsibility of producing and providing means of sustenance and women fulfil their role of propagating mankind by bearing, nourishing and raising children. 16

Therefore, men (not husbands) have the basic responsibility of providing and maintaining a balanced system of sustenance for women (not wives) to flourish. This will of course be done with the help of, and in partnership with, women. Society functions only when both sexes co-operate and work in a complementary manner. Before we study the rest of this important verse, a look at the conservative concepts is in order.

Traditional Islam translates and interprets this verse in the light of its attitude towards women mentioned earlier. It is taken to mean that ,

> 'men are lords over women because Allah has given men superiority over women and also because men spend their money on women. Therefore, good wives are obedient to, and guard their chastity in the absence of, their husbands. If husbands fear disloyalty and ill conduct

> from their wives, they should admonish them first, refuse to share their beds next, and last, beat them...' [17]

That is why Muslim jurists, like Ibn al-Jawzi (d. 521 H / 1201 AD), assert that a wife should consider herself her husband's slave.

> 'It is incumbent upon a woman to know that it is as if she is owned (*ka al-mamlookah*) by her husband, therefore she may not act upon her own affairs or her husband's money except with his permission. She must prefer his rights over her own and over the rights of her relatives, and she must be ready to let him enjoy her through all clean means. She must not brag about her beauty and must not taunt him about his shortcomings...It is incumbent upon a woman to endure her husband's mistreatment as a slave should. [18]

The *Musnad* by Ibn Hanbal records a report by Anas bin Malik stating that the Prophet said,

> 'If a woman prays five [times a day], fasts Ramadan, *obeys her husband*, and guards her chastity, she will enter heaven.' [19]

Now if we interpret the same verse (4:34) within the Quranic perspective, it will doubtlessly appear in a very different light, presenting a picture in line with the Quranic message and theme.

> *Men are protectors of, and providers of sustenance for, women because they both have attributes better than the other; hence the sustenance produced by men is used to maintain women in an environment conducive to the development of women, who are then able to utilise their own capabilities in the best way, i.e. to guard that secret gift (the human foetus).*
> *If then any women shirk unreasonably from this basic responsibility, the society should first try to educate them. Failing that, they may be interned, or in extreme cases, punished (according to due legal process).* [20]

(ii) Share of Inheritance
A woman is entitled to parental inheritance at a rate half that of a man. It is not because she is inferior to man but because of the situation illustrated in 1 above. A man needs more because he is going to be a *qawwam* to a woman. However, the inheritance situation and its laws belong to a temporary phase as has been explained in Chapter 4, Part II, The Quranic Economics. Once the Quranic social system is fully in place, the question of inheritance will no longer apply.

(iii) Testimony in a Court of Law
It is erroneous to infer from verse 2:282 that one man equals two men, therefore one woman equals half a man! The verse in question says:

> '...and get two witnesses from your men; and if you cannot get two

> men, then one man and two women such as you choose, *so that if one of them(women) errs, the other can remind her...'* (2:282) (my emphasis)

As is obvious, two women are needed so that one (the one witness) may lean on the other if need be. That probably is the reason behind having two men witnesses in the first place! Why has it specifically been mentioned in the women's case? The explanation is presented in the following section.

(iv) Women are less eloquent (and intelligent) than men
From verse 2:282 it is popularly inferred that women are naturally born with inferior intellectual faculties than men. But the Quran makes it clear that that particular condition of women is due to social upbringing and engineered environment. About the state of women in the Arab society of the time it says:

> '...the one brought up in trinkets (jewellery) and unable to give a clear account in a dispute...' (43:18)

But, she is not created like that, and certainly does not have to stay in that state for ever. With appropriate social conditions provided, she can, and surely will, realize her full potential. In a paradisiacal life,

> '...she will become eloquent and mature..' (56:37)

7.10. POLYGAMY

In rare particular social situations, the Quran does allow a man to take more than one wife at a time.

> "*If ye fear that ye shall not be able to deal justly with the orphans* [21] *(al-yataama), marry women of your choice, two, or three, or four; But if ye fear that ye shall not be able to deal justly (with them), then only one, or that which your right hands possess. That will be more suitable to prevent you from doing injustice.*" (4:3) (my emphasis)

It is obvious from the rules and regulations regarding marriage (and divorce) we have seen earlier in this paper that the decision for men to take more than one wife at a time is by no means individual or arbitrary. This is a social concern and shall be dealt with and decided upon by society that will formulate proper regulations and procedures for such a social emergency.

One may wonder and ask: What have 'orphans' to do with the question of multiple wives? In normal English (as well as Urdu) usage the term 'orphan' / *yateem* is applied to a child who has lost its father. In Arabic, however, the term has a much wider application. It springs from the three-letter root *ya-ta-meem* with the basic meaning of being lonely and forlorn – *al yuteem* (a sandy piece of land, separate from its surrounding land; *al maitam* (anything which is unique); *durra tun yateema* (a rare and unique pearl); *imraa tun mootim* (a widowed woman whose children become orphans); *teiteem* (a husbandless woman). That is exactly the sense in which the Quran uses the expression *yataama an nisaa* [the orphaned (lonely and forlorn) women] in *An-Nisaa* – 4:127. That should clear the confusion; the Quranic verse in question (4:3) is referring to lonely and forlorn women *not* to orphaned children.

It should also be clear from the pre-condition given in 4:3 that before allowing polygamy, the Quranic society must exhaust all other avenues of amicably dealing with the situation of *al yataama*. It should also be clear from 4:3 that in the Quranic society the norm is monogamy (one wife) and polygamy is an exception.

7.11. REASONS FOR TAKING MULTIPLE WIVES

In the Quranic social order, men are not allowed to take more than one wife at a time for personal reasons such as disobedience, beauty of another woman (2:221), or even being barren. Conception takes place according to laws of Nature and it is *not* the sole (or fundamental) objective of marriage.

> "To Allah belongs the dominion of the heavens and the earth. He creates what He wills. He bestows male or female according to His Will. Or He bestows both males and females, and He leaves barren whom He wills: "For He is full of knowledge and power." (42:49,50)

The only permissible reason, as already mentioned, is a governmental decision on the basis of exceptional demographic situation resulting from social causes (4:3).

7.12. MULTIPLE WIVES IN 'TRADITIONAL' ISLAM

Quite contrary to this Quranic concept, traditional Islam maintains that multiple wives are permissible also because of sexual reasons. Abul 'Ala Maudoodi, in his *Tafheem al Quran*, asserts that the provision of multiple wives is designed to cater for the needs of oversexed men.[22] Incidentally, in traditional Islam, the desire to have multiple partners goes beyond the Quranic maximum of four at a time. In addition to the four legal wives, a Muslim is allowed to have a limitless number of slave girls. The victorious Muslim soldiers are allowed to take the female prisoners of war as sexual partners *without entering a marriage contract*![23] That is not all. Traditional Islam promises Muslim men a harem in Paradise. A Prophetic tradition (*hadith*) states,

> 'For a heavenly resident of a lower status, there will be in Paradise, in addition to the worldly wives, created by the Almighty 72 wives.'[24]

7.13. THE AMOROUS MESSENGER

It is this obsession with sex, to the point of perversion, on the part of Traditional Islam that has led to scandalous misrepresentation of the Quran and also that of the personality of the Messenger. There is no shortage of anti-Messenger literature by non-Muslims depicting Mohammed as a sexually obsessed man.25 A few years before the creation of Pakistan, there occurred in the northern city of Lahore an incident of murder, which shocked the Muslims of the sub-continent. A simple Lahorite, by the name of 'Ilmuddin, knifed to death Rajpal, a Hindu publisher, for bringing out a book titled *Rangeela Rasool* (The Amorous Messenger). The book had depicted Mohammed as a highly amorous man, almost obsessed with sex. People hailed 'Ilmuddin as *ghaazi* (victorious warrior) for glorifying God's name by avenging the assault on the Prophet's personality . Arrested (he actually walked into a police station and gave himself up), he was sentenced to death. Mr Mohammed Ali Jinnah, later known as the *Quaid-e-Azam* (The Great Leader), the founding father of Pakistan, travelled especially from Bombay to legally represent and defend 'Ilmuddin, who was eventually hanged to death. People began referring to the youth as *shaheed* (martyr) for laying down his life for the cause of Islam. To this day, people remember him as possibly the only Muslim in history to be simultaneously known as *ghaazi* and *shaheed*.
Unbelievable as it may appear, the book *Rangeela Rasool* was merely a collection of selected *hadith*!

7.14. POINT OF ORDER – GENDER DISCRIMINATION

It is only fair to say that, strictly speaking, this practice of polygamy in Islam should be termed *polygyny* (having multiple wives) as compared to *polyandry* (having multiple husbands) because Muslim women are *not* allowed to take more than one husband at any given time. This hint of sexual/gender discrimination becomes stronger when one notices that Muslim women are also not allowed to marry men of the 'People of the Book' as Muslim men are, according to 5:5.

Point of interest 1 – Exceptional Prophetic licence?
It appears that the Messenger was given special and exceptional permission to marry women exclusive of his followers– "…this only for thee, and not for the Convinced (at large)…" (33:50). This discrimination in favour of Mohammed has not been justified in the Quran, and as such, it appears contradictory to the repeated prophetic claims of leading by example through proclamation of *ana awwal al muslemeen* – 'I am the first (to become) Muslim' - as in 6:163 (also in 6:14; 27:91; 39:12; 40:66).

Point of interest 2 – *ma malakat aiemaanukum* – slave girls

Literally, the expression is translated as 'those your right hands possessed.' This is commonly taken to mean slave men and women, who were mostly captives of war. The Quran very clearly put a stop to the practice:

> "Therefore, when ye meet The Deniers (in fight) smite at their necks; at length, when ye have thoroughly subdued them, bind (the captives) firmly; therefore (is the time for) either generosity or ransom:..." (47:4)

This is in accordance with the Quranic principle that no man is to be in servitude to another – not even a prophet! This is clearly stated (3:79). Therefore, the expression refers to slaves who already existed from pre-Islam era. Furthermore, the Quran required Muslims to follow the due process of law if they wished to marry any of *ma malakat aiemaanukum*:

> "If any of you have not the means wherewith to wed (*yenkeha*) free Convinced women, they may wed Convinced girls from among those whom your right hands possess..." (4:25)

However, traditional Islam has always presented a view contrary to that of the Quran.

> 'The state reserves the right (in regard to women captured in war) to either free them for a ransom or without; or exchange them for its own Muslim captives; or distribute them to its soldiers for their use.' [26]

In his *Tafheemaat*, Maudoodi asserts that there is no requirement of *nikaah* (a legal marriage contract) to take these women captives of war as sexual partners (p. 315). Further, he states,

> 'Islamic sharia'(religious law) restricts to a maximum of four the number of nikaah, ...but there is no limitation whatsoever in the case of slave girls.' (p. 319) [27]

It is also a tragic reality of our own age that institutionalised slave trade was officially outlawed in a country like the Kingdom of Saudi Arabia only in 1962!

7.15. FORBIDDEN RELATIONS (INCEST)

The Quran provides a long comprehensive list of prohibited (incestuous) relations:

> "And marry not (*wa la tankehoo*) women whom your fathers married,- except what is past: it was shameful and odious,- an abominable custom indeed." [28]

> "Prohibited to you (for marriage) are: your mothers, daughters, sisters, father's sisters, mother's sisters, brother's daughters, sister's

daughters, foster-mothers (who suckled you), foster sisters, your wives' mothers, your step-daughters under your guardianship – born of your wives to whom ye have been intimate – (but) no prohibition if ye have not, wives of your sons proceeding from your loins, and two sisters in wedlock at one and the same time, Except for what is past; for Allah is Oft-forgiving, most Merciful.

"Also (prohibited are) women already married (*al muhsanaat*), except those whom your right hands possess (*ma malakat aiemaanukum*). Thus hath Allah ordained (prohibitions) for you: Except for these, <u>all others are lawful</u>,29 provided ye seek (them in marriage) with gifts from your property, desiring chastity (*muhseneen*), not fornication (*ghair musaafeheen*).30 Give them their dowry for the enjoyment (*fa ma astamta'um*) 31 you have as of duty......." (4:22, 23, 24)

Having seen the Quranic concept, attitude and rules regarding marriage, it will be worth our while to look at the underlying philosophy/ideology of it all if we are to fully appreciate the Quranic standpoint in this regard.

7.16. THE BASIC PHILOSOPHY: IS SEXUAL URGE INVOLUNTARY?

The dominant notion is that the human sexual urge is entirely involuntary; it is a basic need, which has to be met – comparable to another basic urge, hunger (or thirst); it is a basic instinct of the human species. Unsatisfied, this urge causes physical as well as psychological problems, more in males than in females. Traditional Islam holds the same view and agrees with the sexual urge being a totally involuntary instinct - just as saving and protecting one's life is. That is why, as already mentioned, it allows a sexual union *without* witnesses. Again, it is because of this notion that there has existed – and still does – the Muslim tradition of *zawaaj al mut'a* (temporary marriage). The term is derived from *istimta'* from the three-letter root *meem-taa-'ain,* which means 'enjoyment' or 'pleasure'. It refers to an arrangement where a man and a woman enter a marriage contract temporarily for a declared period of time. 32 Although it was outlawed by the Shah (Reza Pahlavi), and also by the present theological state, the practice of *mut'a* is allowed, and still practised, in the Islamic Republic of Iran as an article of the Shia faith. Conservative Islam derives the term *mut'a* from the Quranic verse 4:24 (*fa ma astamtatum behi min hunna* – 'for the enjoyment you have of them'). The concept is derived from the notion that in some original versions of the Quran, the verse also contained the words *ila ajlin musamma* 'for a declared period.' 33 Credence and support for this un-Quranic notion is obtained from *Hadith*.

'Abdullah bin Mas'ud reports: "We used to go on warring missions with the Messenger of Allah and we did not have any means (to satisfy our natural urges). We enquired if it was better to have ourselves castrated. The Messenger refused to allow that and gave us permission to (temporarily) marry women for a dower of a fabric (or something), etc.'" 34

7.17. THE WEDDING NIGHT / HONEYMOON

Interestingly, this notion is also reflected in the almost universal practice of the wedding night. Most arrangements in a marriage are focussed on, and point to, providing opportunity for the newly-weds to have a sexual union. Serious problems may arise if a marriage is not consummated during the couple's first post-marriage meeting. But, is the sexual urge involuntary? Let us look at the issue from the perspective of the Quran.

The human species has been given by Nature several basic needs and urges. Almost all of them may be traced back to one common original *instinct* at the animalistic level – to save one's own life. This is observable in our behaviour in ordinary living, more so in situations of danger. It manifests itself in certain involuntary actions like respiration, heartbeat, digestion, and also when we startle and panic. Nature gave Man the urges of hunger and thirst to preserve life by nourishing the body. The sexual urge is also an extension of the basic instinct of preservation of life. Commonly, sex is likened to hunger and thirst. But, there are important differences.

Imagine a very ordinary and common situation in which you are doing some important and interesting work. Time passes and your body becomes in need of nourishment. You either 'forget' to eat or consciously postpone feeding your body. Your digestive organs (stomach and throat) keep on sending signals to your brain. You keep ignoring them. The signals keep getting stronger and stronger. Your concentration begins to waver but you carry on regardless. Eventually, your body including the brain begins to experience weakness from lack of nourishment and you cannot function properly. Ultimately, you lose the battle and have to stop working and feed yourself. Otherwise, if you persist and carry on an endless fast, it will ultimately result in your illness and eventual death.

But this is not the case with the sexual urge. It differs from hunger and thirst in TWO aspects. In the same scenario of you working, the passage of time *does not* start any signals. Unlike hunger and thirst, sexual signals need *external* stimuli to trigger. Secondly, if ignored, they do *not* cause physical problems. [35] Physiologically, they work in a direction opposite (from the brain to the genitals) to that of hunger and thirst (from the stomach and throat to the brain). Therefore, sex is *not* like hunger and thirst, which are involuntary and not totally controllable. It is entirely voluntary and controllable. [36]

That is why the Quran recognises desperation in case of food but not in sex. As is well known, the Quran prohibits certain foods as *haraam* (as in 6:145, etc), but allows them in a desperate (life-threatening) situation:

"...But (even so), if a person is forced by necessity, without wilful disobedience, nor transgressing due limits,- Thy Lord is Oft-forgiving Most Merciful."   (6:145) [37]

But, in the case of sex:

"Let those who find not the wherewithal for marriage, KEEP THEMSELVES CHASTE (*wal yast'afif*), until Allah gives them means out of His grace..." (24:33) (my emphasis)

That means that in the Quranic Order one has to control one's sexual urge and satisfy it only within the prescribed Quranic limits (*nikaah*). Transgressing those boundaries is not allowed – because there is no question of desperation – and is therefore *haraam* (forbidden). This is because, in the Quranic perspective, Man's sexual ability has a purpose – *procreation* – just as consumption of food has the basic purpose of providing nourishment to the body. Most enlightened people are likely to agree with the assertion that someone giving priority to pleasure (taste) over utility and purpose (nourishment) in food is not being sensible. By the same token, someone preferring pleasure in sex to its basic function (procreation) is not being entirely sensible. The Quran makes a very clear distinction between sex for procreation and sex for recreation. It does that by using two eloquent expressions in several verses. Please refer to 4:24 mentioned earlier:

"...provided ye seek (them in marriage) with gifts from your property, desiring chastity (*muhseneen*), not fornication (*musaafeheen*)." [38]

The word *muhseneen* springs from the three-letter root *haa-saad-noon* with the basic meaning of 'to keep safe and protected.' Some examples are: *al ehsaan* (to keep something safe and under protection); *haseen* (a safe, inaccessible place); *al mehsan* (lock); *hasaan* (a chaste woman; a pearl); *muhsin* (active – a chaste unmarried woman); *muhsan* (passive – a chaste married woman). [39]

Some examples of the term's usage in the Quran are:

1 "... and they thought that their *husoon* (fortresses) would defend them from Allah..." (59:2)
2 "They will nit fight you together, except in *qur am muhassana* (fortified townships) ..." (59:14)
3 "...the making of coats of mail (armour) *le tuhsenakum* (to guard you)." (21: 80)
4 "...except a little which *mim maa tuhsenoon* (you shall have guarded)." (12: 48)

In the same vein, the Quran refers to *muhseneen* (chaste men) and *muhsenaat* (chaste women) in the context of marriage and sexuality. Clearly, it means people – men as well as women–who fortify themselves within the safe and protected environment of marriage (*nikaah*) and guard themselves sexually. As opposed to *hasana,* the terms *musaafeheen* (males) and *musaafehaat* (females) spring from the three-letter root *seen-fa-ha* with the basic meaning of 'to waste away, to spill.' Some examples are: *safaha ad-dam* (he spilled blood); *safah addama'* (he shed tears; tears started rolling); *as-*

safeeh (a blank arrow in a gambling round). In the pre-Islam Arab society, the message *inkaheeni* meant a marriage proposal while *saafeheeni* meant a suggestion for illicit relations. In the Quran therefore, the expressions *musaafeheen* (males) and *musaafehaat* (females) mean people who throw away (spill) their sexual energy and do not use it for its original purpose (procreation).

The Quran, for precisely this reason, forbids fornication, which is clearly a case of *safaha*. 40

The simile of *hars* (tilth) has been eloquently used by the Quran to drive the point home. In the backdrop of what we have discussed so far in this paper, it is hard to think of a better simile to illustrate the concept of *hasana* and *safaha*.

> "Your women are (as a) tilth (*harsun*)unto you, so approach your tilth (*harsakum*) <u>when</u> you will; and do some (good act) for yourselves <u>in advance</u>..." (2:223)

It may be appreciated that this simile represents very adequately the Quranic philosophy regarding marriage and sex. A farmer is naturally expected to take good care of land to keep it fertile and till it when needed for the purpose of cultivating it to get a good crop and to sow seed properly, sensibly and with good planning. He is doing something good *in advance* (2:223, above). He is engaged in *hasana*. On the other hand, any farmer who tills land just for the pleasure of it, and wastes away seed by spilling it aimlessly, is not being sensible and is engaged in *safaha*.

Before we go any further, explanation of the expression '*when* you will' (*anna shei'tum*) in 2:223 is in order. Traditional Islam translates it as '*how*ever you will'. This is clearly based upon the ideas of conservative Islam elaborated earlier. Needless to say, this attitude has had a very negative and disastrous effect on the Muslim men's sexual orientation and attitude over centuries. The fact of the matter is that the word *anna* has multiple uses as employed in the Quran. For example: '*whence* [from where] comes this?' (3: 37); '*how* will that remembrance profit him? (89:23); *when* (or *how*) shall I have a son? (19:8); *wither* are you going (away from the truth)? (6:95), etc.

It may be deduced from this simile that the Quran suggests that human sexual energy be used when required (family planning) for its primary function of producing children by keeping it safe and guarding it (chastity-*hasana*) within the fortified relationship of monogamous marriage. All forms of sexual activity where the intent is to waste away this precious resource and avoid the natural responsibility/consequence (spill-*safaha*) are forbidden (*haraam*). In a nutshell, to the Quran, sex is for procreation not recreation.

It may be concluded from all we have seen so far that the best form of family planning is abstention.

7.18. SEX AND SOCIETY

The basis of this Quranic attitude is the natural fact, as already discussed earlier, that our sexual behaviour is entirely psychological – it is all in the brain – and therefore totally under conscious human control. Sexually, we are what we learn from our social environment and we become what our society makes us. That is why sexual behaviour varies in human societies. There is no natural instinctive sexual behaviour – it is all learnt. As it has been observed by some writers,

> Every society fashions the development and expression of sexuality in a unique fashion. 41

Another writer notes:

> Most of these (gender signals) are imposed on the child by the society in which it lives. 42

The father of modern psychology, Sigmund Freud, is also of the same opinion though he holds the view that the sexual urge is instinctive in the same way as hunger and thirst are. 43 That is why it has been said,

> 'Of course, the brain can override and suppress such reflex activity – as it does when an individual decides that a sexual behaviour is inappropriate.' 44

7.19. INCEST

This phenomenon can be observed in human history as well as our own daily lives. Because their society accepted the practice, the ancient kings of Persia felt no aversion in marrying their own sisters for the benefit of the dynasty. The same is true of ancient Greeks and Egyptians – Cleopatra was first married to her own half brother Ptolemy. We have already mentioned the pre-Islamic practice of men taking their stepmothers as their wives. Some years ago there was a widely known case of a real brother and sister who got separated at a very young age during World War Two. Years later, quite by coincidence, they met and, not knowing their biological relationship, got married, had children like any other normal couple. All this while, they did not have any qualms about their sexual relationship. However, their world was turned upside down when eventually they learnt about their reality. They were devastated. Sometimes, people may decide consciously to engage in incest. There have been cases of that nature on record in sexually 'liberated and advanced' countries like Sweden. Reportedly, certain groups of Hindu men may marry their own nieces but Muslims do not. Christians feel aversion to the idea of marrying one's first cousin whereas Muslims do not. The point is that legitimacy in matters of sex is learnt not instinctive. 45

Why the Quranic limitations?

That should explain why the Quran holds the view that the human sexual urge is entirely controllable. It requires humans to have a social system in which the norm is one marriage partner at a time. Pre-marital and extra-marital sexual activity is a punishable offence. Most of one's close relatives fall in the category of forbidden relations. Even within marriage, Muslims are expected to employ their sexual energy for procreation alone.[46] Sexual intercourse is also forbidden during Fasting.[47] A state of desperation is not recognised in the case of sexual urge.[48] From all these restrictions, it appears that the Quran wants to limit the sexual activity to the absolute minimum.

In fact, it is safe to deduce that the Quran wants a married couple to engage in this activity only when they need to procreate. [49]

But, why does the Quran take such a strict stand on human sexuality?

7.20 SEX AND CULTURE

It does so because there is a definite connection between a society's sexual habits and its achievements as a civilization. The more restrictive a society is on sexual matters, the better its chances of advancement, progress and prosperity. Dr. J. D. Unwin of Cambridge University, UK, observes in his valuable research *Sex and Culture*:

> 'No creative energy can be retained in a society unless every generation is raised with values restrictive of sexual activity to the minimum. If that society keeps up such a system, it will have a brilliant existence.' [50]   *(translated from Urdu)*

Debateable it may be, but it is intriguing to look at great civilizations and empires in history from that perspective. The mighty Greek and Roman civilizations began to crumble soon after they sank in debauchery. The Arabs themselves rose to great heights when Islamic teachings put a clamp on uncontrolled sexual practices. In our own modern times, the British Empire flourished as long as Victorian values of modesty were the norm. The great United States is currently undergoing the same phase. It seems that unbridled sex weakens a nation by sapping a valuable source of energy, which can be channelized to constructive activities. [51]

That is exactly what the Quran says:

> "Those who invoke not with Allah any other god, nor slay such life as Allah has made sacred, except for just cause, nor commit fornication,- and any that does this meets *athaama*." (25:68)

Traditionally, *athaama* is translated as 'punishment' or 'sin' (as indeed done by Abdullah Yousuf Ali in this verse). But, the term actually has meaning much deeper than that. It springs from the three-letter root *alif-say-meem* (AThM), with the basic meaning of 'weakness, exhaustion, depression, and sapping of strength'. *Al aathema* is a very tired she-camel, which walks slowly; *al mu'aathem* is a camel which cannot walk on due to exhaustion. To Ibn Faaris, the term has the basic meaning of being late and to fall behind.52 Some examples of its usage in the Quran are:

> 1. In case of drinking intoxicants and gambling –
> "…and their disadvantages (*ithmuhumaa*) are greater than (*nafe'humaa*) their advantages…" (2:219)
> 2. About heavenly drinks – "…free of frivolity and *(taatheem)* depression (hangover)… (52:23)
> 3. About life in Paradise – people there "Will not hear any frivolity and no *(taatheem)* nonsense." (56:25)

So, this is another of the Quranic permanent values (fundamental principles).

7.21. PERMANENT VALUES AND TEMPTATION

The Quran, as many of us know, bases its system on certain fundamental principles (permanent values) called *aqdaar*. In this chapter we have mentioned a couple of them. One is sanctity of life. One is to preserve life as a matter of obligation. Taking life without just cause is forbidden (25:68). So much so, that one is allowed to miss fasting, even allowed to consume forbidden (*haraam*) food, if faced with a life-threatening situation. What we see here is a clash of values – in this particular example, the value of abstaining from *haraam* food vs. the value of preserving life. It means, in case of tie between two values, the bigger, more important value must be upheld. Chastity is another Quranic permanent value. It is so important that, in the case of a tie between preserving chastity and saving life, it is chastity, which must be preserved.

7.22. THE STORY OF JOSEPH

True to its style, the Quran has an example from real life (history) to illustrate this point. It is in the story of Joseph. A son of Jacob (*Ya'aqoob*), he was cast away in a dried well by his jealous brothers. Rescued by a passing caravan, Joseph was sold into slavery in Egypt. He was bought by an influential Egyptian (probably a high-ranking official). He eventually rose to great heights in that society to become next only to the Pharaoh himself. While in the service of his master, Joseph underwent an experience, which concerns us at the moment. He was young and probably handsome. In the usual decadent ways of the rich and the powerful, his master's wife fell for Joseph and wanted to commit adultery with him. To fully appreciate Joseph's dilemma and his resolve, one has to remember that he was between the rock and a hard place. To one side there was all the temptation of the favours of a beautiful, wealthy woman (and most certainly the prospect of many more of her friends). To the other was the threat of persecution resulting from refusing to comply with his masters' wish (eventually, a prolonged imprisonment did come to him). But, Joseph stood fast and firm. He was faced with making a choice between saving his life or his chastity. He chose chastity:

> "...He said, 'I seek refuge with Allah! Truly, He / he is my sustainer, He/he made my sojourn agreeable! Truly to no good come those who do wrong." (12:23)

In legend, Joseph is famous for his physical beauty and attraction. In fact, Joseph's beauty lies in his character and resolve to uphold the Quranic permanent value of preserving chastity.

Therefore, the Quran asserts that uncontrolled and unbridled sexual activity will result in weakness and depression of body and mind, which will cause the gradual downfall of a society. That is why it recommends a tight control on this valuable human faculty and suggests employing it properly only when required and under careful planning. Only that will ensure an escape from degradation, adversity and downfall.

* * * * * *

Chapter 8

'MIRACLES' IN THE QURAN

All religions, divine or otherwise, have their own respective miracles. In ancient Greek and Roman mythologies we see gods controlling and manipulating the natural elements; in Hinduism, god Arjun works wonders with his bow and arrows; in Judaism, Moses parts the Red Sea to deliver the Israelites out of Egyptian bondage; in Christianity, Jesus raises the dead back to life, and so on. Conventionally, the dominant majority of Muslims still believe in a number of miraculous events associated with Prophet Mohammad. Most of these accounts, as a rule, come from the literature of Traditional Islam. 1 Many, however, claim their authenticity from the Quran. It is believed by most religious-minded people that prophets of God were bestowed with superhuman powers to perform miracles (or they were performed by God for them) as the need arose. These were occurrences which appeared to defy the common laws of Nature and were incomprehensible to ordinary mortals as to the mechanics of these events. I intend to examine some of them in the light of the teachings of the Quran itself.2 I shall begin with establishing the Quran's attitude and stance towards such events as are commonly known as miracles; I shall raise and attempt to address questions like 'Were they really extraordinary, supernatural occurrences violating the laws of Nature? Can they be interpreted and explained from a practical and scientific perspective? What was their aim and purpose in any case? Were those aims realized, i.e. were they successful?'

Since I intend to look at this question from the Quranic perspective, it is imperative to first look at the language used by the Quran in this regard.

8.1. THE LINGUISTIC ASPECT

For the seemingly extraordinary, supernatural occurrences such as are taken to be 'miracles' the Quran has used a number of terms.3

1. From root *'ain-jeem-za* ('JZ)
The Arabic lexicon *Taaj al'Uroos* gives its basic meanings as 'to lag behind' or 'to get something at the last moment'.4 Generally, *'ajzun* means

'be unable to.' To some, it means 'weakness' and also 'the last part/end of'. Therefore, *'ujooz* is 'an old man' and *'al'Ijza'* is 'the last child of an old man.'5 It is also used for the last part of a tree trunk, which connects with soil as in the Quran's *a'jaazu nakhlen* (54:20).6 Again, *a'jaza* means 'to consider weak', 'to render weak or powerless' as in *inna hum laa yu'jezoon*–'they cannot render powerless'–(8: 59).7 Also, *mo'jez* is 'the one who frustrates/defeats' as in (46:32).8 *Mo'aajezeen* means 'those who strive to frustrate' as in 22:51.9

2. From root *seen-Haa-raa* (SHR)
This linguistic root carries the basic meaning of 'to turn/change direction, to misrepresent, to deceive'10 as 'to present falsehood as truth'. Some have said it means 'to turn something from reality to illusion'.11 Also, it refers to all things very subtly deceptive.12 Eventually, the term came to represent deception in the ordinary everyday sense of the word. For example, *sahara hu wa sah-hara hu* means 'he was deceived' as in (26:153, 185).13 *'Anzun mas-hoora* is a goat with big teats but little milk. *Al-mas-hoor* is someone of deranged mind. His adversaries called Mohammed *rajulun mas-hoor* (17:47)14 – a man under deception. In addition to 'deception', *sehr* is also used in the sense of 'falsehood' or 'a lie' as in (11:7).15 Thus the term *saaher* is used for someone who lies, deceives and presents falsehood (evil) in the cloak of truth (good). Indeed, the Deniers called the messengers of God precisely that (51:52).16 For obvious reasons, this term is also used for 'magic'.
Anthropologists, particularly researchers into Man's religious past, have identified an Age of Magic in the human march to civilization. They have shown the strong links between magic and origins of ancient pagan religions.17 The transfer from the Age of Worship to the Age of Magic was mankind's first step towards rational thought. In the former, Man was in awe of Nature whereas in the latter he tried to find some order and logic in Natural phenomena. This was gradually taking him to the current Age of Science.

3. From root *alif-ya-ya* (AYY)
This root is the origin of the word *aaya* (which is commonly translated as 'verse') and carries the basic meaning of 'sign' or 'symbol'. In fact, it is used for any visible part of something, which is partly hidden and serves as an indicator of the whole.18 In the Quran, it has been used in this sense in several instances: for a she-camel by Prophet Saaleh (7:73)19, for Noah's ark (29:15)20, and for a memorial (landmark) in 26:128.21 The Quran uses it for non-concrete things too, such as evidence to promote logic and understanding as for the cycle of day and night in (17:12).22 It is this term that has been used in the Quran closest to the concept of a miracle. For example, we can see (2:118)23, (6:109)24, (13:7)25, and several others.

8.2. THE QURANIC STANDPOINT ON MIRACLES

First of all, according to the Quran, the Universe works on firm and permanent (unchanging) laws. One does not notice any change, not even a detour, in the laws of Nature. That is the firm and reliable basis for our knowledge of our environment (Science).

> "...But no change wilt thou find in (*sunnat* Allah) Allah's Way:
> No turning off wilt thou find in Allah's Way." (35:43)[26]

Not only that, but He does not allow anyone else to do it:

> "...there is none that can alter the Words (and Decrees) of Allah..." (6:34)[27]

So much so that He even follows those laws Himself!

> "...Say: 'To Allah; He hath inscribed for Himself *ar-rahma*..." (6:12, 54)

Secondly, there is no compulsion whatsoever in matters of religious belief (2:256).[28] No one has the right to force a particular philosophy on anyone by coercion or psychological pressure, which is what miracles essentially do. So much so, that Muslims are instructed to stand up against it and fight those who try to compel others (2:193).[29] The Messenger Mohammed himself was rhetorically asked:

> "...Will thou then compel mankind, against their will, to be convinced?" (10:99)

That is why the Prophet of Islam did not have, and did not perform, any miracles to prove his point. In response to demands and challenges for miracles, the Quran said:

> "...But thou art truly a warner and to every people a guide." (13:7)

and,

> "...Say: 'Truly Allah leaveth, to stray, whom He will; but guideth to Himself those who turn to Him in penitence." (13:27)

and,

> "...Say: 'Glory to my Lord! Am I aught but a man, a messenger?" (17:93)

8.3. MUHAMMAD'S 'MIRACLE'

Instead of complying with their demands for a supernatural occurrence, they (the disbelieving Meccans) were told:

> "They say: 'Why does he not bring us a sign from his Lord?' Has not

> a Clear Sign (*bayyana*) come to them of all that was in the former Books of Revelation?" (20:133)

It was further elaborated and spelled out:

> "And is it not enough for them that We have sent down to thee the Book which is rehearsed to them? Verily, in it is *ar-rahma* and a Reminder to those who are convinced." (29:51)

Therefore, Mohammed had only one 'miracle' – the Quran! It contains knowledge, logic and proofs of the truthfulness of its message (6:104). He did not claim to be superhuman and a miracle worker:

> "Say: 'I tell you not that with me are the Treasures of Allah, nor do I know what is hidden, nor do I tell you I am an angel. I but follow what is revealed to me." Say: 'Can the blind be held equal to the seeing? Will ye then consider not?" (6:50)

He presented his message asking people to be convinced of it on the basis of rational reasoning

> "Say: 'This is my Way (*sabeeli*); I do invite unto Allah – with a certain knowledge (*baseera*)..." (12:108)

All the messengers mentioned in the Quran had essentially the same message for mankind and delivered it in likewise manner [Noah (11: 25-26), Hood (11:50), Saaleh (11:61), Shua'ib (11:84), and also in 23:52. Thus it follows that all the other messengers too did not employ the psychological tool of miracles to convince people of their message.

Let us now see how certain 'miraculous' events may be explained or interpreted in a scientific, practical, down to earth, natural way.

8.4. SOME 'MIRACULOUS' EVENTS REPORTED IN THE QURAN

8.4. (i) Abraham (*Ibraheem*) and the birds

There are several 'supernatural' events associated with this great Semite of the long line of monotheistic messengers. His 'sacrifice' of his son Isma'il (Ishmael; but it is Isaac in the Biblical legend) is the basis of the Muslim festival of *Eid al Adhaa*, the day after the annual pilgrimage, Hajj, on the tenth day of the 12th month of the Islamic (lunar) calendar. (Because of its importance and connection to Hajj, it deserves special treatment; please refer to chapter 10, Rituals in Islam, where I have discussed it in some detail). Here, I wish to discuss another episode of Abraham's life; the one involving some birds. It is mentioned thus in sura *Al-Baqara* (The Cow):

> "Behold! Abraham said: 'My Lord! Show me how Thou givest life (*tuhee*) to the dead (*al mautaa*).'
> He said, 'Dost thou not then believe?' [30]
> He said, 'Yea! But to satisfy my own heart.'
> He said, 'Take four birds; (*fa surhunna ileika*) tie them (or, cut them into
> pieces), then put a portion of them (*minhunna juz un*) on every hill, and call to them: they will come to thee (flying) with speed. Then know that Allah is Exalted in Power, Wise.'" (2:260)

Firstly, the expressions *tuhee* (Thou giveth life) and *al mautaa* (the dead) do not have to be taken in their literal meanings of physical life and the end of it. The Quran makes extensive use of figurative and idiomatic expressions, as indeed is the case with any language, especially when dealing with abstract concepts. In fact, the terms *haya* (life) and *maut* (death) are such cases in point. For example:

> "...in the rain which Allah sends down from the skies, and the *life* which He gives therewith to an earth that is *dead*..." (2:164)
> (my emphasis)

It has also been used as the simile for the rise and fall of nations as in the case of the Israelites:

> "Then we raised you up after your death..." (2:56)

It is precisely in this sense that Abraham seems to have wanted to know the logistics of life and death because he had the responsibility of reviving his culturally, socially and religiously 'dead' nation. Secondly, the expression *fa surhunna ileika* needs our attention. It should be translated thus: *fa* – then, *surhunna* - tie them, *ileika* – to you(r direction / side). Why *to you*? If Abraham was to tie the birds up to (or with?) himself, how would they be put on the hills?

Secondly, we must look at the expression *surhunna*. It springs from the three-letter root *saad-raa-raa,* with the basic meaning, among others, of extreme cold. The sense of tying comes from the fact that intense cold renders things motionless (tied up). *Israar* is to be adamant. Thus *surhunna* means tying them up figuratively (hence *to you*), i.e. to attach them to you, make them get used to you. The convention of translating *surhunna* as 'cut them into pieces' results from the classical exegetes interpreting this passage under the influence of *asbaab an nuzool* – Occasions of Revelation (discussed in detail in Chapter 3); traditional accounts interpreting verse 2:260 are based upon the 'miraculous' nature of the episode in which the dead birds come back to life when Abraham beckons. Hence, the translation as 'cut them.'

Thirdly, why should *minhunna juz un* (a portion of them) necessarily be taken as portions resulting from *cutting* them up?.[31] A *juz* (part) of something can be a part *without* cutting, as in a part of a group / class of people. For example:

> "And verily, Hell is the promised abode for them all! To it are seven gates: for each of those gates is a (special) class (*juz un*) (of sinners) assigned." (15:43, 44)

This should enable us to look at the episode of Abraham and birds in a different way. The verse under consideration (2:260) should be interpreted as follows:

> "And when Ibraheem said, 'Lord! Show me how you (your law) can revive dead nations)? God said, 'Are you not sure yet?' He said, 'Of course, but I want to be absolutely certain (of the mechanics of it as I have to carry out this immensely important task). God said, (it is done through education and training in the same way as if you were to) 'Take four birds and get them so used to yourself that they never leave you. Then, even if you divide them in groups and put them far away from you on hills, they will speedily flock back to you at the faintest of calls. Your dead nation can also be revived in the same manner.'"

8.4. (ii) Moses (*Moosa*)

The founding father of Judaism, Moses, is said in the Quran to have been given nine *ayaas*, or signs (17:101). From this and other locations in the Quran (7:130-134), they may be listed as 1.Drought, 2.Wholesale Death (caused by a flood, or a typhoon, or an epidemic), 3.Locusts, 4.Lice, 5.Frogs, 6.Blood, 7.Plague, and the two he carried with him, i.e. 8. Staff, and 9.'White Hand' (7:107-108). The story of The Children of Israel and Moses is one of the most extensively dealt with by the Quran. It merits special treatment of its own. Here, therefore, I shall confine myself to discussing the confrontation between Moses, along with his brother Aaron (*Haroon*), with the pharaoh in his court and the subsequent exodus of the Israelites out of Egypt involving parting of the sea. The events relevant to this story are located in the Quran mainly in Chapters *Tahaa* (20) and *Ash-Shu'raa* (26).

According to the popularly believed version Moses was instructed by God to go to the pharaoh and demand the release of the Israelites from slavery. Moses went to the court with his brother Aaron and was pitted against the royal magicians. They put down their little ropes and rods, which magically changed into snakes. Instructed by God, Moses put his staff down on the floor. It miraculously changed into a huge python and devoured all the little snakes. The magicians bowed down into submission, accepting Moses' call to the One God. This made the pharaoh very angry. Moses rallied the Israelites and began the exodus out of Egypt towards Palestine with the royal forces in hot pursuit. On reaching the Red Sea, Moses used his staff to hit the water, which miraculously parted exposing enough dry ground for them to cross safely over to the other side. As soon as the Israelites had crossed over, the royal forces with the pharaoh at their head reached the sea. Seeing the dry path trodden by the Israelites, the pharaoh and his army followed. But, the water merged again and the royal forces and the pharaoh drowned and were perished.

Part Two: Chapter Eight

The linguistic perspective

Before I present my version of events, it is desirable, for it to make sense, to consider some of the key terms used by the Quran from a linguistic angle.

1. *'Asaa* (staff) stems from the three-letter root *'ain-saad-waow* ('SW) with the basic meaning of 'gathering, coming together. *Al 'asaa* is group, nation, fraternity.[31] *Shaqq al'asaa* means to sow discord in the group; *'aswat al qawm* means 'I rallied the nation.' Staff is called *'asaa* because fingers of the hand have to come together in order to grasp it. Idiomatically, *alqaa al mussafer 'asaahu* (literally, 'the traveller put his staff down) means 'the traveller reached his destination' or 'he broke journey and stayed.' Therefore, the Quranic utterance *idrib be 'asaak al hajar* [32] (literally, 'hit the rock with your staff') can idiomatically mean 'travel with your group to the stony ground.' Similarly, the expression *idrib be 'asaak al bahar* means 'go with your group towards the sea (or river)' or 'go through the water using your staff.'

2. *Habl* (rope, string) comes from the three-letter root *Haa-ba-la* (HBL) with the basic meaning of 'rope, something to tie up with' (plural is *Hibaal*) – *Habala hu* means 'tied him up with a rope.' Standard Arabic lexicons, such as *Taaj al 'Uroos* and *Kitab al Ishteqaaq*, say *Habl* means 'a covenant. To Raagheb, everything that serves as a means to reach something is *Habl*.[33] That is why the Quranic verse *wa a'tasamoo be Habl Allah jamee'an* means 'you all together keep attached to the Covenant of God (the Quran). [34]

3. *Thu'baan* (python) originates from the three-letter root *thaa-'ain-ba* (ThBN) with the basic meaning of 'to (make) flow,' as in *tha'b al maa'* (flowed water). A snake is *thu'baan* because it walks like a line of flowing water.

What most probably happened

In the light of these linguistic points (and also terms like *sehr* and *saaher* discussed earlier), let us consider the following version.

Moses was appointed by God to rise up for the downtrodden, bonded Israelites against the tyrant pharaoh (20:43). Moses was not sure of his own capabilities as an orator and requested that his brother Aaron be sent with him (26:13). They both presented their mission to the king and delivered God's message (20:49). There took place a debate with Moses and Aaron presenting the brilliant Divine arguments in a smooth flowing manner. The king asked for a big debate with his state scholars and priests. They presented their arguments first, which appeared threatening enough to give Moses some anxiety and worry (20:67, 68). Then Moses presented his arguments on behalf of his nation, which decisively negated and destroyed the other side's case (20:69). The state scholars and priests saw the logic and the light of Truth shone on them. They accepted Moses' mission and answered his call to monotheism (20:70). The

The Quran's Challenge To Islam

king was furious and threatened his courtiers with severe punishment (20:71). But they were steadfast and defied the king because they had seen reason (20:72, 73). Then Moses planned an exodus with his people out of Egypt through a part of land which was seasonally dry but normally under water. The royal army was in hot pursuit, but when they reached the area it was time for the return tide of that part of the sea (or river). They did not quite realize this (or ignored it in the heat of the moment) and were drowned. Thus Moses and Aaron led their people out of Egyptian bondage to freedom and open spaces of the Sinai Desert.

8.4. (iii) David (*Daood*) and Solomon (*Suleimaan*)

The two great king-prophets of The Bible[35], the respected messengers of God in the Quran are the subjects of some of the most fantastic stories widely believed by Muslims as well as Jews and Christians. Detailed accounts in the Tradition (based upon the conventional understanding and interpretation of the relevant verses of the Quran) tell miraculous tales about the famous father and son: David could melt iron simply by touching it, he could play music and sing so well that animals and even inanimate matter (hills and trees) listened in trance; Solomon knew bird-speak and controlled winds at will, he had 700 wives and 300 concubines, he could hear and understand ants speak; both controlled invisible giants (spirits/monsters) and fairies, mountains bowed to them and chanted God's praises, etc.

The linguistic perspective

Let us look at certain Quranic terms before we try to see its version of events.

1. *Tasbeeh* stems from the three-letter root *seen-baa-Haa* (SBH) with the basic meaning 'to swim'[36] - *masbah* (swimming pool), *sabah fin nahr* (he swam in the river), *as saabehaat* (boats), *sabbaah* (swimmer – and also, because of the similarity of movement, quick horse or camel); also, *sabhun* (to work hard for livlihood) and *assabhu* (to roam around the earth / world).[37]

Therefore, *sabahu* means to be diligent and work consistently hard towards a goal. In the Quran,

> "It is not permitted to the Sun to catch up the Moon, nor can the Night outstrip the Day: each (just) swims along (*yasbahoon*) in orbit." (36:40)

That is the sense when God said to Mohammad:

> "True, there is for thee by day (*fin nahaar*) prolonged occupation (*sabhan taweela*)." (73:7)

2. *At-Tair* comes from the three-letter root *taa-yaa-raa* (TYR) with the basic meaning of 'to fly'- *taair* (a bird), *at-tair* (birds / bird) as in 68:19 and 3:48, *istataar* (spreading and dispersal), *al mustateer* (high and spread, affecting the environment (76:7), *at taair* (mind/brain power) 38 - figuratively it can be applied to an elevated person. That is the sense of what Jesus said to his people:

> "... "I have come to you with a Sign from your Lord, in that I make for you out of clay *(at-teen)* as it were, the figure of a bird *(k haya at-tair)*, and breath into it, and it becomes a bird by Allah's leave..." (3:49)

Also, *faras un mutaar / tayyaar* is a good fast-running horse39 as in *wat-taira mahshoora* (collection of swift horses) for David (38:19).40

3. *Mantiq* originates from the three-letter root *noon-taa-qaa* (NTQ) with the basic meaning of 'to speak.' *Nutq* ('voice' with meaningful words) is speech of people, whereas animal voice (sound) is *saut*. *Nutq*, by implication, is used for 'making something clear' as in *nataq al kitaab* (the book explained and clarified).41 Examples from the Quran include *in kaanoo yenteqoon* (if they spoke) in 21:63, and *haaza kitaabunaa yentequ 'alaikum bel haq* – 45:29 (this Our Book clarifies everything truthfully to you).

4. *jabal* stems from the three-letter root *jeem-baa-la* (JBL) with the basic literal meaning of 'something high and consolidated'42 such as a 'mountain' but is figuratively used for the high and mighty of a society, as in 18:47.43 Also, *jibilla* in 26:18443 and 36:62 44 means 'a big (or important) group of people.' 45

5. *namla* (feminine) originates from the three-letter root *noon-meem-la* (NML) with the basic meaning of 'ant' and has *an-naml* as plural and *naml* (masculine) as singular. *Taaj al 'Uroos* says that the Valley of Naml is situated between Jebreen and 'Asqelaan.46 But, if it was located on the road to the country of Sheba *(Sabaa)*, it would have been somewhere near Yemen.47 Therefore, *waad en naml* in 27:18 is not a valley full of insects but the abode of the tribe Naml. And that *an-namla* is a female member thereof is clear from the grammar employed by the Quran; verse 27:18 uses the verb *qaalat* – she said – in the singular feminine mode. If it was an ant, it would not have mattered enough for the Quran to specify the gender of the insect – it could equally have been *an naml* (a male ant).

6. *Jinn* 48 comes from the three-letter root *jeem-noon-noon* (JNN) with the basic meaning of 'to conceal / hide'– *jananun* ('grave', because it conceals the dead), *janeen* (foetus), *junna* (a tool for protection and defence) and *mijanna* (shield) as in 58:16, *la jinna be haazal amr* (there is nothing secretive about this matter), *jinnatun* (madness) as in 23:25. To Raagheb, it

means to conceal not only from vision but also from mind (senses) as in *falammaa janna 'aleihel lailu raai kowkaban* – 'when the night hid him, he saw a star' (6:77).

There is the possibility that in the march of evolution there may have been a species suited to very hot conditions of the Earth in its early developmental stages. It may be called *jinn*:

> "We created Man from sounding clay, from mud moulded into shape; and the Jinn race We had created *before* from the fire of a scorching wind." (15:27) (my emphasis)

But obviously, that species is now extinct. At the time of the Quran, the world in general, and the Arabian desert in particular, was sparsely populated (it still is). There were very few cities, which were really small towns according to our current standards. The desert-dwellers (Bedouins) lived and moved deep in the wilderness, away (hidden - *jinn*) from the town-dwellers (social – *ins*). If we consider the various verses in this regard (such as 6:131, 7:35, 72:1, 6:113, 7:179, etc), it is clear that the term *jinn* refers to the desert-dwelling gypsies. They were – as they still are – physically stronger and culturally weaker than the town people. Because of their comparatively unbridled strength, vigour and free style of life, they were also referred to as *shayaateen* (from the three-letter root *sheen-taa-noon* (ShTN), with the basic meanings of 'unruly and fiery.'

What most probably happened:

In the light of the above linguistic points, the following is our most probable version of the stories about David and Solomon.

After Moses led the Israelites out of the Egyptian bondage into the Promised Land (Palestine), they subsequently rose to great heights of civilization reaching their zenith under David and Solomon. David knew the science of metallurgy and was an expert in making armour (21:80). He was endowed with knowledge (27:15) and a stable realm to rule over (38:20) so that he should rule justly (38:26). He was given Divine guidance, which was contained in a book called *Zaboor / Az-Zaboor* – Psalms (4:163 and 21:105). Big chiefs of mountain tribes had submitted to him and worked for him (38:18). Also, he had under him gypsies of the tribe Tair, which constituted swift cavalry (38:19). Solomon was David's son (38:30) and successor (37:16). He was endowed with knowledge and the quality of decision-making (27:15). His armies comprised of town-dwellers as well as desert people with great cavalry (27:17). He had also subdued the aggressive mountain tribes (21:82), who worked for him on huge building projects which were adorned with paintings and statues (34:12, 13). His naval forces were also very strong and his ships roamed the seas at will (21:81). He carried the Divine Message to the country of Sabaa

(Sheba), ruled by a queen, which was eventually conquered (27:20 – 44). On this expedition, Solomon's army passed through the Valley of Naml (27:18, 19); Hudhud was an officer in this army (27:20, 21). He was not the subject of fantastic stories as believed and propagated by the Israelites (2:102).

8.4. (iv) Jesus Christ (*'Eesaa al-Maseeh*) [49]

The founder of Christianity is widely believed by Muslims as well as Christians to have been born miraculously of a virgin (Mary–*Maryam*), to have performed miracles such as raising the dead and curing the ill, and to have been raised alive from the Cross. A dominant majority of the adherents to both religions believe in the Second Coming of Jesus near the time of the world's end. Let us see what the Quran has to say in this regard.

What the Quran says:

Following from what we have seen earlier (2:164, above) in the case of Abraham and the birds, Jesus' so-called 'miracle' of making a bird of clay and infusing life into it should be taken figuratively, not literally. Similarly, following the Quran's style of figurative and idiomatic use of language, healing the sick should also be considered likewise (3:49). As to his birth and ascension, related mainly in Chapter *Maryam* (Mary), 19:16–34, as well as in Chapter *Aal-e-'Imraan* (Progeny of 'Imraan), 3:35-59, one sees the following as the Quranic version.

> A woman of the family of 'Imran vowed to God to dedicate her expected child for the service of the temple (3:35). She was a bit dismayed when she delivered a girl, who was named *Maryam* (Mary), but kept her vow (3:36). Maryam was put under the guardianship of *Zakaria* – Zechariah - (3:38). By the time she attained maturity, Maryam was convinced of the true *deen* (monotheistic religion of Abraham) and decided to initiate dissent against the false, unholy and unreligious Jewish customs of the time for the emancipation of women (3:42, 43). She decided to rebel against the unnatural and ridiculous practice of celibacy imposed by the religious establishment. After much thought, she took courage and got married and decided to start a family who would carry on the Divine Mission (3:45-54 and 19:16-21). For fear of reprisals she went away for the pregnancy. She gave birth to a boy (19:22-26) and raised him away from her people. At length the boy (Jesus) grew into a fine man and was appointed Messenger by God. Then they came back to their people. In the eyes of the religion of the day, she had committed a great sin – no less than fornication, so the community in general, and the priests in particular, were furious (19:28). She asked them to speak to her son. They said, "How can we speak to one who *was* (not a long time ago) just an infant?" (19:29). Jesus said, "I am indeed a servant of Allah: he hath given me Revelation (*kitaab*) and made me a prophet (*nabi*). And he hath made me blessed wheresoever I be, and hath enjoined on me *salaa* and *zakaa* as long as I live."[50]

About the death of Jesus, the Quran clearly and emphatically denies Crucifixion:

> "That they said (in boast), 'We killed Christ Jesus, son of Mary, the Messenger of Allah":- But they killed him not, nor crucified him. Only a likeness of that was shown to them...for of a surety, they killed him not." (4:157)

His ascension, mentioned in 4:158 (*bel rfa'ahu Allah ilaihe* – Nay, Allah raised him up unto Himself) cannot be physical, as everyone has to meet death (21: 7, 8 and 21:34, 35). Furthermore, in the specific case of Jesus, he was told that he would die a natural death - *inni mutawaffeeka* (3:55).

It logically follows that there is going to be no Second Coming of Jesus, or anyone else for that matter. There is no return to this life once we die (32:12-14; 23: 99, 100).

8.5. 'MIRACLES' OF MOHAMMED

As mentioned earlier, in response to demands of 'miracles' Mohammed presented the Quran on the basis of reason and rational thinking. Also, he declared that he did not possess superhuman attributes, as he was just an ordinary human (18:110).[51] Despite this very clear Quranic statement, conventionally the majority of Muslims have always believed that Mohammed *did* perform miracles. Based upon Traditional Islam, Mohammed is believed to have been of such a brilliant physical constitution that he did not cast a shadow.[52] He could cure the ill and feed a thousand people on one kid, etc.[53] Another favourite dogma of Hadith is the pre-existence of the soul of Mohammed, i.e. the soul of Mohammed was the very first one of all humanity created by God. This is commonly accepted by the writers of *sira* (biographies of the Messenger).[54] Among numerous such 'miracles', two stand out, which I have selected to discuss here.

8.5. (i) THE MOON RENT ASUNDER

According to popular legend Mohammed, in response to the Disbelievers' demands, performed this miracle. Gathering his opponents one night he took them out into the open moonlit desert. Pointing to the full Moon, he moved his finger in a vertical action. The Moon split in two semi-circles, which moved away from each other to the opposite edges of the horizon. After having given his awestruck audience enough time to behold the spectacle, Mohammed motioned the rent Moon back to its normal state. After the American landing on the moon in 1969, stories were heard in Muslim circles that Neil Armstrong heard the *azaan* (the Muslim call for prayer) and observed a crack on the lunar surface running throughout its entire body.

This 'miracle' is traditionally based upon verse 1 of sura *Al-Qamar* (The Moon):

> "The Hour (of Judgement) is nigh and (*wan shaqq al qamaru*) the Moon was cleft asunder." (54:1)

What the Quran says:
The term *shaqqa* comes from the three-letter root *sheen-qaa-qaa* (ShQQ) with the basic meaning of 'to split, rent' and derivatives like *shaqqa 'asaa al muslemeen* (he split and divided the Muslims), *shiqqun / mushaqqa* (back-breaking hard work), *shiqaaq* (opposition and breaking up, as in 4:35), and *shaaqun* (to vehemently oppose, as in 4:115).55 *Al-Qamar* originates from the three-letter root *qaa-meem-raa* (QMR), and is applied to the Moon of the 3rd to the 25th of the month; for the rest of the month it is called *al-hilaal*). Pervez reports from *Ghareeb al Quran* that the Moon was the national emblem of the *jahiliya* (pre-Islam) Arabs.56 Therefore, 54:1 is predicting the downfall of the Arabs opposing Mohammed's message by saying that the fall of the people of the banner of the Moon was imminent.

8.5. (ii) ASCENSION TO HEAVEN (Night Journey – *me'raaj*)

The legend of Mohammad's *me'raaj* (nocturnal journey to heaven) is based upon verse 1 of sura 17:

> "Glory to (Allah) Who did take His Servant for a journey by night from the Sacred Mosque (*Masjid al-Haraam*) to the Farthest Mosque (*Masjid al-Aqsa*) whose precincts We did bless,- in order that We might show him some of Our Signs: for He is the One Who heareth and seeth (all things)." (17:1)

It is said that this miraculous episode took place before *hijra* [the Prophet's migration from Mecca to Yathrib (later, Medina)] one night in Mecca. There are various versions of the occurrence,57 but a collective picture may be constructed as follows.

The Messenger was awakened from deep sleep by Gabriel and served with God's summons. The means of transport was an animal called Buraq, a cross between a donkey and a mule.58 The Prophet was taken from Mecca to the Temple of Solomon in Jerusalem where he led in prayers all the previous prophets, who had been assembled especially for the occasion. After that, Buraq flew Mohammed up to the heavens – all seven of them in turn – meeting various past prophets and visiting a number of celestial and divine sites such as Paradise and Hell.59 Eventually, he reached the Seventh Heaven where he 'met' (conversed with but did not see) the Almighty Himself. At the end, he was brought back safely to his bed in Mecca. Entering the house, Mohammed noted that the locking chain on the door was still swinging from the jolt of his exit at the start of the journey.

In the light of the discussion, therefore, verses 1 to 18 of sura 53 (*An-Najm* – The Star) cannot be referring to events of that nocturnal journey that never took place. They refer to the state, condition, and status of Mohammed's mind, personality and mission in a general sense. Here, I present an interpretation, as I see it, of the eighteen verses.

> 1. As real as the universal phenomenon of stars and their life is (it is equally true that);
> 2. Your Companion (Mohammed) is neither astray nor being misled (when he teaches you the universal principles of life);
> 3. (This is because) He says nothing of his own Desire (he speaks but the Truth);
> 4. He speaks only the inspiration that is revealed to him;
> 5. That knowledge has been given to him by one Mighty in Power;
> 6. The one (God) with (real) Wisdom, Who has propped him up with great calibre and qualities (necessary for the job);
> 7. He (Mohammed) is of as high and lofty of status and character as is the Horizon (you see);
> 8. He has observed The Truth from extremely close quarters;
> 9. Closer in fact than two bows joined together in united shooting; 62
> 10. It is that knowledge (acquired thus) which is given as Revelation to God's Servant (Mohammed);
> 11. (Therefore) His mind and heart in no way falsified the information;
> 12. Will you still – after knowing the source and method of Revelation – Dispute what he says?
> 13. He has seen The Truth in a way entirely different (from yours);
> 14. The Truth was of such power and magnitude that he experienced extreme amazement; 63
> 15. As a result, he knows the principles of life which can lead you to a permanent state of peace and happiness;
> 16. That Eternal Truth is so overpowering that it encompasses everything;
> 17 Despite that awesome situation (God made sure that) Mohammed was not perplexed as he had an extremely important mission to accomplish;
> 18 This is the manner in which he has observed the Great Truths of God.

8.6. CONCLUSION

According to the teachings of the Quran, miracles, as we know them in a conventional religious sense, do not happen because it is a form of psychological pressure on an individual to accept a certain point of view under intellectual duress. They are a violation of Nature's Laws. Furthermore, 'miracles' in religion do not have a direct sensible relationship with the validity of the prophetic messages in support of which those supernatural events are supposed to have happened. To take an example from everyday life, if I were to tell you about a fire, which had broken out somewhere, I would not be able to convince you of the truthfulness of my statement if I could perform certain extraordinary acrobatic actions. I would have to provide some *related* evidence

Part Two: Chapter Eight

What the Quran says:

The term *asra* stems from the three-letter root *seen-raa-waow / yaa* (SRW/Y) with *as- surra* (to travel for most of the night), *as-sarriya* (a battalion of soldiers marching at night), etc among certain other meanings.60 The verse almost definitely refers to a nightly journey as it adds the word *lailan* ('by night') for emphasis. The term *aqsa* comes from the three-letter root *qaa-saad-waow* (QSW) with the basic meaning of 'being distant' in its derivatives – such as *qasa 'anhu* (he distanced from him), *al qaswa* (maximum, as in *as-sur'a tal qsawa* – maximum speed limit), and *makaanan qaseeya* (a place far away) in 19:22, etc.

There seems to be no doubt that *Masjid al-Haraam* refers to the K'aba, the sanctuary in Mecca. But the reference to *Masjid al-Aqsa*, commonly taken as the Temple of Solomon in Jerusalem, is in question. It cannot be the Dome of the Rock, also known as the Mosque of 'Umar, which we today know as Masjid al Aqsa. As the name evidently suggests, it is the spot where 'Umar ibn al-Khattaab, the second Caliph, offered prayers after entering Jerusalem triumphantly. The present Masjid al Aqsa was built by Caliph 'Abdul Mullick in 68 AH.60 The verse could not have referred to the Temple of Solomon as it simply did not exist because it had been destroyed for the second time in its history, and 'completely razed to the ground by the (Roman) Emperor Titus in 70 AD'.61

From a theological point of view, it is inconceivable that Mohammed travelled in a certain direction and reached a specific spot in the Universe where God was located at that given moment. This concept negates the fundamental idea of the person of God given by the Quran. He is everywhere at all times – "*...wa huwa ma'kum aina maa kuntum...*" – He is with you wheresoever ye may be (57:4). So much so, that "*...wa nahnu aqrabu ilaihe min habl al wareed.*"- for We are nearer to him (Man) than (his) jugular vein (50:16), but "*...wlaakin laa tubseroon*"- you cannot see Him (56:85). Therefore, the concept of Mohammed meeting God on the seventh Heaven is tantamount to limiting the Omnipotent, the Omniscient, the Almighty God of the Quran within Time and Space. However, it could not have been a dream because Mohammed was not given to hallucinations or stray imagination of his own: "*maa kazab al fuaadu maa raaea*" – His heart and mind in no way falsified that which he saw (53:11).

I find the explanation given by Pervez the most plausible. Verse 17:1 refers to the Prophet's migration (hijra) from Mecca to Medina. It happened under cover of darkness in the wake of threats to his life and to that of the new movement, Islam. Conditions were more promising in the northern oasis of Yathrib. He was one of the last Muslims to emigrate. The Muslims who had gone on before him had doubtlessly allocated a place for their missionary activities – a mosque (*masjid*). Medina is about three hundred miles across a hostile desert from Mecca. It was quite a distance at the time (nearly a millennium and a half ago!). That place was the 'far away' mosque – *Masjid al Aqsa*.

– such as observing smoke, smelling something burning, people running around frantically, fire engines speeding through the streets, etc. Similarly, if Jesus was to convince people of the individual and collective social benefits for them of his message from the One God, he would have to explain the advantages of his system in comparison to the disadvantages of the system current at the time; wonderful acts like healing the ill and walking on water would not have convinced his audience. As David Hume has observed,

> A miracle is a violation of the laws of nature, and as a firm and unalterable experience has established these laws, the proof against a miracle, from the nature of the fact, is as entire as any argument from experience can possibly be imagined.64

8.7. MIRACLES - TO WHAT END?

This view is supported by historical facts. Apparently, the purpose of miracles was to convert people to a new ideology. But, the sad fact is that these extraordinary events proved unsuccessful in meeting their objective. Abraham, despite having performed the 'miracles' of the birds and of his escape from the fire, was expelled from his home town of Ur. The Pharaoh, along with several of his soldiers and officers, chased Moses and his Israelites out of Egypt despite having witnessed his 'miracles' of the Staff and the White Hand. Jesus was a failure in his mission despite raising the dead, healing the ill, and walking on water. He was still arrested and put on the cross. Christianity did not take roots as a faith until the Roman emperor Constantine converted some three hundred years *after* Jesus' death! Above all, having no shadow, the splitting of the Moon, and the Night Journey were of no use to Mohammed. The Meccans were not intimidated and still plotted to take his life and he had to emigrate under cover of night.

It is not what the God of the Quran does to drive His point home.

> "It may be thou (O Mohammed) will kill thyself with grief that they do not become Convinced. If (such) were Our Will, We could send down to them from the sky a Sign, to which they would bend their necks in humility. But there comes not to them a newly-revealed Message from the Most Gracious, but they turn away therefrom."   (26:3, 4, 5)

It is not befitting the Lord of the Universe, the Most Gracious God, the Allah of the Quran to resort to such methodology. In the words of Hospers:

> We believe that most of the alleged miracles are in some way unworthy of an omnipotent being. If god wanted people to believe in him, why perform a few miracles in a remote area where few people could witness them? Instead of healing a few people of their disease, why not all sufferers? Instead of performing a miracle in Fatima [a

Portuguese village where three illiterate children saw visions of "Our lady of the Rosary" in 1917, why not put an end to the enormous slaughter of World War I, which was occurring at the same time, or keep it from happening? [66]

The Quran says that the Universe is full of Nature's miracles (its handiwork)- *ayaatenaa fil aafaaq wa fi anfusehem* - 'Our Signs in the skies and within their own selves' (41:53) for those who care to ponder upon and study it.[67]

It is a pity that:

"*Wa kaa aiyyin min aayate fis samawaat e wal arde yamurroona 'aleihaa* wa hum 'anhaa mo'rezoon."

"And how many Signs in the heavens and the earth do they pass by? Yet, they turn (their faces) away," (12:105)

Chapter 9

RITUALS IN ISLAM

A 'ritual' (or 'rite') is defined as *'the customary or prescribed form or order of conducting especially a religious or solemn ceremony'*. A 'ceremony' is *'a formal act or a conventional social gesture or act <u>with no intrinsic purpose.</u>'*[1] In Arabic, the word is translated as *sha'eera*.[2] Linguistically, the word stems from the three-letter root *sheen, 'ain, ra* (Sh'R) with the basic meanings of 'to conceive and understand through senses'. It comes from the original physical meaning of *sha'r/sha'ra* (hair on the human body).[3] It acquired the applied meanings of understanding most probably because hair give some information about the body. It has derivatives like *ash'arahu* (told or informed him), *shei'r* (poetry/verse), *shaa'er* (poet)[4], *she'aar* (code words, signs, or symbols for soldiers or travellers), *sh'eera* (the animal taken along on the journey to the *Hajj* (Pilgrimage), *ish'aar* (signs and symbols put on such animals, *she'aar al Hajj* (signs, symbols, and rituals of *Hajj*), *mash'ar* (the location of such a sign – with its plural being *mashaa'er* or *sh'aa er*).[5]

Respecting, and preserving the sanctity of, rites and rituals are important in social, political and religious contexts. Since the Quran views life as one whole encompassing all these and other areas, Quranic rituals assume a multi-fold importance for its followers. *Sh'aa erAllah* (5:2) must be respected and followed with sincerity and devotion. But, it must be remembered that they are just that (signs and symbols)! They are formal expressions of some principles. They are not an end in themselves. They can never take precedence over the principles they represent. For instance, the flag of a country represents a nation and/or a geographical territory. When a soldier dies trying to hold it up in battle, he does not lay down his life for the piece of cloth he is holding; he dies for his country/nation. Forms of greeting like a handshake, an embrace, and utterance of words like *as-salaamualaikum* (literally, 'peace be upon you', the standard Quranic greeting) are instances of social rituals. A handshake is a formal expression of the good intentions the two parties involved have for one another. If the parties involved are fully aware and convinced of the good intentions, a handshake becomes unnecessary. In case of one or both parties harbouring bad intentions, the ritual is pointless at best and hypocritical at worst.

Let us look at, and examine, the state of some rituals in Islam. *Sawm* (fasting), *sala* (prayer), *hajj* pilgrimage, *zaka* (sustenance) and *shahaada* (testimony) are the main rituals (popularly known as the pillars of Islam) I have discussed here.

9.1. *AS-SALAA* (PRAYER)

Commonly translated as *prayer*, the word stems from the three-letter root *saad, laam, wao/ya* (SLW/Y), with the basic meanings of 'to cling to something/someone.'[6] Its derivatives include words like *as-sallaa* (the back, the hip where falls and touches an animal's tail), *al-musally* (the horse following another very close behind), *al-musalleen* (the followers)[7], *sallu* (to praise and encourage – most probably by close support),[8] and *as-salaa* (formal, ritual gathering of Muslims).[9]

As may be apparent therefore, the Quran has used the word *salaa* and other derivatives of the root not only in the meanings of the customary gatherings of prayer but also for a variety of other applications. In a comprehensive figurative sense the Quranic concept of *as-salaa* is applied to a social system where God's law is followed in every walk of life at all times. In Chapter 24, it says:

> "Seest thou not that it is Allah whose praises all beings in the heavens and on earth do celebrate, and the birds with wings outspread? Each one knows its (own mode of) *salaa* and *tas beeh;* and Allah knows well that they do." [10]

Obviously, *salaa* here is not the ritual Muslims are supposed to perform five times a day. It is to follow the course Nature has set for them. Inanimate matter and the entire animal kingdom (plants and animals, with the exception of Man, are programmed by Nature to behave in a certain manner.[11] That is their mode of *salaa* and *tasbeeh*.[12] But Man, born free and with a clean slate, has to learn his programme of action (*salaa*), and according to that, his behaviour (*tasbeeh*) through experience. The Quran claims to give mankind their desired code of behaviour with a suggested plan of action, which includes practical aspects of life such as economics. The comprehensive term used for this is *as-salaa*:

> "They said: 'O Shu'aib! Does thy *salaa* command thee that we leave off the worship which our fathers practised, or that we leave off doing what we like with our property (wealth)? ...." [13]

That is why the Quran makes Muslims responsible for establishing the system of *salaa* after they have been entrusted and blessed with political power on Earth:

> "(they are) those who, if We establish them in the land, establish *as-salaa*, and give *zaka* ..."

and,

> "Those who respond to their Lord, and establish *as-salaa*, and conduct their affairs by mutual consultation; and spend out of what We bestow on them for sustenance." [15]

They do it because the Quran wants them to follow God's Law and not their own desires through man-made laws:

> "But after them there followed a posterity who wasted *as-salaa* and followed after lusts; soon, then, will the face Destruction." [16]

Such an important concept needed a formal expression (ritual) to keep Muslims in a state of psychological readiness to establish the Quranic social order on Earth. Since it is a social system, there can be no individual establishment of *as-salaa*. That is why Muslims are required to do it *collectively*:

> "Those that (collectively) turn (to Allah) in repentance; that serve Him, and praise Him; that wander in devotion to cause of Allah; that bow down and prostrate themselves..." [17]

Clearly, bowing down (*ruku'*) and prostrating (*sajda*) are symbolic of submitting to the Law of God:

> "O, ye who believe! Bow down, prostrate yourselves and obey your Lord; and do good; that ye may prosper." [18]

To establish this system (*as-salaa*), they naturally need to be guided by the Book:

> "And to those who hold fast by the Book and establish *as-salaa*, never shall We suffer the reward of the righteous to perish." [19]

Symbolically, Muslims turn their faces in the direction of the Ka'aba (in Mecca in modern Saudi Arabia), "the first House of God erected for mankind and guidance for all" [20]

> "So from whencesoever thou startest forth, turn thy face in the direction of the Sacred Mosque; and wheresoever ye are, turn your face thither....." [21]

To prepare for these formal meetings, the Quran suggests ritual washing (ablution):

> "O, ye who believe! When ye prepare for prayer, wash your faces, and your hands (and arms) to the elbows; rub your heads (with water); and wash your feet to the ankles...."

The same verse continues to make provision for scarcity of water in Arabia:

> "... and ye find no water, then take for yourselves clean sand or earth,

and rub therewith your faces and hands..." (5:6)

But remember: this ritual of *as-salaa* is NOT the real thing:

> "It is not righteousness that you turn your faces towards East or West, but righteousness is to be convinced of Allah (and His system and laws), the Last Day, and the angels, and the Book, and the Messengers ; to spend of your subsistence, out of love for Him for your kin, for orphans, for the needy, for the wayfarer, for those who ask, for the ransom of slaves, to be steadfast in prayer, and give *zaka*, to fulfill the contracts which you have made, and to be firm and patient in pain (or suffering) and adversity and throughout the period of panic. Such are the people of truth, the law-abiding." (2:177)

Lastly, we come to the two very important questions of MODE and TIMING of these ritual gatherings. It is widely believed that the Quran has only given the principle of *as-salaa* while the details of its mode and timing are there in *Hadith* (the Prophet's Tradition). It is correct that the Quran has not recommended a specific mode of prayer (except for the direction, as we have seen earlier), and it has left both of these areas to the discretion of Muslims (collectively, not individually).

> "Establish *as-salaa* at the Sun's rise till the darkness of the night..." [22] (17:78)

and:

> "Establish *as-salaa* at the two ends of the day and at the approaches of the night..." (11:114)

Interestingly, it should be noted that the details of mode and timing may *not* be found in *Hadith*.[23] While there is a possibility that the Prophet ascertained the mode and timing according to the requirements of the day, there have been suggestions that the origin lies elsewhere. One is that the number five and the times have been taken from the ancient Zoroastrian text *Avista*. Another, points to the Jewish/Christian tradition.[24]

In view of all the discussion thus far, the summary is that *as-salaa* is a term applied to comprehensive implementation of God's Law. It is formally expressed in ritual meetings and gatherings. The mode and times are to be decided by the central government of all Muslims according to circumstances of a given era and area. [25]

9.2. *AL-HAJJ* (THE PILGRIMAGE)

The word stems from the three-letter root *ha, jeem, jeem* (HJJ) which basically means 'to intend'- especially for a noble, sacred purpose; 'to intend repeatedly'; 'to stop, prevent or forbid.' [26] Some of the derivatives are: *al-hajju* (to intend), *hajajtu fulaanan* (I intended that), *al-hijja* (one year –

with *hijaj* as its plural,27 *al-muhaajja* (to quarrel), *hujja* (argument, reason).28 Linguistically, therefore, *Hajj* (2:196), which has also been called *hijj ul Bait* – visit to the House – in 3:96, in the Quranic concept is the visit to the House of God to participate in an annual gathering of Muslims in order to ponder upon, and seek solutions to, the various issues facing the nation in the light of reason and arguments. This is done so that people "may witness the benefits (provided) for them ..." 29 The consultation aspect comes from the Quranic principle given in 42:38. It is applicable in smaller gatherings of *as-salaa*, on a daily or weekly30 (*juma'*) basis, as well as larger gatherings (*al-Hajj*).

The Quran claims that the tradition and practice of an annual visit to the House of God in Mecca was first established by Abraham (Ibrahim) under Divine guidance.31 The father and son team of Prophet Abraham and Prophet Ishmael built the Ka'aba, the first House of God on Earth, at Mecca situated in a barren and non-arable valley.32 Because of scarcity of food in the area, visitors were asked to bring food along for themselves as well as for others (22:36). In the absence of modern facilities of storage and refrigeration that we enjoy today, meat could only be useful if animals were brought alive. The livestock was only meant to be a source of food. That is why they are to be slaughtered (only) near the House of God.33 The visitors are to express equality in the sameness of dress (*ahraam*). They are to circumambulate the Ka'aba to express their will to lead their lives keeping God's Law in view all the time.34 The stay in the plain of 'Arafat near Mecca, is a meeting to get acquainted with others (*'arafa* means 'to know'). The stoning of the three statues ('devils') has no basis in the Quran. It probably is a remnant of a pre-Islamic custom. The two hills of *As-Safaa* and *Al-Marwa* near the Ka'aba are not sacred.35 It is popularly believed that Prophet Abraham left his infant son Ishmael and his wife Haajera (Hagar) behind (abandoned?) in the wilderness. The mother searched frantically for some water for the crying infant who dug up the sacred well of Zamzam with his tiny heels. Later in life, the father, under influence of a dream in which he was instructed by God to sacrifice his son, tried to realize his dream when he *actually* laid Ishmael face down to slaughter him. Instantly, God 'spoke' to him accepting his devotional gesture and miraculously sent down a sacrificial lamb to be slaughtered instead of Ishmael.

This traditional view, in my opinion, is erroneous for various reasons. Firstly, the chronology of events is confusing. It is believed that the sacrificial episode occurred when Ishmael had become a youth. It is nowhere explained why or when he returned to Palestine (that, according to the story, is where Abraham had gone back after abandoning his wife and infant son in the barren hills of what was still to become Mecca). And, if the episode took place in Mecca, did Abraham specially travel down for this sacred mission of sacrificing his son? No Tradition (*hadith*) or historical reports identify Mecca as the location of the incident. Furthermore, the reason cited for Abraham abandoning his family in such an irresponsible manner is ridiculous – jealousy on the part of his first wife Sarah of Hagar who had borne a son before she could. Such behaviour is not at all worthy of great people like divinely-appointed prophets and their household. Even if we accept the jealousy saga, why remove Hagar so far away? She could be set up in another house in the same city, or another town of the same district for that matter. And then, why abandon a vulnerable woman with an infant in an unpopulated spot in a dry, barren wilderness without food or even water? It is inconceivable that a normal husband of a sane mind would behave in such a heartless manner, let alone a noble prophet of God. It seems likely that, if this episode at all happened, Abraham set up a grown-up Ishmael in this remote area, which was already populated in the form a small settlement by a natural spring (Zamzam) with a purpose; most likely, it was for Ishmael to propagate the message of monotheism in the Hejaz while his father carried on God's work back in Palestine.

Secondly, the incidence of 'sacrificing' Ishmael by intending to literally slaughter him does not match the Quranic theological framework. The Quran's God appears to be very different from ancient pagan deities who could be pleased by making offerings. The Quranic message was aimed at eradicating such practices of old. The Quran's God is a legal god who can be 'pleased' only by following His natural laws.

Seen in this light, therefore, the Quranic verse commonly believed to be the basis of this view should be interpreted thus:

> "Then, when (the son) became of (age to) work, he (Abraham) said, 'O son! (My) vision (of the next step of this Divine mission) is that I (put you through circumstances which will be just like I am) slaughtering you. So what do you say?' (The mature and grown-up young man) said, 'O father! (since I agree with this mission of yours, it is imperative that you) Do what you have been ordained to do. According to God's will (and law), you will find me to be steadfast and brave.' Then, when both of them submitted (to the plan according to the Divine scheme of things) and he (Ibraheem made) him (Ismail)– (in a manner of speaking)- bow down his forehead (carried out his duty in God's Way), We called out to him, 'O Ibraheem! (Consider that) Your dream (of this Divine Mission) has (already) been realized (since you have begun the journey, your destination is that much closer!).'
>
> This is how We (ask to do, and consequently) reward those who (do noble deeds for mankind and surely) are the doers of right. This was a clear (example of the) rigorous (training and) testing (time).
>   Surely, we had asked of him (Ibraheem to do) something greatly excruciating !"
>
> (*As-Saafaat* - Wings Outspread, 103-108)

9.3. *AZ-ZAKAA* (THE POOR TAX, OR THE DUES OF THE STATE?)

The institution of *az-zakaa* has not been ritualized as such in the Islamic world but it certainly has been reduced to the status of a ritual. Hence I

Part Two: Chapter Nine

have decided to present it in its true Quranic perspective.

It is derived from the three-letter root *za, ka, waow* (ZKW) with the basic meanings of 'to grow, to thrive.' Some examples of other derivatives and their uses are: *zakaa al maal wa(l)zzar'u* (thriving growth of cattle and farming); *zakaa ar-rajlu yazku* (the man became prosperous and well-off); *tazkia tun nafs* (thriving growth of personality).36 In the Quran, an example cited by Raagheb37 is: "...Be on the look out for nutritious food..." (18:19). It can also be used in the sense of 'clean and pure' as a secondary meaning. The basic meaning remains 'to grow, to thrive.' In a Quranic verse two separate words have been used for growth (*azkaa*) and pure cleanliness (*atharu*). 38

It is commonly accepted that *zakaa* is the amount of money (or equivalent in kind) paid annually to the poor and the needy. It is a certain percentage of the wealth which lies unspent at the end of a given year. The percentage varies with the particular tradition of any given sect but the most widely known figure is 2½ %. Although in some Muslim countries there is a rudimentary central system in place for collection and spending this amount, it is in principle left to the discretion of the individual. In the Quran, however, the picture is very different. There are three important points to be considered before we can fully appreciate the Quranic concept of *az-zakaa*.

1 *Surplus Wealth* In the Quranic scheme of things, no individual is allowed to have, let alone keep for a year, any surplus money. In fact, no Muslim is allowed keep *anything* which is superfluous (more than what is needed):

> "They ask what (how much) should they keep open (to be spent in God's Way); Say, 'that whatever is surplus of (your) needs!'" (2:219)

Hoarding of wealth is a heinous crime:

> "...and those who hoard gold and silver, and spend it not in the way of Allah; announce unto them a most grievous chastisement. On the Day when it will be heated in the fire of Hell, and with it will be branded their foreheads, their flanks, and their backs – 'This is (the treasure) which ye hoarded for yourselves; taste ye, then, the treasure ye hoarded.'" 39 (9: 34, 35)

So much so, that this crime is not absolved even by *as-salaa*.
> "So woe to the worshippers who are neglectful of their *salaa* – those who (want but) to be seen but refuse that (which should be kept) flowing (the system of neighbourly needs)." (107: 4-7)

2 *Zakaa and the State.* According to the Quranic system, the State and the citizen enter a contract whereby the State gets jurisdiction over an individual's potential in return for ensuring his/her comprehensive welfare:

> "Allah hath purchased of the Believers their persons and their goods; for theirs (in return) is the Garden (of Paradise); ..." (9: 111)

3   This covenant is taken because it is basic responsibility of the state to establish the systems of *as-salaa* (the Quranic Code) and *az-zakaa* (the comprehensive system of nourishment for the citizens to grow and thrive).

> "(They are) those who, if we establish them in the land, establish *as-salaa* and *az-zakaa,* and enjoin the right and forbid the wrong..." (22: 41)

Practically, this covenant takes place between the citizen and the people representing the State, actually representing God.

> "Verily who plight their fealty to thee plight their fealty to Allah; the Hand of Allah is over their hands..."   (48:10)

To summarize, *az-zakaa* is a comprehensive system of economy. This is a term applied to all commercial and financial activity under the laws of the Quran. The State has the right of access to all the wealth produced. In return, it is completely responsible for the comprehensive development, growth and welfare of the citizens. It includes their physical, mental, psychological, and other needs and requirements- also that of their children. [40] Therefore, the entire mechanism of collecting revenue, taxation, benefits, welfare etc. is collectively known as *az-zakaa*.

9.4. *AS-SIYAAM* (FASTING)

The annual month of fasting in Islam is *Ramadan,* the 9th month of the Muslim calendar. Traditionally, it is a time for practising self-discipline and refreshing one's conviction of the Islamic system by special prayers and revising the Quran. This lasts for the entirety (29/30 days, because it is based upon the appearance of the Moon) of the month during which every adult Muslim is expected to exercise self-control by abstaining from consuming food and having sex during daylight hours and offering special prayers at night.

Historically, fasting (abstention/self-control/self-denial) is nothing unique to Islam. It was, and still is, practised in as ancient a religion as Zoroastrianism (circa 1,500 B.C.). It is not, however, clear whether the aim of fasting for Zoroastrians is self-control or salvation.[41] Fasting is also a standard religious practice in other ancient religions like Hinduism and Jainism. In Hinduism, for instance, the month of *Jeth* (May/June) contains an important three-day fast, which is observed by women to ensure marital happiness. This fast culminates in special worship for the goddess *Savitri*.[42] Some of my readers may be familiar with the practice of *Karva Chowth*. This is a fast observed regularly by Hindu wives for the welfare and long life of their husbands. The philosophy behind this practice is that a woman is held to be an equal partner in *dharma* with her husband, and is thought to share his destiny.[43] Fasting in Hinduism usually means refraining from consuming non-vegetarian food and alcohol.44 In Jainism, the practice of fasting appears to have a more social than spiritual purpose:

> The most important festival of Jainism is held at Pajjusana, the solemn season which closes the Jain year. For eight days or longer, during the wet monsoon period, usually in August, devout Jains fast and attend special services [.....] On the closing day of the festival, every Jain abstains from food and water [....] asks forgiveness of his neighbours for any inadvertent offence and determines to carry no grudge or quarrel over into the next year.' 45

There is a strong tradition of fasting in Judeo-Christian religious systems. In Judaism, for example, ten days after the New Year is the Day of Atonement (*Yom Kippur*). This is a twenty-five-hour fast day beginning at dusk (sunset) and lasting till nightfall on the following day. All food and drink is forbidden. So is wearing leather shoes (because they are a sign of comfort). Also, no sexual relations are allowed.46 There appears here an element of self-denial as well as self-control.

Incidentally, the Judaic (and also, to some extent, the Christian) fast has strong resemblance with the Muslim. We learn from early Muslim history (most notably, *Hadith*) that:

> 'During the first year after the *hijra* Muhammad instituted a one-day, twenty-four hour fast called the *ashura* ('tenth'). This was apparently the name used by the Jews of the Hijaz for the fast on the Day of Atonement, which falls on the tenth day of Tishiri. The Ramadan fasting seems to have been related to the Muslim victory at Badr in Ramadan, 624 AD. 47

Some researchers have even suggested that the tradition of fasting in the month of Ramadan pre-dates Islam. As noted by Serge Trifkovic:

> 'Fasting during the month of Ramadan combined the traditions of brief Jewish fasting during Yom Kippur (the Day of Atonement) and the Sabeans' month of fasting that had been adopted in Mecca some time before Muhammad's birth.' 48

Christians practise fasting for forty days before Easter. It is called Lent (Old English for Spring; generally, the term used is Latin *Quadragesima,* meaning forty days). During this period of forty days, Christians of ages 18-60 fast and abstain on Fridays and also on Good Friday (mourning for Crucifixion) but not on Sundays (rejoicing for Resurrection). The fast is limited to having one single meal and two small snacks a day. Those with medical conditions can be easily dispensed by their pastor. Catholics of age 14 and over abstain from meat though fish and dairy products are allowed in the Western Rites (but not in the Eastern Rites). During the forty-day period, Christians are also expected to do acts of mercy to others and offer prayers. The number forty has its basis in the

Old Testament, Book of Exodus (24:18 and 34:28) according to which Moses spent 40 days on the Mountain. More importantly, Christ spent 40 days in the wilderness praying and fasting before beginning his mission.[49] The basis for fasting and denying oneself what one likes, to experience empathetically what some prominent religious figures went through, and to repent and become better Christians is to be found in the *Old Testament*, Book of Daniel:

> "In the third year of Cyrus king of Persia.... 'I, Daniel, mourned for three weeks. I ate no choice food, no meat or wine touched my lips; and I used no lotions at all until the three weeks were over.'" [50]

It is now time to consider what the Quranic viewpoint on fasting is.

9.5. FASTING AND THE QURAN

The word for 'fasting' in Arabic comes from the three-letter root *saad, waow, meem,* (SWM) which basically means 'to abstain, to stop or to hold oneself'. Some of the derivatives are: *sawm* (fast), *saama* (he fasted), *siyaam* (fasts), *sayyaam* (one who fasts a lot), *saaem* (a male who fasts), *saaema* (a female who fasts), *masaam* (place to stop), etc. Some common uses of the expression are: *saam al maa* (the water stopped), *saama 'an en nikaah* (he did not marry), *saama an al kelaam* (he abstained from speaking), etc.[51] Incidentally, in English the word used for this activity (fasting) is taken not for its meaning of *speed* but for another application of the word, i.e. *to be strong and resilient* as in acid-*fast* or stead*fast*.

In the Quran, the regimen of fasting is dealt with in Sura *Al-Baqara* (The Cow):

> "O, you who are convinced! Fasting is made obligatory to you as it was obligatory to those before you, so that you may become law-abiding (self-resilient)."   (2: 183)
> "(It is for) Fixed number of days; but if any of you is ill, or on a journey, the number is (to be made up) from later days. For those who can do it with hardship, is a ransom – the feeding of one who is indigent ; but whoever will give more of his own volition, it is better for him ; and it is better for you all that you fast – if you only knew."   (2: 184)
> "The month of Ramadan is the one in which I sent down the Quran for guiding mankind, also clear (signs) for guidance and standards (of right and wrong), so whoever of you comes upon this month should fast. But, if anyone is ill or on a journey, the number (should be made up) from later days. Allah intends every facility for you and does not intend hardship for you, so that you can complete the number (of days), so that you can help prevail (over non-divine systems) what He has guided you with, so that you can be grateful (that your efforts have borne fruit). (2:185)

> "Permitted to you on the night of the fasts is the approach to your women – they are your garments and you are their garments; Allah knows what you used to secretly do among yourselves ; but He turned to you and forgave you (saved you from the ill effects of your misdeeds), so now associate with them (women) and seek what Allah has ordained for you – eat and drink until the white thread of dawn is distinct for you from the black thread (of dusk); complete the fast till night ; do not approach women while you are in retreat in the mosques.52 Those are the limits of Allah, so do not approach near those (limits). Thus Allah makes (His signs) clear to Man so that they may become law-abiding (self-controlling)." (2: 187)

9.6. SIGNIFICANCE OF RAMADAN

In fact, according to the Quran, each and every human action – good or bad – bears result for the doer; it does not affect God.

> "Whoever works righteousness benefits his own soul (self); whoever works evil, it is against his own soul..." 53 (41: 46)

As to the philosophy of fasting, the Quran states that its purpose is "...that you may become law-abiding (self-resilient)–*la 'allakum tattaqoon.*" (2: 183)

And moreover, as mentioned earlier:

> "...so that you can help prevail (over non-divine systems) what He has guided you with, so that you can be grateful (that your efforts have borne fruit). (2:185)

Therefore, the annual month of fasting is really a refresher course of training in discipline and self-control so that Muslims stay mentally, emotionally and physically ready to lead the Quranic life in the best possible manner.

Another significance of the month of Ramadan, as already mentioned, is stated as:

> "The month of Ramadan is the one in which I sent down the Quran for guiding mankind, also clear (signs) for guidance and standards (of right and wrong), .." (2:185)

Muslims are expected to rejoice over the fact that God bestowed mankind with His bounty – the Quran!

> "O mankind! There hath come to you an admonition from your Lord and a healing for the (diseases) in your hearts,-and for those who are convinced (of its message), a Guidance and a Mercy. Say: 'In the Bounty of Allah, and in His Mercy,-in that let them rejoice': that is better than the (wealth) they hoard." (10:57, 58)

Here, I would like to make two minor points in connection with the practice of fasting.

1 *Eid al Fitr*

It is evident, in the light of the teachings of the Quran, that the festival at the end of the month of fasting (Ramadan) should be a time for rejoicing over the fact that mankind received this Divine Guidance (The Quran) in its darkest hour. Perhaps it should be renamed *Eid Nuzool al Quran* (Festival of Revelation of the Quran) instead of *Eid-al-Fitr* (Festival of Breaking Fast).

2 *Laila tal Qadr* (Night of Values)

The mention of mankind's darkest hour brings us to another important point – the popular notion, and celebration of, a very special night during the last ten days of Ramadan. It is believed that during that special night – also known as *Shab e Baraat* (Night of Destiny) in Persian – God decides on the destiny of all beings for the coming year; it is therefore in one's own interest to remain busy in prayer through the night in order to please God and win His favour. In addition to special prayers, many Muslims also celebrate this night with putting on special lights, candles and fireworks.

This view is not in accordance with the teachings of the Quran. Firstly, the notion of pre-destiny is anti-Quranic. Man makes his own destiny according to the actions he takes exercising his freedom of choice. Secondly, it is obvious for its ancient Zoroastrian influence in the practice of illumination and fireworks, which reflect fire-worship.

From the Quranic perspective, this night (mankind's darkest hour – when Man needed Divine Guidance) is the time when Man was given a set of values (*aqdaar*) to live his life by:

> "Ha Meem
> By the Book that makes things clear;-
> We sent it down during a blessed night:
> For We (ever) wish to warn (against Evil).
> In that (night) is made distinct every affair of wisdom,
> By command from Us.
> For We (ever) send (revelations).   (44: 1-5)

And more clearly, using the expression *Laila tal Qadr*, it says:

> "We have indeed revealed this (Message) in the Night of Power (Values):
> And what will explain to thee what the Night of Power (Values) is?
> The Night of Values is better than a thousand months.
> Therein come down the angels and the Spirit by Allah's permission on every errand: Peace!....This until the rise of Morn!"   (97: 1-5)

Finally,

9.7. AN IMPORTANT QUESTION – THE TIMING

The duration of the daily fast, as we have seen in the Quran, is from sunrise to sunset. This is most obviously for the equatorial regions of the globe, which have a normal day of about 12 hours. These timings most certainly cannot be applied universally. It will be unthinkable to have a 'normal' fast on the Moon where a day is equivalent to 14 Earth days. Even on Earth the Polar Regions present a real problem. It has been suggested, and in some cases even implemented, that such areas should liaise with Mecca in Saudi Arabia. This is one way to resolve the situation. Regardless of the merits of this solution, it *does* clearly accept the principle of amendment in the timings of a fast day. It accepts, inadvertently and grudgingly perhaps, that the duration mentioned in the Quran is bound by time and culture, as of course are a number of other things in this great book. (Please refer to Chapter 3 for more on this point).

It may be suggested that this very important question should be the exclusive privilege of the ultimate global Quranic government, whenever in the future it is established. Till then, Muslims should carry on fasting on a personal level, as they have so far been doing for nearly a millennium and a half, to the best of their intentions, knowledge and satisfaction.

9.8. *ASH-SHAHAADA* (THE TESTIMONY)

It is commonly believed that to become a Muslim, or to affirm one's conviction of Islam, one has to say, *'I testify that there is no god but Allah, and I testify that Mohammed is His messenger.'* Normally, one is expected to utter this statement aloud in Arabic. But, like so many other Quranic principles, this foundation stone of the Quranic Order has also been degraded to the position of a ritual. Here is a view of its Quranic perspective.

The Quran requires a would-be Muslim to be convinced of certain realities:

> "It is not righteousness that ye turn your faces towards East or West; but it is righteousness to be convinced of Allah, and the Last Day, and the Angels, and the Book, and the Messengers..." [54] (2:177)

Like any other ritual, oral testimony is worthless unless supported by action:

> "Of the people there are some who say: 'We believe in Allah and the Last Day,' but they are not really convinced. Fain would they deceive Allah and those who are (really) convinced; but they only deceive themselves!" (2: 8, 9)

Action comes from firm conviction, which in turn comes from knowledge. That is why Mohammed presented his Message not on the basis of blind faith but knowledge and thought:

> "Say, 'This is my Way; I do invite unto Allah ('s Way) with *baseera* (knowledge gained through thought process) ..." [55] (12: 108)

That is why The Quran makes a distinction between a Muslim (one who submits his/her will to the Law of God) and a Momin (one who is convinced, on the basis of conscious choice, of God's message to Man):

> "The Desert Arabs say: 'We believe (*aamannaa*).' Say, 'Ye have no faith; but ye (only) say, 'We have submitted (*aslamnaa*) our wills to Allah,' for not yet has conviction entered your hearts..."

You can call yourselves Momin only

> "... if you OBEY Allah and His Messenger, He will not belittle your deeds: for Allah is Oft-Forgiving, Most Merciful." (49: 14)

Ash-Shahaada, therefore, is the testimony by the tongue and, more than that, by the heart and deeds.

Chapter 10

TERRORISM OR *JEHAAD*?

The shocking events of September 11, 2001 in the United States of America rocked the entire world as never before. It has been the topic of the day ever since, dominating media reporting all over the globe. The USA, Britain and their allies have formed a global coalition and have bombed heavily the suspected strongholds of Osama bin Laden in Kandhar, Kabul and other parts of Afghanistan. Iraq, though apparently for different reasons but also for its terrorist activities, was invaded and stands devastated. Meanwhile, terrorists are busy blowing up key Western cities such as Madrid in Spain and London. This is the burning issue, figuratively as well as literally, of the day and warrants our attention. It becomes even more desirable when considered in the light of the fact that a vast number of people in the West equate such terrorist activities with Islam. Literature establishing links of the inhuman practices of terrorists with the Islamic concept of *jehaad* have flooded the market. [1] Muslim states in general and radical countries such as Saudi Arabia in particular have been rightly or wrongly accused of producing or harboring terrorists. Since the destruction of the twin towers of The World Trade Center, Muslim agitators have taken the front seat in the arena of violent global politics; they have taken over from the Irish or the Basque terrorists. Consequently, the term 'terrorist' has become synonymous with 'jehaad' (unfortunately, the English-speaking world has already accepted 'holy war' to be the correct translation of *jehaad*); and the Islamic world finds itself in a semi-permanent state of war-like tension with the Western civilization of the Judeo-Christian world, very much a reminder of the Crusades of a millennium ago. Muslim writers have been trying to put across a different view. [2] I, too, propose to present my own view of the situation. However, I do not wish to attempt to evaluate, let alone justify, Muslim politics in today's world – this is out of scope of this work. I certainly do not desire to present an apology for Muslim activists. Rather, keeping with the declared objective of this book, I intend to present to non-Muslims, as well as Muslims, the Quranic viewpoint, as I see it, of concepts like *jehaad*, holy war, and specifically, terrorism. The sad fact of the matter is that while the West does not appear to have the real picture from the Quranic angle, a vast majority of Muslims too do not appear to have grasped it. I hope to present the Quran's stance, which is the correct one in my opinion, and appeal to both sides to exercise use of reason rather than blind passion. Let us look at this issue intelligently, and more important than anything, coolly and level-headedly from the standpoint of the Quran.

As it has been so aptly remarked, more than half of the issues in a discussion are automatically addressed if the terminology involved is agreed upon before hand. Let us, therefore, determine what we mean by TERRORISM.

Linguistically, 'terror' is described as:

> '1 intense, overwhelming fear. 2 Something, as a terrifying object or event that instills intense fear. 3 Ability to instill intense fear. 4 Violence promoted by a group to achieve or maintain supremacy. Also, (informal): One that is annoying or difficult to manage, especially a child (NUISANCE).
> - *Webster's II, New Riverside Dictionary* (1984).

This may be expressed in Arabic by the word *khawf*. Lexically, *khawf* springs from the three-letter root *kha, waao, fa* (KhWF) which basically means 'to apprehend an imminent danger.' [3] In the Quran it is mentioned in Sura *An-Nisaa* (The Women):

> "If a woman fears transgression from her (quarrelling)[4] husband, ..." (4:128).

In Sura *An-Nahl* (The Bees), it says:

> "They fear their Sustainer's supremacy and do as they are told .." (16:50).

Therefore, 'fear of Allah' means to follow the right (Allah's) path for fear of the ill effects which will result by abandoning it. As we can see, *khawf* is just like the apprehension one has if one is to touch a naked flame. That is why *al-khafa* is the protective overall of the bee-keepers.[5] Incidentally, *khawf* has also been used in the Quran in the applied meanings of armed combat.[6] It also means to reduce or decrease.[7]

Fear, therefore, is a negative feeling which can be avoided by following God's way as laid down in the Quran.[8]

It can be deduced, therefore, that firstly, fear (terror) is not desirable and is to be avoided and averted. It just cannot be right for anyone to live in terror. Thus, the tactics used by any single person, or a group, or a state to try to achieve or maintain supremacy by instilling intense fear is wrong.

Secondly, one of the fundamentals of the Quranic teaching is that one cannot adopt negative (wrong) means to achieve an aim, even if it is positive (right). In other words, the end does not justify the means. The Quran says:

> 'We have shown him (Man) the (right) way – to take it or leave it.' 9

It also declares:

> 'The right path leads Man to the right end, the wrong to the wrong…' 10

Therefore, according to the Quran, instilling fear just cannot be accepted as legitimate – even it is for the noble and exalted purpose of upholding Islam (God's law).

Thirdly, the terror tactics aimed at people who are not directly involved in, or responsible for, the conflict can *never* be justified from the Quranic viewpoint. It says very clearly: 'No one shall bear someone else's burden.' 11 So, punishing innocent people for the misdeeds of men in power is totally anti-Quranic. Furthermore, such unjustifiable and misplaced killings are seen by the Quran as gigantic acts of murder: 'A single unjustified killing is tantamount to annihilating the entire human race …' 12

By the same token, bombing the helpless and innocent civilians in the poverty-stricken villages and towns of Afghanistan and Iraq for the crimes of one person and his group cannot be justified from a Quranic perspective.

Fourthly, the Quran has laid down rules of conduct in times of both war and peace. Generally, you *must* be fair to everyone at all times:

> 'Be just and fair, even to your enemies.' 13

Elsewhere, it says:

> 'If you fear violation of an agreement by a nation, throw it away on the basis of equality…..'

Again, it reminds Muslims:

> 'In confrontation, remember a lot more, and adhere more strongly to, the Law of God – so that you come out benefited.' 15

Clearly, then, Muslims must conduct themselves fairly, honestly and openly, even in times of war. So, how can killing of innocent people, taking the hostages, etc. in times of peace be justified?

10.1. 'HOLY WAR'

The term *jehaad* comes from the three–letter root *jeem, haa, daa* (Jhd), with the basic meaning of 'to strive.' Some commonly used derivatives are:

Al-jahdu (to achieve with utmost diligence); *juhd* (strength and extent); to some both *jahd* and *juhd* are used for 'strength and extent' while *jahd* is only for painstaking hard work, but the Quran has used *jahd* for the latter in 9:79. *Jihaad* thus means 'to employ one's extreme efforts to the fullest towards achieving a goal.' *Jahaad* is 'a grassless barren piece of land'; *al-ijtehaad* means 'to spend all disposable energy with backbreaking effort to do something'; *al-jaahed* (one who does not sleep).

In the Quran, we find *mujaahedeen* (those who work with their full capacity) in contrast to *qaaedeen* (those who just sit idly). Therefore, *jihaad* is 'constant perseverance in the work of God to establish and maintain the Quranic social order, even at the cost of one's life.' Armed combat in the cause of God's Law is but a portion of a Muslim's *jihaad*, for which the specific term used by the Quran is *qitaal* as *kuteba 'alaikum ul qitaal* [Fighting is prescribed upon you (all)]' in 2:216; also in *allazeena kuteba 'alaihemul qatl* [those for whom fighting is made obligatory] (3:154).[16] In principle, armed combat is to uphold God's Law:

> 'Those who are convinced of God's Message (*allazeena aamenu*) fight in the cause of Allah (*fi sabeel Allah* – 'in the path of Allah), and those who reject (it) fight in the cause of Evil (*fi sabeel at-taaghoot*): so fight ye against the friends of Satan: feeble indeed is the cunning of Satan.' (4:76)

So, any situation which threatens the rule of God's Law either by attempts to abolish or undermine an established Quranic system or by endeavours to impose a non-Quranic system against people's will shall demand *qitaal*. Furthermore, it is permitted in self-defense and as a last resort; it is *never* to be initiated according to 22:39 and 2:190. War is waged to eradicate evil and must be stopped as soon as the objective has been met (2:193 and 8:39); Muslim fighters must always keep within the bounds of ethical bahaviour dictated by the Quran and never transgress (2:190). During war times, and also during circumstances leading to war, all treaties and agreements are to be honoured and all pledges fulfilled (2:177, 5:1, 16:91); so much so, that a treaty cannot be disregarded even if Muslims living in a non-Muslim country are suffering (8:72). The sanctity of a treaty is paramount; even when the Islamic government fears treachery from any group, the covenant must be properly revoked on equal terms *before* any action is taken (8:58). Armed combat is also allowed to help the downtrodden and the oppressed but only when all peaceful means have been tried and exhausted ((4:75). Above all, the purpose of *qitaal* is to eliminate the causes of hostilities; Muslims must fight so that, and only so long when, '...*hatta tada'al harbu awzaarehaa*...- until war lays down its weapons...' (48:4).

Part Two: Chapter Ten

It is clear from the teachings of the Quran that a Muslim must engage in *qitaal* if need be only to establish, defend and uphold God's Law enshrined in the Quran. Any other reason – political, social or other – to take up arms, especially against the innocent, is just not Islamic and cannot be condoned, approved or justified from the Quranic perspective.

Chapter 11

THE PERMISSIBLE (*HALAAL*), THE FORBIDDEN (*HARAAM*)

In the Muslim world at large, in the non-Muslim world in general, and, in the western world in particular, the mention of the two terms *halaal* and *haraam* almost invariably turns one's mind to food. It is my intention to not only deal at length with the question of permissibility of food from the Quranic standpoint, but also to show that *halaal* and *haraam* extend beyond, and mean much more than, food. But first let me examine the two terms linguistically.

11.1. HALAAL

The word *halaal* stems from the three-letter Arabic root *Haa-laam-lam* (HLM),[1] with the basic meaning 'to open a knot; to untie'. In Sura *Tahaa*, Moses prays to God: *'wa ahlul uqda min lisaani'* - "..and remove the impediments from my speech" (20 :27). In simpler words, Moses was asking God to 'open the knot' in his tongue. Similarly, when something is melted, it is termed *hallun* – that its knot was opened (was untied). *Hall al ahmaal* means 'to untie (unpack) luggage', which led to its application as *hall al makaan* – to arrive at a place and stay. From this comes the expression *haleel* (husband) and *haleela* (wife) as they stay together at the same place.[2] Hence, the figurative meaning of *halaal / helaal, al-hellu / al-haleel* is 'permissible / allowed'.

Some other examples of the use of the term and related expressions as in the Quran are: 1) *laa tuhillu* ('violate not the sanctity') in 5:2; 2) *fa yahilla 'alaikum ghazdabee* ('lest My Wrath should descend on you') in 20:81; 3) *thumma mahilluhaa ila al-Bait-el-Ateeq'* ('in the end their place of sacrifice is near the Ancient House') in 22:33 [i.e. They (the animals brought as gifts on the occasion of *al-Hajj* – the pilgrimage) become permissible –*halaal*- near the Ka'ba].[3] 4) *hillun* (an inhabitant) in (90:2).

11.2. HARAAM

The word *haraam* stems from the three-letter Arabic root *Haa-ra-meem* (HRM). It has the basic meaning of 'to forbid; to stop.'4 *Al-haraam* – all that has been forbidden. This is the opposite of *al-halaal* (to allow; to permit). *Ahram al-haaj* means 'the pilgrim reached a stage where several restrictions were imposed'. This is the status of *ahraam*, the symbolic ritual garb of Muslim pilgrims. *Ash-hurul haramu* were the four months (*Moharram, Rajab, Dhulqa'da, Dhulhijja*) during which armed conflict was forbidden. *Al-Mahroom* is the one whose needs are no longer met. *Al-Haram* is a common reference to the enclosed area of the Grand Central Mosque in Mecca (*Al-Masjid al-haraam*), which contains the Ka'ba. The Messenger's Mosque in Medina is referred to as *Al-haram an-Nabavi ash-shareef*.

Some other examples of the use of the term and related expressions as in the Quran are: 1) *wa antum hurumun* ('while you are in the Sacred Precincts') in 5:1; 2) *al-hurumaat* ('all things prohibited') in 2:194; 3) *muharramun 'alaikum* ('unlawful for you') in 2:85; 4) *baitek al-moharram* ('Thy Sacred House') in 14:37; and 5) *al-mahroom* ('the deprived') in 51:19.

Hopefully, this makes the basic meanings and concepts of the terms *halaal* and *haraam* clear according to the Quran. Let us now look at these terms in a wider Quranic sense. The fact of the matter is that the Quran has employed these terms to a variety of things in addition to food. In Sura *Al-A'raaf*, it says:

> 'Say: Who hath forbidden the beautiful (gifts) of Allah which He hath produced for His servants, and the things, clean and pure, (which He hath provided) for sustenance? Say: They are, in the life of this world, for those who believe, (and) purely for them on the Day of Judgment...' (7:32)

This is a very significant verse with regards to our topic. Firstly, it says that there are things in life, in addition to food, to which the terms and conditions of *halaal* and *haraam* are applicable. Secondly, the authority of deeming something as *halaal* or *haraam* rests only with Allah. To drive this particular point home, the Quran says in Sura *An-Nahl*:

> 'But say not – for any false thing that your tongues may put forth,- "This is lawful, and this is forbidden," so as to ascribe false things to Allah. For those who ascribe false things to Allah, will never prosper.' (16:11)

Again, in even stronger and clearer terms, in Sura *Younis*:

> 'Say: "See ye what things Allah hath sent down to you for sustenance? Yet ye hold forbidden some things thereof and (some things) unlawful." Say: "Hath Allah indeed permitted you, or do ye forge (things) to attribute to Allah?" (10:59)

Part Two: Chapter Eleven

And then the Quran delivers its final and categorically ultimate verdict on the subject in Sura *Aal-e-'Imraan*:

> 'It is not (possible) that a man, to whom is given the Book, and Wisdom, and the Prophetic Office, should say to people: "Be ye my worshippers rather than Allah's": On the contrary, (he would say):"Be ye worshippers of Him (Who is truly the Cherisher of all) for ye have taught the Book and ye have studied it earnestly."   (3:79)

Clearly, whatever is permissible / forbidden is to be found only in the Quran. That is exactly why the Messenger was ordered in the Quran to say in Sura *Al-An'aam*:

> 'Say: "I find not in the Message received by me by inspiration any (meat) forbidden to be eaten by one who wishes to eat it, unless....'
> (6:145)

The verse goes on to list the things (of food) which are forbidden:

> '... unless it be dead meat, or blood poured forth, or the flesh of swine - for it is an abomination - , or what is impious, (meat) on which a name has been invoked, other than Allah's....' [5]   (6:145)

Therefore, as far as food is concerned, only what is mentioned in the Quran is *haraam* – everything else is *halaal* if one finds it desirable to be consumed. It is a matter of individual taste and preference. That is why the Quran qualifies the permissible with the adjective *tayyaban* : Sura *Baqara*:

> 'O ye people! Eat of what is on earth, lawful and good,......'   (2:168)

11.3. *AL HAJJ* - SLAUGHTER OF ANIMALS

It is time now turn to an important point in this regard, which was referred to earlier in connection with the slaughtering of gift animals on the occasion of *Al-hajj*. The dominant concept current in the Islamic world of *halaal* meat is that the animal must be 1) slaughtered with a knife at the throat, and during that 2) the words *Allahu Akber* (God is the Greatest) must be recited.

This notion has developed as a result of mixing the following:

1. The verses (2:173, 5:3, 6:145, etc) which prohibit consumption of blood.
2. The same verses mention as *haraam* anything on which a name other than that of Allah has been invoked. To fulfill this condition, there started the practice of invoking God's name on the animals being slaughtered. [6]
3. The legend of Abraham offering to slaughter his son Ismail in God's way and ending up in slaughtering a lamb instead. [7]

All these ideas and notions have been mixed up over the centuries and confused into the current idea of a *halaal* animal whereas, as we have seen, what makes an animal permissible is:

(i) That its blood has been completely drained, [8]
(ii) It is not invoked under a name other than that of Allah,
(iii) Most importantly, it must not have been obtained by any means of earning deemed HARAAM by Allah. [9]

Pig's meat, even if slaughtered in the traditional way with *Allahu Akber* recited, remains *haraam* ! Also, the most clean and healthy chicken even if slaughtered in the traditional way with *Allahu Akber* recited does NOT become *halaal* if it is obtained by theft or cheating !

Lastly, let us see some of the things, other than food, for which the Quran has employed the two terms.

Haraam

1. '... indecent deeds – whether open or secret (7:33)
2. '... sins...(7:33)
3. '... trespasses against truth or reason (7:33)
4. '... saying things about Allah on which ye have no knowledge.' (7:33)
5. 'Nor take life which Allah has made sacred... (17:33)
6. 'The adulterer cannot have sexual relations with any but an adulteress, none can have sexual relations with her but an adulterer or an idolater; To the believers such a thing is forbidden.' (24:3)
7. '...usury...' (2:275)
8. '...Ye are forbidden to inherit women against their will..' (4:19)
9. 'Prohibited to you (for marriage) are .....' (4:23-24)

Halaal

1. The forbidden foods are allowed in case of desperation. [10]
2. '...Lawful unto you (for food) are all beasts of cattle ...' 5:1 and 22:30
3. '...Say: "lawful unto you are (all) things good and pure....' 5:4
4. 'This day are (all) things good and pure made lawful unto you. The food of the People of the Book is lawful unto you and yours is lawful unto them. (Lawful unto you in marriage) Are (not only) chaste women who are believers, but chaste women among the People of the Book, revealed before your time,-.... (5:5)
5. '... Allah has permitted trade...' (2:275)
6. '.... what ye took in war...' (8:69)
7. Remarrying the same spouse after three divorces - (2:230)
8. 'Permitted to you on the night of the fasts is the approach to your wives...' (2:187)

11.4. THE LOGIC OF IT

A lot has been written on the philosophy behind foods forbidden by the Quran. Curious and inquisitive minds have been asking questions, and trying to find satisfactory answers. Muslim writers have endeavoured to come up with explanations (as to why a certain food is forbidden). Intoxicants, such as alcohol (not mentioned in 'clear' verses referred to above) seem to be the only item with some explanation offered by way of justification. Verse 2:219 says, 'They ask thee concerning wine 11 and gambling. Say: "In them is great sin, and some profit, for men, but the sin is greater than the profit.."' In 5:90-91, we find, '..Intoxicants and gambling, sacrificing to stones and (divination by) arrows, are an abomination, of Satan's handiwork: eschew such (abomination) that ye may prosper. Satan's plan is (but) to excite enmity and hatred between you, with intoxicants and gambling, and hinder you from the remembrance of Allah, and from prayer: Will ye not then abstain?'

Apart from intoxicants, justification or explanation for prohibition of any other item of food is not very clear. Sadly, Muslim scientists have not as yet researched into the reasons for abstention from dead meat or blood (most probably harmful medically) and above all, swine. Some half-baked theories (without any hard evidence of scientific enquiry) have been presented about pig's meat. Apparently, they do not stand the test of logic and factual knowledge. It has been said that pork/bacon/ham 1) carries bacteria harmful to humans (but so do several *halaal* animals, such as sheep); 2) is fed on all kinds of rubbish and waste matter (but so do several other 'allowed' animals such as chicken, specially in under-developed parts of the world; 3) carries over to humans the filthy habit of the swine indulging in indiscriminate sexual activity (but such habits are also present in people *not* consuming pig's meat; furthermore, no animal is known to be modest in their sexual behaviour. Also, this theory rests on the notion that meat of a particular animal carries over to human consumer the characteristics of that animal; it should follow that consuming chicken would make one timid and 'chicken-hearted' and eating lion's meat would instil courage and aggression!) It is significant that prohibition of swine is an ancient article of religious law dating from Judaism or before. Perhaps, in Islam it was kept as a sympathetic gesture to continue with the monotheistic tradition of the Semitic religions of the Middle East.

It may be concluded from our discussion that, according to the Quran,

1. The authority of deeming and declaring something permissible or forbidden rests with Allah alone.
2. Whatever Allah intended to declare so has been mentioned in the Quran.
3. Outside of that, anything is permissible provided it has been obtained by means deemed lawful by the Quran.

AFTERWORD

Let us look back at the journey we have just made through this work and reflect upon the various notions presented.

* * * * * *

Religion is a very strong and influential force in human life. Most religious-minded people adhere to it fervently and believe strongly in the validity of their respective faiths. At the same time, they attach themselves to their value-systems emotionally enough to be upset at even the slightest criticism aimed at their thoughts. Few care – or dare – to cast a critical and academic glance at the set of beliefs inherited from their ancestors. There have been countless conflicts – often violent and bloody – over disagreement between the followers of different religions. The Crusades – a lengthy string of fierce battles between the Islamic and the Judeo-Christian worlds for the custody of ancient sacred sites in the Middle East – stand as a stark example in history. The current geo-political set up of the globe and the recent wave of terrorism – which shows no sign of abating – has helped to re-trigger old enmity. Man's eternal and basic desire to live a peaceful and happy life begs a calm, serious and sincere stock-taking on the part of both sides. One of the ways to do that is to coolly assess our own value-systems to look for probable sources of the problem and, at the same time, open our minds and hearts to the probable merits on the other side.

In the course of this book we have seen that, as far as Islam is concerned, there *are* issues worthy of our attention in the areas of its sources, namely, the classical literature [the scripture (The Quran) as well as the extra-Quranic literature (Hadith, history and exegesis) which forms the basis of the faith. Such issues are often the basis of non-Muslim criticism on the theory and practice of Islam. It is desirable that Muslims accept the utility of responding to criticism in a rational, non-emotional manner.

At the same time, we have seen that the Muslim holy book – The Quran – despite its very genuine problems for the unbeliever is not without merits. Based upon its own particular philosophy, it suggests a comprehensive social system for human societies, which may be summarised as follows.

* * * * * *

Islam – meaning peace for all through submitting to the eternal laws of the Creator, which are enshrined in the Quran – is a value system for human life (*ad-deen*) for all mankind (3:19). It presents the same monotheistic principles which were suggested to mankind by earlier divine messengers through the

Creator's Message in scriptures like the Torah and the Bible (2:41) – only in its pristine, unadulterated form (11:110, 2:253, 10:93). Islam addresses the entire human race (114:1-5) and suggests a universal human fraternity on the basis of absolute equality transcending all barriers of prejudice (2:213, 3:103); it goes beyond internationalism and wishes to create universalism. It wants to create an environment which is conducive to the development of human personality, both physically as well as spiritually (1:2). The aim is to prepare Man for the next stage of existence in the evolutionary ladder (84:19). It wants to achieve that goal by establishing a global community which takes complete and indiscriminate care of its members by means of a comprehensive cradle-to-grave welfare system (1:3, 8:4, 6:151, 17:31). It wants to eradicate the notion and practice of one man's rule over another (3:79). Sovereignty belongs to the One and Only Creator God (18:26, 17:111). Dignity and respect in the Quranic society must be earned on merit not through inheritance (2:124, 4:58, 27:39, 46:19). Apart from the physical slavery, the Quran also wants to do away with spiritual, mental and psychological subjugation of Man by Man. Islam has no place for priesthood – Man and God do not need intermediaries (9:31,34; 2:166) . Knowledge of both the outer as well as the inner Universe is available to, and should be desired by all (2:88, 28:80). Islam stands to abolish all systems which exploit mankind economically. It suggests a universal and comprehensive socialistic economy where everyone works according to their capacity and gets according to their needs (53:39). Sources and means of production of all wealth are to be the personal property of no one – they are to be kept under communal control (9:111). Private ownership in general and of land in particular is anathema to Islam (2:255, 19:40). With its arrival a millennium and half ago, Islam emancipated women, elevating them to a status absolutely equal to that of men (33:35). It gives them equal rights of marriage, divorce, work, business and running and managing human social systems. Islam teaches fair play even with the enemy (17:34, 5:1, 8). It wants tolerance and the spirit of peaceful co-existence as the fabric running through human societies. To Islam, *jihad* is not indiscriminate killing of opponents, nor it is hostage–taking of innocents, nor it is the culture of terrorism; it is to strive with all one's heart to eradicate exploitation and injustice to create a universal, peaceful and blissful society for all mankind for all times.

* * * * *

With that this book makes a heart-felt plea to both the Muslim and the non-Muslim worlds to start earnestly working towards a peaceful co-existence on this small but fragile planet we call Earth, which is our common home. Let us strive together to usher in the new dawn which mankind has yearned ever since its creation, which in the Quranic expression will be the time when 'the Earth will shine with the light of its Lord' (39:69).

Endnotes

NOTES AND REFERENCES

FOREWORD

1. The term 'Crusade' comes from 'the Cross' (in connection to the execution of Jesus) and refers to a series of bloody, armed encounters, begun in 1095, between the Christian and the Muslim worlds to stake claim over control of the Holy Land. The saga has left us with bitter memories of Christian-Muslim conflicts, clashes, rivalries and mutual hostile enmity. It has also given history legendary personages of Salaaheddin Ayubi (Saladin), the Muslim ruler at the time and Richard the Lion-Heart, the king of England.
2. Tariq Ali (2002) *The Clash of Fundamentalisms,* Verso, UK.
3. Samuel Huntington (1993) *The Clash of Civilizations?,* article in the journal Foreign Affairs, USA.
4. Daniel, N (1960 & 1993) *Islam and the West – The Making of an Image,* Oneworld Publications Ltd., Oxford, UK.
5. A few years before the partition of British colonial India into the two modern sovereign states of India and Pakistan, a book titled *Rangeela Rasool* (The Amorous Messenger) was published in Urdu by a Hindu publisher Rajpal. The slanderous work – aimed at degrading Mohammed by publicising his sex life – created a furore among the Muslims of the sub-continent. A simple, young man from the northern town of Lahore (now Pakistan's second biggest city) named 'Ilmuddin knifed Rajpal to death. People hailed 'Ilmuddin as *ghaazi* (victorious warrior). Arrested (he actually walked into a police station and gave himself up), he was sentenced to death. Mr Mohammed Ali Jinnah, later known as Quaid-e-Azam (the Great Leader), the founding father of Pakistan, travelled especially from Bombay to legally represent and defend 'Ilmuddin, who was eventually hanged to death. People began referring to the youth as *shaheed* (martyr). To this day, people remember him as possibly the only Muslim in history to be simultaneously known as *ghaazi* and *shaheed*. Unbelievable as it may appear, the book *Rangeela Rasool* was merely a collection of selected *hadith* (The Prophetic Tradition).
6. For details please refer to chapter 3, The Quran.
7. Sura *Sabaa* (Chapter on [the city of] Sabaa) in the Quran records God instructing Mohammed to say, 'Say: "I do admonish you on one point: that ye do stand up before Allah – (it may be) in pairs, or (it may be) singly – and reflect (*tatafakkaru*)."' Translation of verse 34:46 from *The Holy Quran – English translation of the meanings and Commentary* by Abdullah Yousuf Ali, revised and edited by The Presidency of Islamic Researches, IFTA, CALL AND GUIDANCE, Riyadh, Saudi Arabia.
8. Some modern researchers have disagreed with the notion that Mecca lay on that trade route (Patricia Crone and M Cook, for instance, in works like *Hagarism* [1977] and *Meccan Trade and the Rise of Islam* [1987]).
9. Muslim legend has it that the *K'aba* in Mecca was originally built by patriarch Abraham and his son Ishmael, the ancestor of Arabs. However, some researchers have questioned the possibility of Abraham ever visiting the Hejaz, the district in which Mecca is situated.
10. The name *Muhammad* is an adjective meaning 'the praised one' and is thought to have been given to Mohammed as an honorific title later in his life. Some early Muslim sources have reported his birth name as *Qutham* (Ibn al Jawzi in *Wafa* and Maqrizi in *Imta,* among others).
11. J B Glubb (Pasha) in *History of Arabs.*
12. For a detailed discussion of these works please see chapter 2 (Extra-Quranic Sources of Islam) in the first part of this book.
13. The biggest faction of Shiites is *athna 'asharie* (the Twelvers), who believe the divine leadership of Ali's house carried on till the 12th Imam, who was raised to Heaven in Jesuit fashion. Known as the *Mahdi* (the Promised One), he is the current leader-in-'hiding' and will reappear just before the Dooms Day to work along Jesus to establish a just, universal social

order on Earth. Another big Shia sub-sect is the Sixers – the *Ismailie*. They hold that the leadership after the sixth Imam was inherited by another son (Ismail) of the 5th Imam, Ja'afer, the Truthful, and continues to this day in the person of Aga Khan (Prince Karim, residing in Paris, is the current [50th] Imam).

14 *The New Testament,* Matthew 21:22: "Render unto Caesar, the things that are Caesar's; and unto God the things that are God's."

15 I have dealt with the Muslim rituals in the second part of this book.

Part I: OVERVIEW

Chapter 1: The Extra-Quranic Literature of Islam

1 Ibn Warraq (1995), *Why I am Not a Muslim,* Prometheus Books, Amherst, New York, USA.
I have used the adjective 'derogatory' in view of Ibn Warraq's general, self-declared attitude towards Islam. He is decidedly (by his own admission) anti-Islamic and is one of the group of writers who have written polemically about Islam. He is popularly viewed as an apostate and lives in fear of his life enough to write under a pen-name. But, that must not discredit him, or anyone else, for making rational, critical and realistic statements about Islam or anything else, for that matter.

2 Ghulam Jilani Barq's works in Urdu (circa 1950's), Campbellpore in Pakistan.

3 Incidently this situation is the same in Christianity and Judaism

4 That is why *Hadith,* especially the most authentic compilation *al-Jaame' as-Saheeh* by Bokhari, is often referred to as *mithluhu ma'hu* (literally, 'Like It, With It' -; something which is the Quran's companion and is just like the Quran itself; in other words, the two are equal partners.

5 Rashid-ud-Daula, P. (c. 1935), *Kufrzaar e Islam* (The Infidel Land of Islam), Lahore/Delhi, British India. The Urdu article was published as issue 10 in a series of critical writings titled *Maulvi ka Ghalat Mazhab* (The Religious Errors of Priests) under the auspices of Inayatallah Khan al-Mashriqi, popularly known as Allaama Mashriqi, the founder of the famous *Khaksar* Movement in the days of the British Raj in India.

6 Bokhari, *Al-Jaam' as-Saheeh.*

7 Maudoodi, A A. (1973), from an article in magazine *Asia* (an organ of *Jamaat e Islami*), Lahore, Pakistan.

8 Doi, A Rahman (1980), *Hadith: An Introduction,* Kazi Publications, USA.

9 Humphreys, R S (1991), *Islamic History – A Framework for Inquiry,* I B Tauris & Co. Ltd., UK.

10 *Fiqh Ja'fafariya* is the declared state religion of the Islamic Republic of Iran.

11 Also see 3: 164 and 62: 2. It is said that 'the book' refers to The Quran and 'Wisdom' refers to what the Messenger gave by way of explaining and interpreting the Book, i.e. *Hadith.*

12 From *Tadween e Hadith,* p.259, as in *Maqaam e Hadith,* Pervez, quoted in a paper *Hadith al Hadith* (1981) by Asif Jaleel, Riyadh, Saudi Arabia (unpublished).

13 Ibid.

14 It is said that the verse means the Quran (Allah), Hadith / Sunnah (the Messenger) and laws enacted by the government of the day (those charged with authority).

15 Heikel, M H, *Life of Abu Bakr,* Egypt.

16 *Lectures,* Dr. Mohammed Iqbal.

17 Heikel, M H, *Life of Abu Bakr,* Egypt.

18 In fact, Maulana Abul 'Aala Maudoodi, in recent times the best known scholar of Sunni (Hanafi) Islam from the sub-continent, referred to earlier in this work, remarked that if God had decided to give all those details - missing in the Quran and found in *Hadith* – the Book would have grown to the size of Encyclopaedia Britannica! The absurdity of this argument does not merit any comment.

19 The concept of *az-zakaa* is crucial to Quranic ideology. Due to its importance I have dealt with it in detail under a separate chapter *The Economic System of the Quran* elsewhere in this book.

Endnotes

20. As mentioned earlier in the main text of this chapter, Bokhari is reported to have gathered 600,000 original reports out of which he selected about 7000 items to include in his compilation [Ref. *Islam* by A S Tritton, (1951), Hutchinson & Co. Ltd., London – p. 32]. Repetition reduces this number to nearly 3000. Bokhari lived for about 65 years (b. 190 H, d. 256 H). He must have spent the first two decades of his life growing up and educating himself. Of the 40 odd years left, he must have used at least 10 (one quarter, although for most normal people it is roughly one third of a lifetime) in sleeping, eating and other daily chores. He was not entirely desk-bound for the work; he is reported to have physically travelled to distant places in all parts of the Islamic empire to meet narrators to determine authenticity of his material. It was the 3rd/9th century; a few hundred miles took weeks, if not months, to cover. Even if he was working non-stop, he was sifting through that gigantic mass of material at the rate of 20,000 a year, 1,600 a month, 50 odd a day, and about 2 every hour. That does not leave any time for writing the material down at a time when typewriters, computers, even the printing press, did not exist! Bokhari must have been a workaholic of extremely exceptional stature, almost superhuman (he must have taken time, even if occasionally, off work due to illness). Was he, really?
21. *Hadith al Hadith* (1981) by Asif Jaleel, Riyadh, Saudi Arabia (unpublished).
22. *Sunan*, Ibn Maajja. The punishment of stoning takes its legitimacy from a hadith, which reports: '…Ayesha (rta) reported: "The verse for *rajm* (stoning) and the verse for breast-feeding the older (children) were in a document kept under my settee. When the Messenger of God died, and we were preoccupied with it, the domestic goat walked in and ate that document up (thus those verses were lost for ever)."' Where does that leave the Quran's claim of being complete and uncorrupted?
23. Maudoodi, A A, *Tafheem al Quran,* footnote on verse 24:2, Lahore, Pakistan.
24. *Qurani Faiseley*, 2nd edition (1987), Idara Tolu-e-Islam, Lahore, Pakistan.
25. Bokhari, *al-Jaame' as-Saheeh* chapters on self-washing and menstruation *(baab al ghusl, baab al haiz)* etc.
26. Fazlur Rahman (1979) *Islam* (2nd edition), note 31, chapter 3, p. 268, University of Chicago Press, Chicago and London.
It is a pity that a writer and academic of Fazlur Rahman's stature is confused about this particular group. He equates *Ahl al Quran* with the non-sectarian, intellectual movement called *Tolu e Islam,* founded in 1938 by one Choudhary Ghulam Ahmed, who wrote under the pen-name of Perwaiz. Both movements were eventually based in, and operated from, the city of Lahore in northern Pakistan but had very little in common. Perwaiz stood for a re-evaluation of the approach and methodologies applied to study the Quran and the Islamic Movement. He did *not* reject *Hadith.* His stance was to advocate an assessment of all Tradition according to the yardstick of the Scripture. To Perwaiz, the Quran must have the last word in any conflict or confusion. He regarded the Prophetic Tradition as a precedent – what Mohammed and his companions did in their time. But, he very rightly pointed out - as I have tried to illustrate in the main text of this chapter – that only reports which do not clash with the Scripture should be accepted as having a real possibility of being true historical record, even then just as a precedent and not as articles of Faith on par with or overriding the Quranic injunctions. In his approach to *Hadith,* Perwaiz was no different from people like the jurist Abu Hanifa of the past or Abul a'la Maudoodi of the present in being selective on the basis of the Quran.
27. Goldziher, *Muslim Studies* (1889-90), vol. 2 – first published in German, as quoted in Ibn al-Rawandi in *Origins of Islam: A Critical Look at the Sources* in Ibn Warraq (2000) ed. *The Quest for the Historical Muhammad,* Prometheus Books, Amherst, New York.
28. Abiu Dawood, *Sunan* 24:3.
29. Bokhari, *al-Jaame' as-Saheeh*, 3:39.
30. Fazlur Rahman (1979) *Islam* (2nd edition), University of Chicago Press, Chicago and London.
31. Muhammad Ali, Maulana (1936), *The Religion of Islam,* 6th ed. (1990), p. 47, The Ahmadiyya Anjuman Isha'at Islam (Lahore) Ohio, USA.
32. Ibid, p. 48.
33. Watt, W M & Bell, R (1970 / 1994), *Introduction to the Qur'an*, Edinburgh University Press.

34 This is more than mere hypothesis. The Arab society has traditionally been authoritarian and dictatorial to the point of being violently intolerant to opposition. Even in today's 21st century Saudi Arabia, for instance, the Press is not free and no publication, especially of a religious/political nature can make its appearance without prior approval of the government. It is not difficult to imagine the state of affairs in the Arab society of more than a millennium and a half ago.

35 *Sunni* comes from *ahl al-sunna* (People of the Sunna [model] of the Prophet). It is the name for the most numerous mass of Muslims. *Shia'* comes from *Shia'an Ali* (The Partisans of Ali), named after the Prophet's cousin and the fourth Caliph.

36 Haykal, M. (1976) *The Life of Muhammad*, translated from the 8th edition by Isma'il al Faruqi, North American Trust Publications. Originally from Abu Ja'afer Mohammad Ibn Jareer at-Tabari (839-923 AD), *at Taareekh ar Rusul wal Mulook*.

37 Tabari, in part IV, vol. 1 of his *at Taareekh ar Rusul wal Mulook*, reports the incident in some detail.
Here, I translate the excerpt from an Urdu article in *Qurani Faiseley*, 2nd edition (1987), Idara Tolu-e- Islam, Lahore, Pakistan by G A Perwaiz.
'Now people swarmed Abu Bekr to take an oath (of allegiance) and nearly trampled S'ad over. One of his men called out to protect and save him. 'Umar said. "May God kill him. Slay him," and came and stood over him saying, "I want to trample you to death." S'ad grabbed 'Umar by the beard. 'Umar said, "Let go. If I lose even one hair, you won't have any teeth left." Abu Bekr said, "Be quiet, 'Umar. This is the time for mellowness." 'Umar let go. S'ad said, "If I had the ability to rise, I would fill the streets of Medina with my supporters to the shock of you and your supporters. By God, I would hand you over to the ones I would obey. Now, take me out of here." He was not pursued for a few days. After that, he was sent a message to come and declare his allegiance [to Abu Bekr] as everyone, even his [S'ad's] men already had. He replied back, "Never. Not until I empty my quiver against you, dip my lance in your blood, use my sword indiscriminately, and fight it out with my tribe and family against you!" From then on, S'ad would not offer congregational prayer under Abu Bekr, nor perform *Hajj* [the Pilgrimage] alongside him. He continued to behave in this manner till Abu Bekr's death.'
In contrast, the Quran gives a very different picture of mutual relations of the people of the like of 'Umar (a migrant from Mecca) and S'ad (a host from Medina), both Companions of Mohammed.
About the Companions of the Messenger, the Quran says: " *Muhammad is the Messenger of Allah; and those who are with him are strong against Unbelievers, (but) compassionate amongst each other"* (48:29). About the Migrants and Helpers in particular, see (59:8, 9).

38 Such reports are favoured more by Shia literature than Sunni.

39 Maudoodi, A A. (circa '60s) *Khilafat aur Mulookiat*, Lahore, Pakistan.

40 This was a faction who took a neutral position in the Ali-Mu'aawiya conflict. They later became a philosophical school of thought called *al Mu'tazela*, who promoted rationalism.

41 It is also reported that the tension between the two clans dates back to pre-Islamic times. Umayya, a real nephew of Hashem, the Messenger's ancestor, harboured feelings of jealousy and ill-will against Hashem over his prestige as the custodian of the Ka'ba.

42 Literally, 'People of the House' – the members of the Messenger's family.

43 This explains the presence and establishment of Shiaism in Iran.
The Persian support to the Hashemites probably was not so much for their love as much it was for the hatred of the Arabs (Muslims). Their reasons were historical and driven by patriotic feelings and wounded pride, which had resulted from Arab invasion and occupation of their coveted land. I have the intention of dealing with this subject more comprehensively whenever an opportunity arises and the time is right.

44 I translate this rather lengthy report from the Urdu work *Qurani Faiseley* (Verdicts from the Quran), 2nd edition (1987), Idara Tolu-e-Islam, Lahore, Pakistan by G A Perwaiz.

45 The part of the story in parentheses has not been reported by Bokhari but Allama 'Ainy has from a work titled *Maraseel Sha'by*.

46 Heikel, M H, *Life of Abu Bakr,* Egypt.
47 Ibn Qutaiba, *al-Imaama w as-Siyaasa* as in *Qurani Faiseley* (Verdicts from the Quran).
48 Tabari in his *Taareekh,* vol. 2.
49 Taloot is Saul of the Bible, who fought against Goliath at the head of the Israelite army under David.
50 Goldziher, I, *Muslim Studies,* vol. 2, pp. 18-19 as in Ibn al-Rawandi, Origins of Islam:A Critical Look at the Sources, *The Quest for the Historical Muhammad* (2000), Prometheus Books, New York, USA.
51 M J de Goeje et al (ed) 1879-1901, E J Brill, Leiden as in Humphreys, R Stephen (1991), *Islamic History – A Framework for Inquiry,* I B Tauris & Co. Ltd. London and New York.

Chapter 2:PROBLEMS of LANGUAGE, TRANSLATION & INTERPRETATION

1 Fairclough, N., *Language and Power* (1989), p. 43, Longman, UK.
2 Holmes, J., *An Introduction to Sociolinguistics* (1992), p. 246, Longman, UK.
3 Husain, S S Azfar, *The Indianness of Rudyard Kipling: A Study in Stylistics* (1983) chapter 3: Style and Context, Cosmic Press, London.
4 *The Old Testament,*Genesis 11:9, '…because the Lord there made a babble of the language of all the world.'
5 29:45, and several others.
6 In Arabic, the First degree 'great' should be translated as *kabeer* (m) and *kabeera* (f); from *A Dictionary of Modern Written Arabic* by Hans Wehr (ed. J M Cowan 1974), Librairie du Liban, Beirut and Macdonald & Evans Ltd., London.
7 See work by Abdallah Yousuf Ali, among others.
8 *Webster's New Collegiate Dictionary* lists the following:
   1: one having power and authority over others: **a**: a ruler by hereditary right or pre-eminence to whom service and obedience is due, **b**: one of whom a fee or estate is held in feudal tenure, c: an owner of land or other real property, d: the male head of a household, e: husband, f: one who has achieved mastery or who exercises leadership or great power in some area.
   2 cap **a**: GOD 1 **b**: CHRIST
   3: a man of high rank or position: as **a**: a feudal tenant holding directly of the king **b**: a British nobleman: as (1): BARON (2) : an hereditary peer of the rank of marquess, earl, or viscount (3): the son of a duke or a marquess or the eldest son of an earl (4): a bishop of the Church of England **c**: *pl cap*: HOUSE OF LORDS
   4: used as a British title: as **a**-used as part of an official title (*Lord* Advocate) **b**-used informally in place of the title for a marquess, earl, or viscount **c** – used for a baron **d**-used by courtesy before the name or surname of a younger son of a duke or a marquess
   5: a person chosen to preside over a festival.
9 *A Dictionary of Modern Written Arabic* by Hans Wehr.
10 From *Al-mufredaat fi Ghareeb al-Qur'aan* by Raagheb Esphahaani (d. c 502 H), printed in Egypt in 1324 H, as in *Lughaat al Quran* by G A Pervez.
11 Abdallah Yousuf Ali in his (translation of) *The Holy Quran* translates this single Arabic word with two of English – "Men are the protectors and maintainers of women,…" Obviously, Ali felt the need for *interpreting* the original Arabic term instead of *translating* it.
12 *Muheet al Muheet* by Peter Bustani (1870), Beirut, Lebenon, as in *Lughaat al Quran* by G A Pervez.
13 By Ashraf Ali Thaanewi (1390 H), Farid Book Depot, near Jaame Masjid (Grand Mosque), Delhi.
   Interestingly, *haakem,* too, is Arabic meaning 'judge, one who decides, arbiter.' But the translator was thinking of the specific connotation of it in Urdu ('ruler, one in power') because of the traditional concepts of Islam as handed down by *Sunna* (history and *Hadith*).
14 Pervez, GA, *Taahera kay naam khutoot* ('Letters to Taahera'), pp. 49-50, (1972), Idara Tolu-e-Islam, Lahore, Pakistan.

15 Ibid.
16 See Urdu translations of the Quran by writers like Shah Abdul Qadir and Shah Rafiullah.
17 As in note 14 above.
18 *Taaj al 'Uroos* and *Raagheb*, as in *Lughaat al Quran* by G A Pervez.
19 The punishment for theft is among those in the Quran which have been prescribed by the Scripture. Other examples are flogging for fornication (24:2) as well as for defamation of character (24:4). Such prescribed punishments are called *hudood* (sing. *had*) in Islamic jurisprudence while *t'azeeraat* (sing. *t'azeer*) is the term used for punishments not prescribed in the Quran, such as consumption of forbidden (*haraam*) food or non-payment of *zakaat* (the dues of the State). Please see *Shariah: The Islamic Law* by 'Abdur Rahman I Doi (1984), Ta Ha Publishers, London.
20 Sura *Al-Maaeda* – 5:38-39.
21 Khaled Ahmed, *Pakistan*, article 27 on Justice Alvin Robert Cornelius (1903-1991), Chief Justice of the Supreme Court of Pakistan (1960-1968). Khalid refers to Ralph Braibanti's *Chief Justice Cornelius of Pakistan* (OUP), in which Braibanti praises Cornelius's 'reformism' by citing a conversation between Braibanti and Cornelius, in which the Chief Justice suggested that 'the hand of thief should be cut (disabled temporarily through surgical operation).'
22 *Deen-e-Islam,* an Urdu translation of *The Religion of Islam,* (1961) Mohammed Ali, Ahmedia Anjuman, Lahore, Pakistan, p.189. Ali refers to *Lisaan al 'Arab,* the famous lexical work for the example *qata' lisaanahu* (literally, 'he cut his tongue off') meaning 'he silenced him.'
23 Guillaume, Alfred, *Islam* (1954), reprinted 1990, Penguin Books, London.

It must be said, however, that this particular situation is by no means unique to the Quran. Any piece of literature from any language will experience the same problems of linguistic shortcomings. My own experience testified to that when I was translating some Urdu short stories into English. Conversely, for example, a translation of any part of Shakespearian masterpieces into Urdu would doubtlessly lose at least some of the beauty and appeal of the original. Such an experience, one may add, can only be appreciated by a reader equally well-versed in both the languages concerned.

24 Izutsu, T. (1964) *God and Man in the Koran – Semantics of the Koranic Weltanschawung (world-view)*, Keio Institute of Cultural and Linguistic Studies, Keio University, Tokyo, Japan.
25 Ibid. p. 12.
26 *Lughaat al Quran* by G A Pervez, vol. 1, p.11.
27 The Quran claims to be *'...burhaan min rabbekum'* – a clear argument from your Lord' (4:175).
28 As in note 23, above.
29 *Tasreef* comes from the three-letter root *sawd, raa, faa* (SRF) with the basic meanings of 'to bring back, to repeat, to substitute, to change.' *Saraf assibiaan min al maktab* is 'the kids were turned back from the school'; *tasaareef al umoor* (shuffling and rearranging matters); *sarf al khamr* and *tasreef ul khamr* (to have a neat drink); *assareef* (pure silver); *assrraaf* (money-changer).

In the Quran, we see *'wa laqad sarrafnaa fi haazehel Qur'aan le yazakkaroo-* And We have repeated (things in various ways) in this Quran so that they (the people) may remember and retain them' (17:41 and 17:89 as well as 18:54).

30 Edward Lane and *Taaj al 'Uroos*, as in *Lughaat al Quran* by G A Pervez
31 Ibn Faaris as in *Lughaat al Quran* by G A Pervez.
32 As in Abdallah Yousuf Ali.
33 It must be noted, however, that *sebr* has also been used by the Quran in the ordinary meaning of 'being patient,' as in 18:68 and 49:5.
34 Izutsu, T. (1959) *The Structure of Ethical Terms in the Koran – A Study in Semantics*, p. 20, Keio Institute of Cultural and Linguistic Studies, Keio University, Tokyo, Japan.
35 The figure of 120 million was quoted in the 1986 publication of *The Arabic Alphabet – How to read and write it* by Nicholas Awde & Putros Samano, Al Saqi Books, 26, Westbourne Grove, London.
36 Yule, George, *The Study of Language* (1987, 1985), Cambridge University Press, UK.

Endnotes

37 *An Introduction to Language* by Victoria Fromkin & Robert Rodman (1978, 1974) Holt, Rinehart and Winston), p. 260.

38 *A Dictionary of Modern Written Arabic* by Hans Wehr.

Part II – THE QURANIC ISLAM

Chapter 4: MAN, GOD and the SUPERNATURAL

1 The human population of the Earth today may be roughly divided into two equal halves of believers (divine as well as non-divine religions) and non-believers (atheists such as Marxists).

2 J. Courtney Murray, *The Problem of God*, New Haven and London, 1964, pp. 120-21 as in Patrick Masterson, *Atheism and Alienation*, Pelican Books, London, 1973, p. 13.

3 Friedrich Nietzche (1844-1900), *Thus Spoke Zarathustra* (1969), Penguin Books, UK.
Nietzche describes the prophet Zarathustra coming down from his mountain retreat and marvelling that the people he encounters do not yet recognise that God is dead.

4 Jaynes, J., (1984) *The Origin of Consciousness in the Breakdown of the Bicameral Mind*, Houghton Mifflin Company, Boston, USA.

5 Ludwig Feuerbach (1804-1872), *The Essence of Christianity*, Harper Torchbooks 1957 (from a translation by George Eliot) as in John Hick, *The Existence of God*, Collier Macmillan Publishers 1964, London.

6 Karl Marx (1818-1883), *Introduction to the Critique of the Hegelian Philosophy of the Right* as in Mel Thompson, *The Philosophy of Religion*, (1997) Hodder Headline, London.

7 Alan F Alford, *Gods of the New Millenium* (1996), Hodder & Stoughton, London.

8 From Mel Thompson, *The Philosophy of Religion*, (1997) Hodder Headline, London.
Ontology is the philosophical study of the nature of being.

9 John Hick, *The Existence of God*, Collier Macmillan Publishers (1964), London, p. 23.

10 Ibid, p. 33.

11 Mel Thompson, *The Philosophy of Religion*, (1997) Hodder Headline, London.

12 Ibid. Teleology is the philosophical study of design and purpose in natural phenomena.

13 Ibid. Ibid, p.10.

14 More recently, the horrific Tsunami disaster around the Indian Ocean on Boxing Day (December 26, 2004) left many religionists wondering with the question: Why does God allow all that suffering?

15 Ibid.

16 Sura *Al-Baqara* (The Cow), verses 155-157, translation by Abdallah Yousuf Ali.

17 2:117. Also see 6:14, 80, 101; 12:101; 14:10; 35:1 and 42:11. The divine attributes (adjectives) used in these verses are *badee'* and *faater*, both meaning 'originator' with a slight difference in shade.

18 10:4. Also in 10:34; 27:64; 29:19-20 and 30:11, 27.

19 The term 'tract' is the translation of *taraaeq* (plural for *tareeq* – a path). The number seven in Arabic is used idiomatically for 'several' (see E Lane's *Arabic Lexicon*).

20 21:30.

21 41:11.

22 31:29. Also see 35:13; 39:5; 46:3.

23 21:30. Also in 24:45

24 6:38.

25 30:20 and 40:67. Elsewhere, non-living matter such as *teen* – clay (6:2), *sulaala min teen* - quintessence of clay (23:12), *teenen laazeb* – sticky clay (37:11), and *salsaal min hamaa masnoon* – sounding clay from mud moulded into shape (15:26 and 55:14) have been mentioned.

26 4:1 and 6:98.
The term *nafsen waaheda* – single Person (as translated here by A Yousuf Ali) needs comment. It is commonly taken to refer to the first ever man – Adam – created in Biblical fashion. But,

writers like Pervez and, before him, Inayatullah Khan al-Mashriqi, prefer 'unitary cell' or 'a single soul,' respectively [please refer to their Urdu works – *Iblees o Aadam* (Pervez, Idara Tolu-e-Islam, c. 1960's, Lahore, Pakistan), and *At-Tazkera* (Mashriqi, At-Tazkera Publications, 1980, Lahore, Pakistan)]. Even Ali's translation – 'single Person' – cannot be taken to refer to the orthodox Biblical view because according to that, mankind spread forth from *two* persons – Adam and Eve -, whereas verse 4:1 addresses man in the plural (*khalaqakum*) who were all created from one single being. In fact, Ali, in his explanatory note to this verse asserts that the particle *min* ('from') in pronoun *minhaa* ('from her') refers to "a species, a nature, a similarity."

In 31:28, we find the same expression with a slight variation:

'And your creation or your resurrection is in no wise but *as* an individual soul (*knafse waaheda*)...'

27 6:98 and 11:6.

In the next verse (6:99), the birth and growth of Man has been likened to that of vegetation, which supports the idea of evolution. It is stated more clearly in 70:14: '...it is He that has created you in diverse stages (*atwaaraa*) and reinforced in 84:19: 'You shall surely travel from stage to stage.'

28 51:49. Also, 4:1 and 53:45. See note 26 above.

29 84:19.

30 17:49. Also, 32:10.

31 21:104. Also, 20:55; 29:19; 30:11 and 50:3.

32 Please refer to the Glossary for the etymology of 'Adam.'

33 W. Montgomery Watt, *Islamic Philosophy and Theology – An Extended Survey* (1985) chapter 5: God's Determination of Events, Edinburgh University Press, UK.

34 Please refer to the Glossary in this book for the Quranic concept of 'angel'.

35 A very significant verse in this regard is quite noteworthy: 'Then He fashioned him in due proportion, and breathed into him of His spirit; and He gave you hearing and sight and understanding...' (32:9).

The verse compactly states the natural faculties given to mankind. Lexically, it is very significant that the verse uses the *third* person *singular* to refer to Man in the first part, but in the second half – after having 'breathed into him of His spirit' – uses the *second* person *plural*. It means that breathing the divine spirit gave Man a personality and thus became capable of being addressed.

35a *Asmaa* is plural of *ism* (name; an attribute which distinguishes something/one from others). Since a name is the means to 'know' about something, simply knowing its name (without knowledge about it) is useless. Therefore, when Man was taught to name 'things', by implication, he acquired the capacity and ability to obtain knowledge.

36 The defiance of Satan (Man's own fiery rebellious sentiments) is also mentioned in 7:11, 15:31, 17:61, 18:50, 20:116, and 38:73-74.

37 Please refer to the Glossary in this book for the Quranic concepts of '*Iblees*'- the Devil and *Shaitaan* (Satan).

38 Contrastingly, as we see in the case of Man, the right attitude is not of arrogance but of gracefully accepting responsibility of one's actions if one is to learn from mistakes. When Man erred (20:121), he admitted full responsibility: 'They said: "Our Lord we have wronged our own selves: if Thou forgive us not and bestow not upon us thy Mercy, we shall certainly be lost." (7:23).

39 This respite, being for the entire duration of human existence, practically means that God (Nature) does not interfere in human affairs as far as deliberate actions are concerned.

40 *Shajara* (tree) springs from the three-letter root *sheen, jeem, raa*, which is applied to something which starts as one but divides up into parts later. In the Quran, differences and clashes among men have been termed *shajara baynahum* in 4:65.

41 Also in 20:120: 'But Satan whispered evil to him: he said, "O Adam! Shall I lead thee to the Tree of Eternity and to a kingdom that never decays?"'

42 For further discussion on the position and status of women in the Quran and more references, please see chapter 8, 'Women, Sex and Marriage', in this work].

43 Lexically, the Arabic text in this verse (2:36), as well as in 2:38, uses the verb (*ehbetoo*- 'get down') in the Second Person *Plural*, indicating that there were more than two people involved. It is reinforced in 2:38 with the adverb *jamee'n* ('together').

44 Also see 7:35, 7:49, 10:62.

45 Attached to this notion is the popular Muslim idea that Islam is a system best suited to the human make-up; hence it is called *deen al fitra* (the 'Religion'/System of Nature or the Natural System). Added to this is the assertion: 'Since Islam is the Natural System, every human child is a Muslim because it is born with natural instincts.' That is why it is fashionable to refer to a non-Muslim's conversion to Islam as 'reversion.' This notion of Man being born with 'natural' instincts appears to have come from the Biblical notion of Adam having been 'created in God's own image.' In view of mankind's mostly atrocious behaviour so far, God's 'own' image does not appear very comforting.

46 As in *Lughaat al Quran* (1961), vol.3, by Pervez, Lahore, Pakistan.

47 In addition to *fitra* and/or *bida'* (creating from non-being), there is another Quranic term used for 'create' – *khalq*; it is applied to the act of creating (making) from material already existing as in '*khalaq al-insaan min nutfa* – He has created man from a sperm-drop' (16:4). God is the only *faater/dadee'* whereas He is *ahsan al khaaleqeen* – the best of creators (23:14, 37:125).

48 For example, see the following Quranic comments on human behaviour: 'Truly, Man was created very impatient' (70:20); '...Man is indeed unjust and foolish' (33:72); 'Woe to Man! What has made him reject Him?' (80:17); '...Man is given to haste.' (17:11); '...Man is, in most things, contentious.' (18:54); and '...he (Man) is an open adversary.' (36:77).

49 I must request my readers to note my disagreement with this very conventional translation by A Yousuf Ali under the influence of Traditional Islam. The lexical background to key terms such as *taqwa, salaa* and *muneeb*, given in the Glossary and chapters on the rituals should enable us to arrive at the following interpretation of 30:31: 'Refer constantly to His law, be careful to avoid wrong deeds, and establish a social system comprehensively based upon God's law exclusive of all other laws.

50 Please refer to Chapter 7, 'The Economic System of the Quran' in this work for *anfaaq*.

51 Also in 40:11.

52 In the past some civilizations believed in life after death. In ancient Egypt, the royal tombs were stocked with food, clothing, utensils, etc. – even, according to some accounts, slaves. Similarly, in ancient Greece, food was poured into graves. (See Encyclopaedia Britannica, the article on *Death*). But, in view of this verse – and others, it is clear that according to the Quran, the belief of the second coming of Christ is erroneous. So, for that matter, is the Muslim belief of the second coming of Mohammed al-Mahdi, the twelfth *Imam* of the Shia sect. It is also clear that the Quran negates the Hindu belief of Reincarnation.

53 'Until ye visit the graves.' (102:2)

54 23:15, 16.

55 37: 58,59

56 35:36.

57 32:17

58 Please refer to the Glossary for the etymology of *janna* and *jahannum*.

59 (3:133)

60 (3:133)

61 13:35

62 3:10

63 104: 6,7

64 87:12,13

65 14:17

66 Please refer to the Glossary for the etymology of *al-qayaama*.

67 It is very clear from this verse that 'the Day' will be a new era for mankind in this life because it is going to occur on Earth.

68 That is exactly why, they say, one should be 'resigned to one's fate' and not complain about one's financial state (it is God's infinite wisdom behind that allocation one becomes guilty of complaining against!).

69 It is believed that special prayers on special occasions, such as *laila-tal-Qadr* (most popularly thought to be the 27th night of Ramadam, the Muslim month of Fasting), can do the trick surely and quickly.
70 It is believed that the intensity and magnitude of a good deed can wipe out even a lifetime of sins.
71 That is why people beseech historical figures known as *awliyaa Allah* (Friends of God) – living or dead!
72 It is popularly believed that 'marriages are made in Heaven' and that the number and sex of the children one is going to have is also pre-decided by God.
73 'We have indeed revealed this (Message) in the Night of Power.' (97:1).
74 'Ramadan is the month in which We sent down the Quran…' (2:185).

Chapter 5: THE QURANIC POLITICAL SYSTEM

1 The military – or other – dictatorships and the developing countries aside, even in the industrialized and developed West the situation is not very pleasant. The current US president George W Bush is notorious for his lack of general knowledge; he has been reported, in a pre-election interview, to be ignorant of the current leaders of India and Mexico! In Britain, John Major, a Conservative prime minister, had only GCSEs to his educational credit.
2 Interestingly, some politicians have admitted to that fact. Some years ago, an English secondary school girl did a project asking a number of politicians one question: "Why did you enter politics?"
  The responses – compiled and published in the national Press – made amusing reading. A junior minister of Sports actually said that he had chosen politics as a career as this was the only field *not* requiring any training or qualification for entry. More revealing was the response of another minister who said that he wanted to see "…what life was like on the other side of the fence."!
3 Potter, S and Hanks, P., *A Dictionary of English*, Beirut, Lebenon.
4 *Arth Shaastra,* from Encyclopaedia Britannica.
5 *Summa Theologica* by St. Aquinas, as in Encyclopaedia Britannica.
6 *A History of Political Thought,* Chapter 'The Middle Ages.'
7 The clergy, as it is, have historically been inflexible in their views and stance. This attitude breeds dictatorial disposition, which really comes into its own when supported by political power. The Iranian Revolution of Ayatollah Khomeini provided a stark example of the stubborn, ruthless and hypocritical behaviour of the mullahs (clerics). The new 'Islamic' government executed at least hundreds of its past and present opponents while completely forgetting, or ignoring, the exemplary conduct of the Prophet of Islam who declared general amnesty when he made his triumphant entry into Mecca.
8 *The New Testament,* Matthews 21:22
9 Tawney, R H., *Religion and the Rise of Capitalism*, p. 20
10 The last two sets are typical of Semitic religions, especially Islam.
11 Article *Political Systems,* Encyclopaedia Britannica.
  The common origins of ancient Persian (Zoroastrian) and Hindu religious philosophies may be noted in some strong similarities between the two, such as the caste system and fire worship; also, the terms *Arya* (for ancient Hunduism) and *Iran* spring from a common linguistic base.
12 Maxime Rodinson, *Islam and Capitalism,* p.22.
13 Also, *Al-An'aam* – 6:57 and *Beni Israel* – 17:111.
14 In the same sura (*Al-Maaeda*), there are two more adjectives used for such people – *az-zaalemoon*
  (wrong-doers) in 5:45 and *al-faaseqoon* (rebels) in 5:47.
15 *The Republic,* (378 B.C.)
16 *Politics* (335-332 B.C.).

Endnotes

17 *Summa Theologica*, 13ᵗʰ century AD.
18 *Policratrice*, 1159 AD.
19 Encyclopaedia Britannica.
20 The Constitution of the United States of America, 1776.
21 *Democracy in a World of Tension*, UNO (1947).
22 Professor Alfred Coben, *The Crisis of Civilization*.
23 Professor A C Ewing, *The Individual, The State and World Government*, Cambridge
   Notes 21, 22, 23 as in the Urdu work *Saleem kay naam Khutoot*, vol. 3, Islam ka Siyaasi Nizaam, by G A Pervez, Idara Tolu-e-Islam, Lahore, Pakistan.
24 *The Prince* by Nicolo Machiavelli.
25 *Religion and the Rise of Capitalism*, p. 24.
26 *Shahraah-e-Inqalaab* (The High Road to Revolution), Dr. Mubasshar Hasan, Lahore, Pakistan.
27 *The Crisis of the Modern World* as in *Saleem kay naam Khutoot*, vol. 3, p.305, by G A Pervez, Idara Tolu-e-Islam, Lahore, Pakistan.
28 *Islam and Capitalism* by Maxime Rodinson, p. 22. Rodinson reports that, by the time of the birth of Mohammed, Nowsherwaan the Just, following his father, had implemented a number of socialist reforms in Persia according to the teachings of Mazdak. Rodinson takes as very significant the many similarities between Mazdak's socialist philosophy and the Quran's economic system, especially about private ownership. He deems it quite possible that Mohammed was influenced by Mazdak's teachings. This notion is supported by certain Prophetic Traditions praising the neighbouring king of Persia (reported by Sir Syed Ahmed Khan in his *Maqalaat*, part 9, p. 20). It is echoed in Iqbal's poetry when he puts words to that effect in Abu Jahl's mouth: '*een masaawaat, een mawaakhaat, a'jami ast - khhob mee daanem ke Salman mazdaki ast*' - *Javed Naama*, Abu Jahl's Wailing in the Ka'ba
29 As we have seen, the Quranic concept of opposites is different from all the concepts we have come across so far.
30 *The Communist Manifesto*, as in Communism and Economic Progress (Urdu) by Hussain Ahmed Khan in journal *Charagh e Raah* (special Socialism issue). Sadly, Marx's wish is yet to come true.
31 *Why I Am Not A Christian*, Part WHAT I BELIEVE, section on Moral Principles.
32 Quoted by Murray in *The Individual and the State* as in *Saleem kay naam Khutoot*, vol. 3, by G A Pervez, Idara Tolu-e-Islam, Lahore, Pakistan.
33 Quoted by Susan Stebbings in *Ideals and Illusions* as in *Saleem kay naam Khutoot*, vol. 3, by G A Pervez, Idara Tolu-e-Islam, Lahore, Pakistan.
34 Article *Foreign Affairs* (1952) as in *Saleem kay naam Khutoot*, vol. 3, by G A Pervez, Idara Tolu-e-Islam, Lahore, Pakistan.
35 *On Education*, London, UK.
36 Also in *Ar-Ra'd* – 13: 21, 25.
37 As in *Saleem kay naam Khutoot*, vol. 3, Letter 41, by G A Pervez, Idara Tolu-e-Islam, Lahore, Pakistan.
38 *A Learner's Arabic-English Dictionary*, Librarie du Liban, Beirut, Lebenon.
39 Also, 10:104; 6:56; 40:66; 13:36; 27:91; 39:11 and others.
40 *Maqalaat Sir Syed*, Part 9, Article: Hindustan aur English Government, p. 19-20, Lahore, Pakistan.
41 Ibid, Part 1, Article: Khilaafat aur Khalifa, p. 168.
42 As is common knowledge, the compilation of Hadith began only in the second Muslim century. Ironically, one Tradition reports the Messenger as prohibiting Muslims to report and record from Him anything other than the Quran! – *Saheeh Muslim*, as in the article *Hadith e Hadith* by Asif Jaleel, Karachi, Pakistan (unpublished).
43 Heikel, M H, *Life of Abu Bakr*, Egypt.
44 *Lectures* by Dr. Mohammed Iqbal.
45 Heikel, M H, *Life of Abu Bakr*, Egypt.
46 It does not follow that a capable candidate shall be ignored because of the 'drawback' of family connections. Solomon succeeded his father David not because of being his son but due to

attributes required for the job.
47 This particular point has special relevance to the creation of Pakistan in 1947. The issue is important and extensive enough to warrant a separate paper. Please refer to my articles *The Ideology of Pakistan* and *What is ad-Deen* for a detailed discussion of the subject.

Chapter 6: THE ECONOMIC SYSTEM OF THE QURAN

1 The basics of capitalism can be studied in books like *The Wealth of Nations* by Adam Smith.
2 'Money' may be in the form of cash (coins or bank notes) or otherwise (cheques, perks, articles, etc).
3 The fact is that nowhere in the world is capitalism completely free in the true sense of the word.
4 The basics of socialism may be studied in books like *The Communist Manifesto* by Karl Marx.
5 Actually, no socialistic economy today can claim to be totally 'controlled'.
6 *Lughaat-al-Quran*, Pervez, G A (1961), Idara Tolu-e-Islam, Lahore, Pakistan.
7 Conventional interpretation of *nafsin waaheda* refers to Adam, the legendary first man created. Progressive writers, however, take it to mean 'a single cell.' Please refer to *At-tazkera*, an excellent commentary on the Quran by Inayatullah Khan Al-Mashriqi and *Iblees aur* Aadam, a very informative treatise on the human evolution, by Ghulam Ahmed Pervez.
8 As I have previously pointed out in these papers/lectures, the English translation I have used is by the renowned scholar Abdullah Yousuf Ali and is the authenticated version approved by the government of Saudi Arabia. But, I would quickly like to register my disagreement with it at several places. Here is one case in point. I would like to replace the word 'judgement' with 'uprising'. At a more opportune time, I will deal at length with the issue of translation.
9 *An-nafs* may be best translated in English with 'ego' or 'self.'
10 Please see verses 7-10 of this chapter.
11 Also, 'Nor will they there taste death, except the first death;...' *Ad-Dukhhaan* (44:56).
12 Fear is a negative attribute the absence of which is a characteristic of paradisaical life. Here, the translation should be: 'Follow the law of Allah (beware of the consequences of breaking it).'
13 This may also be interpreted as 'throwing (firing) arrows.'
Rizq is mainly, but not only, food. In *Al-Hajj*, it says: 'Those who leave their homes in the cause of Allah, and are then slain or die,- on them will Allah bestow verily a goodly Provision; ... (22:58).
14 It clearly means sustenance in the Hereafter. So, *rizq* is applied to all means of growth and development. What is more, this sustenance must be provided with no loss of dignity and self-respect. In *Al-Anfaal*, it
is called *rizqun kareem* – the dignified sustenance (8:4).
15 Because God is *Rabbul Aalemeen* - Provider of All Worlds (*Al-Baqara* – 2:1)
16 The Euphrates river in modern day Iraq; it was the farthest limit of the Islamic nation at the time.
17 Quoted from Taufiq ar Rahmaan of Egypt by Pervez, G A in *Shahkaar-e-Risaalet*, Idara Tolu-e-Islam, Lahore, Pakistan.
18 Please refer to the earler part of this chapter where *anfaaq* has been discussd.
'Those who spend their wealth for increase in self-purification (*zakaa*).' *Al-Leil* (93:18)
19 The first part of the verse is my translation; I do not agree with the version given by A Yousuf Ali.
20 The Arabic word for gambling used in this verse is *al-maisara*, which comes from the basic root *ya-seen-ra* with the meanings of 'easy, without difficulty'. *Yasaar* is 'left' as opposed to *yemeen* meaning 'right.' So, *al-maisara* is money which can be made with the left hand, i.e. easily made.

Endnotes

Chapter 7: WOMEN, SEX & MARRIAGE

1. The words *mawadda* and *rahma* are commonly translated – as indeed done by A Yousuf Ali – as 'love' and 'mercy', respectively, which do not entirely represent the Quranic concept of the terms.
   Mawadda originates from the three-letter root *waow-da-da* which means intense love and desire to the point of fixation steadfastly (*al wadd* is 'nail') – *ya waddu* – he/she desires (3:96); *wuddan* – love and attraction (19:96); *Al Wudood* – the very loving (God – 85:14).
   Rahma springs from *ra-ha-meem*, which is womb where a human foetus receives all the nourishment and protection it requires to adequately develop into a human infant. See *ar hamhumaa* (nourish the two of them) - 17:34; rain – 42:28; crops – 30:46; bounties of life – 11:9, 10, etc. *azwaaj* is plural for *zowj* (m) and *zowja* (f) meaning 'complementary' such as a pair of shoes or opposite, such as day and night. *Sukun* comes from *seen-ka-noon* (motionlessness): *as sikkeen* (12:31) is knife probably because it tranquillises the slaughtered animal; *ja'l al lail sakana* – 6:97 – the night provides you with tranquillity; *inna salaatuka sakan lahum* – 9:103 – your supplication gives them comfort; etc.
2. *An-Nisaa* – 4: 21
3. The word *nikaah* stems from the three-letter root *noon-ka-ha* with the basic meaning of mixing to integrate and absorb. For example, *nakaha an-nu'aas* (sleep integrated in eyes); *nakaha al-matar ul ardh* (the rain got absorbed in the earth).
4. Both men and women are not to engage in secret liaison as is obvious from 4:25 (…wa la muttakhezat e akhdaan..) as well as 5: 5 (…wa la muttakhezi akhdaan..).
5. See 2:236-237
6. Also: *Al-An'aam*-6:98; *Al-A'raaf*-7:189; *Az-Zumr*-39:6, etc.
7. Abou El Fadl, Khalid, (2001) *Speaking in God's Name,* Oneword Publications, Oxford, UK.
8. Also: *Al-Ahzaab*-33:4. *Zihar* is the unreasonable oath one takes in a moment of senseless anger. It does not break a marriage contract.
9. Also: *An-Nisaa*-4:128; *Al-Mujaadela*-58:1; *At-Talaaq*-65:1
   It is to be noted that the Quran has used the term *talaaq* for both partners and nowhere has the term *khul'* been used to distinguish (discriminate) between the applications of husband and wife.
10. See *Al-Baqara*-2:228. Incidentally, this is the only one advantage which men have (mentioned in this verse) over women. Otherwise, the two are absolutely each other's equal.
11. Pervez, G A (1979), *Mataaleb al Furqaan,* Vol. 3, pp.385-395, Idara Tolu-e-Islam, Lahore, Pakistan.
12. Ibn Warraq (1995), *Why I Am Not A Muslim,* Prometheus Books, New York, USA.
13. Ibn Hajar al-'Asqalani in *Fath al Bari* as in Abou El Fadl, Khalid, (2001) *Speaking in God's Name,* Oneworld Publications, Oxford, UK.
14. Abou El Fadl, Khalid, (2001) *Speaking in God's Name,* Oneworld Publications, Oxford, UK.
15. It may be worthwhile to see the two verses dealing with divorce in their entirety.
    "A divorce is only permissible twice; after that, the parties should either hold together on equitable terms, or separate with kindness. It is not lawful for you (men) to take back any of your gifts (from your wives), except when both parties fear that they would be unable to keep the limits ordained by Allah. If ye (the judges) do indeed fear that they would be unable to keep the limits ordained by Allah, there is no blame on either of them if she give something for her freedom. These are the limits ordained by Allah; So do not transgress them. If any do transgress the limits ordained by Allah, such persons wrong (themselves as well as others).
    So if a husband divorces his wife (irrevocably), he cannot, after that, re-marry her until after she has married another husband and he has divorced her. In that case there is no blame on either of them if they reunite, provided they feel that they can keep the limits ordained by Allah. Such are the limits of Allah, which He makes plain to those who know." (2: 229, 230)

16. It is to be noted that the verse refers to men (*ar rijaal*) and women (*an nisaa*) in general and not in their capacity of marriage partners.
17. This is the gist of (not verbatim) the translation by Abdallah Yousuf Ali.
18. Abou El Fadl, Khalid, (2001) *Speaking in God's Name,* Oneworld Publications, Oxford, UK.
19. Ibid.
20. Adapted from Pervez, G A (1979), *Mataaleb al Furqaan,* Vol. 3, pp.364, Idara Tolu-e-Islam, Lahore, Pakistan
21. Pervez, G A, *Lughaat al Quran,* Idara Tolu-e-Islam, Lahore. That is exactly the sense in which the Quran uses the expression *yataama an nisaa* (the orphaned- lonely and forlorn women) in *An-Nisaa* – 4:127.
22. From my Urdu paper *Quran mein jinsiyaat* (Human Sexuality as in the Quran), unpublished '80. We are expected to marvel at the benevolent Divine logic behind this provision: it is to prevent sexual crimes like fornication and rape! One wonders if Nature has really put a limit of simultaneous four sexual partners on the male desire. What about men who want more? Further, is an oversexed female non-existent? What provision is there in Islam for such women?
23. Maudoodi, Abul 'Ala, *Tafheem al Quran* and *Jihad fil Islam,* Lahore, Pakistan.
24. From *Jame' as Saheeh* (Bokhari), as in *Maut ka Manzar* by Khwaja Mohammed Islam, Lahore, Pak.
25. Even some Muslims have also come to the same conclusion, e.g. Ali Dashti (*Twenty-three Years*), Ibn Warraq (*Why I Am Not A Muslim*), and of course, Salman Rushdie (*The Satanic Verses*).
26. Maudoodi, Abul 'Ala, (1951) *Tafheem al Quran,* Vol. 1, p. 340, Lahore, Pakistan as in Pervez, G A (1979), *Mataaleb al Furqaan,* Vol. 2, pp.359, Idara Tolu-e-Islam, Lahore, Pakistan
27. Ibid.
28. Refers to the pre-Islam practise of inheriting one's father's widows (except one's own biological mother) and taking them as one's wives.
29. The Quran does *not* appear to agree with the Western-Christian notion of risking medical problems resulting from marrying first cousins. Otherwise, it may be assumed that, the Quran would have included it in its list of prohibited relations. If the Quran appears to be wrong-or guilty of omission-Muslims must conduct serious scientific research in genetics to prove the contrary.
30. I shall deal at length with these very important terms *muhseneen* and *musaafeheen* later on.
31. The term *muta,'* traditionally used for 'temporary marriage' is derived from the expression in this verse. I shall deal with it later.
32. A variation of *zawaaj al mut'a* exists in Saudi Arabia, known as the *misyar* marriage, in which ' a man marries a woman with the intent of divorcing her after a particular period of time, but without disclosing to her his latent intent.' The Grand Mufti of Saudi Arabia, Ibn Baz, deems such a marriage as lawful, which 'does not in any way reproach the male partner for his fraudulent behaviour' (p. 179, *Speaking in God's Name*).
33. From *Tafseer* of Ibn Jareer at-Tabari, as in Pervez, G A (1979), *Mataaleb al Furqaan,* Vol.3, p. 401, Idara Tolu-e-Islam, Lahore, Pakistan.
34. *Al-Jaam' as-Saheeh,* Bokhari, from Pervez (as in 33, above). This is supported by several other Prophetic traditions from compilations like *Saheeh Muslim, Kanz al 'Ammaal,* etc.
35. Of course, there *may* be psychological problems. But, that exactly is my point. Sex is primarily and predominantly psychological. I have not heard of any deaths resulting from lack or absence of sexual
activity. In fact, the reverse is true.
36. Leonore Tiefer asserts in *Human Sexuality – Feeling and Function*: 'Thus in a very real sense, the brain is the major sex organ of the body.' (p. 80, Chapter: The Nervous System).
37. Also in 5:12.
38. Linguistically, the two expressions in this particular verse refer to men, according to Arabic grammar and vocabulary. Keeping true to its stance regarding equality of sexes, the Quran uses identical terms for females (*muhsanaat* and *ghair musaafehaat*) in the very next verse (4:25).

Endnotes

39 Pervez, G A (1961) *Lughaat al Quran,* Idara Tolu-e-Islam, Lahore, Pakistan.
40 The Quran takes such a serious view of the matter that fornication is punishable (*An-Noor* – 24:2).
41 Leonore Tiefer, Human Sexuality – Feeling and Function. P. 18.
42 Desmond Morris, *Manwatching,* p. 23.
43 *On Human Sexuality,* Penguin Publishers, UK.
44 Encyclopaedia Britannica, Article: *Human Sexual Behaviour*
45 'There is certainly no innate aversion to intercourse with sister or daughter.' – Article Kinship, Encyclopaedia Britannica.
46 That is why copulation is banned during menstruation (2:222).
47 2:87.
48 24:33.
49 I am sure this statement may sound harsh, extreme and too radical to many. But, I have come to accept and agree with it in the following of Ghulam Ahmed Pervez of the Tolu-e-Islam Movement, Gulberg, Lahore, Pakistan. In my view, in time, and with further research and resulting enlightenment, and with the emotional maturity of mankind as a whole, this notion will be accepted just as we accept the validity of the notions like junk food vs. nourishing food. It is of interest to note that the philosophy of 'sex is for procreation and not recreation' may have come from the Hebrew religious custom in Christ's time. The Jewish religious establishment required that a couple engage in sexual union only when a child was desired. Laurence Gardner, in *The Magdalene Legacy* (2005, Harper Collins, London), observes:
'As we have seen, the rules of dynastic wedlock were no ordinary affair. Explicitly defined parameters dictated a celibate lifestyle except for the procreation of children at regulated intervals.' (p. 156)
50 From *Letters to Saleem,* vol. 3, p. 429, by Pervez, G A, Idara Tolu-e-Islam, Lahore, Pakistan.
51 The Quran refers to this phenomenon of sublimation in relation to channelization of anger: "…and who channelize anger… (*wal kaazemeen al ghaiz*)…" (3:134).
52 Pervez, G A (1961) *Lughaat al Quran,* Idara Tolu-e-Islam, Lahore, Pakistan.

Chapter 8: 'MIRACLES' in the QURAN

1 I make the distinction between what I call the 'Quranic' Islam (contained in the Muslim holy book, the Quran) and 'Traditional' Islam (contained in the extra-Quranic Muslim literature such as *tafseer* – exegesis, *rawaya / tareekh* – historical accounts, and above all, *hadith* – the Tradition, which is the record of Mohammed's sayings and deeds). It is the purpose of this work to illustrate the stark differences between them in order to show how different the two are.
2 Restraints of time and space do not allow an exhaustive list from the Quran to be examined. Therefore, I have made a selection of them on the basis of popularity.
3 The Urdu term *mo'jeza* (miracle) is nowhere used in the Quran. However, there appear a number of derivatives of the original linguistic root *'ain-jeem-za.*
4 Also, in another great work by Raagheb, from *Lughaat al Quran* (1961) by Pervez, Lahore, Pakistan.
5 See my unpublished Urdu paper *Quran mein Mo'jezaat* (1979) for an academic circle in Riyadh, Saudi Arabia.
6 Chapter *Al-Qamar* (The Moon): "Plucking out men as if they were roots of palm trees…"
7 Chapter *Al-Anfaal* (The Spoils of War): "Let not the Unbelievers think that they have escaped (or triumphed), they will never frustrate."
8 Chapter *Al-Ahqaaf* (The Winding Sand-tracts): "If any does not hearken to the one who invites to Allah, he cannot escape (defeat God's plan) in the earth…"
9 Chapter *Al-Hajj* (The Pilgrimage): "But those who strive against Our Signs to frustrate them…"

10 Pitras (Peter) Bustani in his important lexicon *Moheet al Moheet* (1870), Beirut, Lebanon – as in *Lughaat al Quran* (1961) by Pervez, Lahore, Pakistan.
11 From *Tehzeeb* as in *Lughaat al Quran* (1961) by Pervez, Lahore, Pakistan.
12 From *Taaj al 'Uroos* as in *Lughaat al Quran* (1961) by Pervez, Lahore, Pakistan.
13 Chapter *Ash-Shu'raa* (The Poets): "They said: 'Thou art only one of those bewitched.'"
14 Chapter *Beni Israaeel* (The Children of Israel): "…ye follow none other than a man bewitched."
15 Chapter *Hood* ([The Prophet] Hood): "…But if thou wert to say to them, 'Ye shall indeed be raised up after death", the Unbelievers would be sure to say, 'This is nothing but (*sehrun mobeen)* obvious sorcery (a lie).'"
16 Chapter *Az-Zaariaat* (The Winds that Scatter): "Similarly, no messenger came to the peoples before them, but they said (of him) in like manner, 'A sorcerer (*saaher*) or one possessed (*majnoon*)."
17 *The Golden Bough* (James Fraser) is a fascinating study on the subject.
18 *Taaj al 'Uroos* . Also Raageb and *Moheet* as in *Lughaat al Quran* (1961) by Pervez, Lahore, Pakisan.
19 Chapter *Al-A'raaf* (The Heights): "…This she-camel of Allah is a Sign unto you…"
20 Chapter *Al-'Ankaboot* (The Spider): "…and We made it (the Ark) a Sign for all peoples!"
21 Chapter *Ash-Shu'raa* (The Poets): "Do you build a landmark (sign) on every high place to amuse yourselves?"
22 Chapter *Beni Israaeel* (The Children of Israel): "We have made the Night and Day as (*ayatain*) two (of Our)Signs…"
23 Chapter *Al-Baqara* (The Cow): "Say those without knowledge: 'Why speaketh not Allah to us? Or why cometh not unto us a Sign?…"
24 Chapter *Al-An'aam* (The Cattle): "They swear their strongest oaths by Allah, that if a Sign came to them, by it they would believe…"
25 Chapter *Ar-R'ad* (The Thunder): "And the Unbelievers say: 'Why is not a Sign sent down to him from his Lord?…"
26 Also in 17:77, 33:62, 40:85, and 48:23.
27 Also in 6:116, 10:64, and 18:27.
28 Chapter *Al-Baqara* (The Cow): "Let there be no compulsion in *Deen*…" 2:256
29 Chapter *Al-Baqara* (The Cow): "And fight them on until there is no more persecution and the *Deen* becomes Allah's…"
30 To some it raises theological questions about discrepancies in the Quranic image of a chosen messenger of God, especially of the stature of Abraham. Why was he not as yet convinced of the powers of God? Why was he given the responsibility of teaching and conveying a Divine message he himself was not convinced of? Sadly, Traditional Islam does not help. In fact, it paints Abraham in a bad light. One of the most famous and prolific narrators of Hadith, Abu Huraira, reports: '*The Messenger of Allah said that we have a greater right than Ibrahim (ahs – salutations be to him) to be doubtful – when he asked Allah to be shown how He revives the dead*' – Bukhari, Kitab at Tafseer. In *Fath al Baari,* an interpretation of Bukhari, Ibn Abbas is reported to have said, '*Ibraheem did under the influence of the Devil.*'
31 The verse in question (2:260) makes *no* mention of *cutting*. It is a classic example of the dependence of most translators of the Quran on Tradition. It is sad that even a scholar of Abdullah Yousuf Ali'stature succumbs to this practice.
31 From *Taaj al 'Uroos* and Raagheb as in *Lughaat al Quran* (1961) by Pervez, Lahore, Pakistan.
32 Chapter *Al-Baqara* – 2:60
33 As in *Lughaat al Quran* (1961) by Pervez, Lahore, Pakistan.
34 Chapter *Aal-e-'Imraan* – 3:103. Also, in 3:112.
35 The Old Testament, Book of Kings I and II.
36 From *Taaj al 'Uroos* as in *Lughaat al Quran* (1961) by Pervez, Lahore, Pakistan.
37 *Lataaef al Lugha* as in *Lughaat al Quran* (1961) by Pervez, Lahore, Pakistan.
38 From *Taaj al 'Uroos* as in *Lughaat al Quran* (1961) by Pervez, Lahore, Pakistan.

Endnotes

39 *Moheet al Moheet* as in *Lughaat al Quran* (1961) by Pervez, Lahore, Pakistan.
40 Chapter *Saad*.
41 From *Moheet, Taaj,* Raagheb, and Ibn Faaris, as in *Lughaat al Quran* (1961) by Pervez, Lahore, Pakistan.
42 From *Moheet,* and *Taaj* as in *Lughaat al Quran* (1961) by Pervez, Lahore, Pakistan.
43 Chapter *Al-Kahaf* (The Cave). It is clear from the preceding two verses (18:45, 46) and the succeeding verse (18:48) that *jibaal* and *al-ard* cannot be taken literally here.
43 Chapter *Ash-Shu'raa* (The Poets)
44 Chapter *Yaseen.*
45 Translated as such by Abdallah Yousuf Ali.
46 *Lughaat al Quran* (1961) by Pervez, Lahore, Pakistan.
47 I can recall from my personal experience in Saudi Arabia a student of mine with the tribal surname of Namla. He came from the southern parts of the country.
48 *Jinn, shaitan, iblees* and *adam,* etc are terms relating to the Quran's concept of Evolution of Life and merit special treatment. Hence, the brevity in this paper.
49 The importance of Jesus deserves an extensive paper of its own, which I shall endeavour to do when the time is more opportune. Here I confine myself to a couple of most prominent 'miracles' – his virgin birth and rising from the Cross.
50 Jesus, or anyone for that matter, could not be born of a virgin (without a physical father) as it is against the law of Nature (35:11), which never changes (17:77). Even God would need a consort (*saahiba*) to produce children! (6:101). To God, the birth of Jesus was just like the birth of an ordinary human being (3: 58).
51 Chapter *Al-Kahaf* (The Cave): "Say: 'I am but a man like yourselves...'"
52 This was taken from "We have sent you a *light* and a perspicuous Book" (5:15), etc. 'This was applied to the living person of the Prophet. Hence his body emitted luminous waves, rendering him visible in the thickest darkness. One night this miraculous light enabled Aisha to find a needle she had lost.' Lammens, H, *The Koran and Tradition* (1910), translation by Ibn Warraq (2000) in *The Quest for the Historical Muhammad,* Prometheus Books, New York, USA.
53 Ibn Warraq (1995), *Why I Am Not a Muslim,* Prometheus Books, New York, USA.
54 Ibn al-Jawzi, *Wafa* as reported by ' Lammens, H, *The Koran and Tradition* (1910), translation by Ibn Warraq (2000). Interestingly, Lammens also reports that this legend is of 'Platonic and Gnostic origin' on the authority of a paper (1908) given in Copenhagen by Professor Goldziher.
55 *Lughaat al Quran* (1961) by Pervez, Lahore, Pakistan.
56 *Lughaat al Quran* (1961) by Pervez, Lahore, Pakistan.
57 *Islam and the Divine Comedy,* Miguel Asin (1926) – trans. & abridg. by Harold Sunderland (2001), Goodword Books, New Delhi, India.
Asin reports that the legend of the Nocturnal Journey by Mohammed is not an original in the world of religion. Similarities exist between the Prophet's ascension and older historical sources, Christian as well as others. The Persian culture and literature also had a strong hand in developing this legend as we know it today.
58 Bukhari, *Sahih;* Muslim, *Sahih;* Hanbal, *Musnad* from Lammens, H. (1912), *Fatima and the Daughters of Muhammad,* translation by Ibn Warraq (2000) in *The Quest for the Historical Muhammad,* Prometheus Books, New York, USA.
59 The Tradition finds the Quranic basis for the details of the heavenly journey in sura 53 (*An-Najm*), verses 1–18.
60 *Lughaat al Quran* (1961) by Pervez, Lahore, Pakistan.
61 Abdallah Yousuf Ali, trans. of the Holy Quran, printed in Saudi Arabia, explanation of verse 17:1, note 2168, p. 774.
62 *Qaab* is the piece between the handle and one end of a bow; *qowsayen* is 'two bows'. This refers to the pre-Islam Arab practice of shooting one arrow from two bows put together. This expressed solidarity and closeness – from *Lughaat al Quran* (1961) by Pervez, Lahore, Pakistan.
63 *Sidra* stems from the three-letter root *seen-daa-raa* meaning Lote tree and / or fruit-laden and heavily shaded tree as in *fi sidrin makhdood* (56:28). It also the origin of *sadera* (he was

amazed), *as saader* (the one who is bewildered because of intense heat. Therefore, *sidra tul muntahaa* in this verse should be taken to mean 'extreme amazement' - *Lughaat al Quran* (1961) by Pervez, Lahore, Pakistan.

64 From Ibn Warraq (1995), *Why I Am Not a Muslim*, p. 143, Prometheus Books, New York, USA. This refers to another 'miracle' attributed to Abraham in the Quran. The great patriarch is reported to have miraculously escaped unscathed from a fiery oven he was cast into by Nimrod (21:69). This notion may have resulted from confusion created by a linguistic mistake in translation. In the Bible, it says "I am the Lord that brought you [Abraham] out of Ur of the Chaldees" in Genesis 15.7. 'Ur' in Babylonian means 'a city' as in Ur-Shalim (Jerusalem) – 'the city of peace.' Ur closely resembles in speech another word 'Or' meaning 'light' or 'fire.' As reported by W St. Clair-Tisdall in his *The Sources of Islam* (c. 1901, SPCK, London), '...many years later, a Jewish commentator by the name of Jonathan ben Uzziel translated Gen. XV.7 as: "I am the Lord that delivered thee out of the Chaldean fiery oven.' Clair-Tisdall supports this explanation with an example from the English language – that of the word 'post.' A Persian noticing the departure of an Englishman's post may note in his diary that 'the gentleman had lost his skin (which is what the word means in Persian)!'

66 *An Introduction to Philosophical Analysis*, Hospers, J (1973), London as in Ibn Warraq (1995), *Why I Am Not a Muslim*, p. 143, Prometheus Books, New York, USA.

67 Also in *Az-Zariyaat* (The Winds that Scatter) – 51:20, 21.

Chapter 9: RITUALS IN ISLAM

1 Webster's II, New Riverside Dictionary, 1984
2 *Al-Mowrid al-Qareeb,* Ba'albaki's Pocket Dictionary, Beirut, Lebanon, 1979.
3 *Lughaat-al-Quran*, G A Pervez, vol. 2, p. 955. Hair of camel is *wabar* while that of sheep is *soof.* All the three words occur in *An-Nahl* – The Bee 16:80
4 Occasionally, this word (*shei'r*) was figuratively used for 'a lie' or 'falsehood'. This is why his opposition labeled Mohammed as a *shaa 'er* (poet). *Taaj-alUroos*, from *Lughaat-al-Quran*, G A Pervez, vol. 2, p. 955
5 "O ye who believe! Violate not the sanctity of the rites of Allah ….." Al-Maaeda – The Meal, 5:2
6 *Taaj-al-Uroos*, from *Lughaat-al-Quran*, G A Pervez, vol. 3, p. 1035
7 "They will say: 'We were not of those who followed.'" 74:43
8 "Allah and His angels send blessings on the Prophet; O ye that believe! Send ye blessings on him with all respect." *Al-Ahzaab* – The Parties 33:56, also, *Al-Ahzaab* – The Parties 33:43, and, "Of their wealth take alms that so thou mightest purify and sanctify them, and praise them; verily, your encouragement is a source of (peace and) security for them……" *At-Tauba* – Repentance 9:1034 " O ye who believe! When ye prepare (get up or rise) for *as-salaa* …." *Al-Maaeda* – The Meal 5:6, also, " O ye who believe! Approach not *as-salaa* in a state of intoxication…." *An-Nisaa* – Women 4: 43, and : " And when thou (O Messenger) art with them, and standest for them for *as-salaa..*" *An-Nisaa* – Women 4:102
10 *An-Noor* – Light 24:41
11 Even Man's exceptional freedom from Nature's laws is not comprehensive. It is selective in that he has the capacity to consciously go against Nature, but he has to bear the consequences of break-ing the law. He enjoys relatively wider freedom in the social world. Man's behaviour, both in the physical as well as social context is not pre-programmed by Nature as it is dictated in the case of all other creation.
12 *Tasbeeh* in the Quranic sense is radically different from the common concept of chanting God's names on a string of rosary beads. It comes from the three-letter root *seen, ba, ha* (to swim swigtly) – " It is not permitted to the Sun to catch up the Moon, nor can the night outstrip the day: each just (swims) along in (its own) orbit (according to Law)." *Yaseen* – 36:40
13 *Hood* – (a prophet) 11:87

Endnotes

14 *Al-Hajj* – Pilgrimage 22:41
15 *Ash*-Shoora – Consultation 42:38
16 *Maryam* – Mary 19:59
17 *At-Tauba* – Repentance 9:112
18 *Al-Hajj* – Pilgrimage 22:77
19 *Al-A'raaf* – The Knowings 7:170
20 *Aal-e-Imran* The Family if Imran 3:14
21 *Al-Baqara* – The Cow 2:150
22 The expression *dulook ash-shams* is generally translated as 'the Sun's decline.' But lexically, it can, and does, include the rise of the Sun (see *Lughaat al Quran,* G A Pervez, vol. 2, pp. 664-5)
23 *Al-Jaame' al-Saheeh* by Bokhari, the most authentic and respected compilation of *hadith* gives the number, not the times of daily prayer meetings.
24 The Gospel of Barnabas: 100, 131, 133, 146, and 182; and the Qumran Manual of Discipline from the Dead Sea Scrolls.
25 For instance, the normal requirement of FIVE daily prayers can never be met in the polar regions.
26 *Taaj-al-Uroos* from *Lughaat-al-Quran,* G A Pervez, vol. 2, p. 474
27 *"thamnaa hijaj* meaning 'eight years' in *Al-Qasas* –Retributions 28:27
28 *al-hujja tal baalegha"* – strong, weighty argument – *Al-An'aam* –Bounties 6:149
29 *Al-Hajj* – The Pilgrimage 22: 28
30 This takes place on Friday, whose Arabic equivalent is *yowm al-juma'*–'the day of gathering.'
31 *Al-Hajj* – The Pilgrimage 22:27
32 *Al-Baqara* – The Cow 2:127 and *Ibraheem* – Abraham 14:37
33 *Al-Hajj* – The Pilgrimage 22: 33. The concept of slaughtering livestock as an offering has no basis in the Quran. As I shall presently show, the verse quoted in support of 'offering' has sadly been mis-interpreted.
34 The significance of number SEVEN in circumambulating the Ka'aba is traditional and appears to have been adopted because of the aura attached to the number since ancient times. The Arabs also used the number 7 to show plenty or sanctity. Look, for instance, at the Biblical creation of the Universe in seven days, and the Quranic 'seven heavens.'
35 "Behold! Safa and Marwa are among the symbols of Allah. So if those who visit the House in the season, or at other times, should compass them round, it is no sin in them..." (2:158)
36 Taaj-al-Uroos from Lughaat-al-Quran, G A Pervez, vol 2, p. 808
37 *Lughaat-al-Quran,* G A Pervez, vol 2, p. 808
38 "... that is most thriving and pure for you..." (2:232)
39 Also, "(Hell) Inviting (all) such as turn their backs and turn away their faces (from the Right), and gather (wealth) and hide it (from use) !" (70: 7,18) Also: "Woe to every (kind of) of scandal-monger and back-biter, those who pile up wealth and layeth (counting) it by." (104 :1,2)
40 "Do not kill your children for fear of penury; We provide sustenance to you, and for them." *Al-An'aam* – Bounties 6 : 152, also, *Beni Israel* – The Children of Israel 17 : 31
41 A New Handbook of Living Religions, Penguin, London, (p. 250).
42 Ibid, (pp. 292-3).
43 Ibid, (p. 305).
44 Ibid, (p. 741).
45 *The World's Religions,* A Handbook, Lion, London.
46 A New Handbook of Living Religions, Penguin, London, (p. 25).
47 A New Handbook of Living Religions, Penguin, London, (p. 192).

Many Muslims the world over seem to have carried over the practice of fasting on 'the tenth' – only there appears to have a confusion crept in by later Islamic history. Now many Muslims fast on the 10th of Muharram, the day Hussain, the Messenger's grandson was killed in Kerbala, Iraq.

The Quran's Challenge To Islam

Many of us are also familiar with the issue of *Qibla Awwal* (the First Aim / Direction for prayer) as well as with the story of the number of (five) daily prayers mandated with the help of Moses during Muhammad's *me'raaj* (journey to the heavens). As one can very clearly see, Judaism has had a very significant influence on Islam.

48 *The Sword of the Prophet* – p. 56.

49 The significance of number 'forty' has been discussed in detail in chapter 3 (The Quran).

50 Daniel- 10: 1-3.

51 From *Taaj al 'Uroos* as in *Lighaat al Quran* by G A Pervez.

52 Retreating in mosques in the Quranic sense is very different from the traditional 'Islamic' practice of shutting oneself up inside a mosque in complete isolation for marathon personal prayer. *Masjid* is any place which is used to remember, follow, and uphold God's law as laid down in the Quran -"O Children of Adam! Wear your beautiful apparel at (near) every time and place of prayer (masjid) ; eat and drink, but waste not, for Allah does not like wasters." (*Al-A'raaf* – The Knowings 7:31). *Sajda* (touching the ground with one's forehead) springs from *sa ja da* (to bow, to droop – as in *nakhla saajeda* (drooping date/palm). Figuratively, *sajda* is submitting oneself to the Divine law (the Quran). It is much more important than, as a matter of fact it takes precedence over, the physical ritual carried out in traditional prayer – "It is not righteousness that you turn your faces towards East or West, but righteousness is to be convinced of Allah (and His system and laws), the Last day, and tha angels, and the Book, and the Messengers ; to spend of your substsnce, out of love for Him for your kin, for orphans, for the needy, for the wayfarer, for those who ask, for the ransom of slaves, to be steadfast in prayer, and give zaka, to fulfill the contracts which you have made, and to be firm and patient in pain (or suffering) and adversity and throughout the period of panic. Such are the people of truth , the law-abiding." (2:177)

'*Aakefeen* comes from ' *aka fa* (root : *'aen-fa-ka*) meaning to hold something together, to stop from disintegrating, e.g. *sh'ar m'akoof* (well-groomed hair); *al-huda m'akoofen* (gift animals held) in *Al-mo;menoon* (The Convinced – 48;25); also, in *Taaha* (20:91) *'aakefeen* is used in the meanings of those who hold on to what is being done (steadfast). Therefore, *'aakefeen* means those who are held specially to help in the grand design of things in a Quranic society during the obligatory month of fasting in Ramadan.

53 Also: *Al-Jaasia-* 45:15

54 See also *An-Nisaa* – Women 4:136

The Arabic word *eemaan* is usually translated as 'faith' or 'belief'. It is not truly representative of the Quranic concept of it. Derived from the three-letter root *alif, meem, noon*, it has the basic meanings of 'being safe from fear, having a sense of security'("...when you are at peace.." 2:240; "balad un ameen – a city which offers security - *At-Teen* – The Fig, 95:3; "I am surly a Messenger providing security" – *Ash-Shu'raa* – The Poets, 26:162). Obviously, 'faith' or 'belief'do not carry the same sense of certainty and surety. That explains why one of the attributes of God in the Quran is *Al-Momin* – One Who provides peace and security!

55 The analytical thought process is so essential that the Quran describes *momeneen* (the Convinced) thus : "Those who, when they are admonished with the Signs of their Lord, drop not down at them as if they were dead or blind." (25:73) Naturally, there is no compulsion in case of adopting a value system. (2:256)

Chapter 10: TERRORISM OR JEHAAD?

1 For instance, see *Hatred's Kingdom: How Saudi Arabia Sponsors the New Global Terrorism* (2003) by Dore Gold, Regnery Publishing, Washington, USA. The book, as do others like it, chronicles the history and rise of the Wahabi Movement in the desert kingdom with *Ikhwaan al Muslemeen* (the Muslim Brotherhood) as its muscle since the 18th century.

2 See *The Place of Tolerance in Islam* (2002) by Khaled Abou El Fadl, Beacon Press, Boston, USA

3 Raagheb, quoted by Prevez in *Lughaat-al-Quran,* Vol. 2, p.624

4 My parentheses.

Endnotes

5 Lughaat-al-Quran, Vol. 2, p.624
6 *Al-Ahzaab* (The Battles – 33:19)
7 *An-Nahl* (The Bees – 16:47). The word *takhfeef* is widely used in standard Urdu to mean a discount.
8 *Al-Baqara* (The Cow – 2:38); *Al-An'aam* (The Cattle / The Bounties – 6:48), etc.
9 *Ad-Dahr* (The Times – 76:3)
10 *An-Nisaa* (The Women – 4:88; 4:137; 4:143) ; *Al-Furqaan* (The Distinguisher – 25:9)
11 *Al-An'aam* (The Cattle / The Bounties – 6:165)
12 *Al-Maaeda* (The Meals – 5:32); *Al-An'aam* (The Cattle / The Bounties – 6:152); *Beni Israeel* (The Children of Israel – 17:33)
13 *Al-Maaeda* (The Meals – 5:8)
14 *Al-Anfaal* (The Revenue – 8:58)
15 *Al-Anfaal* (The Revenue – 8:45)
16 Some translators, such as A Yousuf Ali, render this piece from 3:154 as '...those for whom death was decreed...' which is incorrect for two reasons: one, that *qatl* is used for both 'to kill' as well as 'be killed'; two, the notion that those people were destined to be killed is contrary to the Quran's basic philosophy of human free will and confirms the non-Quranic concept of Pre-destiny.

Chapter 11: THE PERMISSIBLE (halaal), THE FORBIDDEN (haraam)

1 *Taaj-al-Uroos* as in *Lughaat-al-Quran,* (1960) Pervez, G A; Idara Tolu-e-Islam, Lahore, Pakistan.
2 *Halaael* (wives of) *abnaaekum* (your sons) – Sura *An-Nisaa* (4 : 23)
3 This is a significant point in the scheme of this chapter. It will be referred to, and dealt with, later on.
4 *Ibn Faaris* as in *Lughaat-al-Quran,* (1960) Pervez, G A; Idara Tolu-e-Islam, Lahore, Pakistan.
5 The same list of forbidden foods has been repeated in the Quran, as in 2:173 and 5:3 etc.
6 It is indeed strange to note that there is no practice of reciting *Allahu Akber* on foods other than meat.
7 This legend, incidentally, has created the practice of 'sacrificing' livestock on the occasion of *Al-Hajj*. But, this notion is erroneous as is evident from verse 22:33 mentioned above. I have dealt with *Al- Hajj* in detail in the chapter *Rituals in Islam*.
8 Obviously, using a knife to slit an animal's throat is not the only way to drain its blood.
9 That, in my view, should be and is, the sense of invoking Allah's name not only on meat but on ALL food ! And not only food but, in fact, EVERYTHING, be it an object or an action.
10 See 2:173, 5:3, 6:146, 16:115.
11 It is noteworthy that the Arabic word *al-khamr* – intoxicant – has been translated as such by A Yousuf Ali in 5:90-91, but apparently inexplicably, as 'wine' (which is exclusively used for fermented alcoholic drinks) in 2:219. Muslims generally take *al-khamr* to mean alcoholic drinks but it actually applies to *all* intoxicants. Interestingly, 'alcohol' itself is a borrowed term from Arabic *al-kuhul*.

BIBLIOGRAPHY

A Learner's Arabic-English Dictionary, Beirut, Lebenon.

A New Handbook of Living Religions, Penguin, London.

Abou El Fadl, Khaled (2001) *Speaking in God's Name* (note 33, p. 167, chapter 5), Oneworld, Oxford, UK.
- (2002), *The Place of Tolerance in Islam,* Beacon Press, Boston, USA.

Abu-Hamdiyyah, M (2002) *The Quran – An Introduction,* Routledge, London, UK.

Ahmed, Mirza Ghulam, *Roohaani Khazaaen,* founder of the Ahmediya Movement in Qadiyan, India.

Ali, Maulana M (1936), *The Religion of Islam,* 6th ed. (1990), p. 47, The Ahmadiyya Anjuman Isha'at Islam (Lahore) Ohio, USA.

Ali, T (2002) *The Clash of Fundamentalism,* Verso, UK.

Al-Mashriqi, Inayatullah Khan (1924) *At-tazkera,* reprinted 1980, At-Tazkera Publications, Ichchra,

Anderson, B W (1988) *The Living World of the Old Testament,* Yale University Press, N.Y., USA.

Aquinas, St. Thomas, *Summa Theologica.*

Aristotle *Politics.*

Asin, M (1926) *Islam and the Divine Comedy,* translated & abridged by Harold Sunderland (2001), Goodword Books, New Delhi, India.

Avesta, the sacred book of Zoroastrianism.

Balbaki, Muneer *Al-Mawrid al-Qareeb,* Daar al Ilm wal Malaaeen, Beirut, Lebenon.

Balyaawi, Abulfazl (1950) *Misbaah al Lughaat,* an Arabic-Urdu lexicon, Maktaba Burhaan, Delhi, India.

Barq, G J (circa 1950's), *Do Islam* (in Urdu), Campbellpore, Pakistan.

Briffault, R (1919) *The Making of Humanity,* George Allen & Unwin, Cambridge, UK.

Bucaille, M Dr. (1997) *The Bible, The Quran and Science,* translated from the French by Alistair D Pannell, published by Kitab Bhavan, New Delhi, India.

Chaanakiya (Kautalliya), *Arth Shaaster.*

Charaagh e Raah, Urdu magazine, special 'Socialism' issue (c. 1970's), Pakistan.

The Quran's Challenge To Islam

Conrad, Lawrence I (1987) *Abraha and Muhammad* – Some Observations apropos of Chronology and Literary *Topoi* in the Early Arabic Historical Tradition, BSOAS, Oxford University Press.

Crone, P (2004) *Meccan Trade and the Rise of Islam,* Gorgias Press, New Jersey, USA.
    - with Cook, M (1980) *Hagarism: The Making of the Islamic World,* Cambridge University Press, Cambridge, UK.

Daniel, N (1960 & 1993) *Islam and the West-The Making of an Image,* Oneworld Publications Ltd., Oxford, UK.

Dashti, Ali (1994) *23 Years,* translated by FRC Bagley, Mazda Publishers, California, USA.
    - *Do Quran* (in Urdu), Campbellpore, Pakistan.

Doi, A Rahman (1980), *Hadith: An Introduction,* Kazi Publications, USA.
    - *Shariah: The Islamic Law* (1984), Ta Ha Publishers, London.

Encyclopaedia Britannica.

Fairclough, N., *Language and Power* (1989), p. 43, Longman, UK.

Fraser, J (1993), *The Golden Bough,* Wordsworth Editions, Herts., UK.

Gardner, Laurence (2005) *The Magdalene Legacy,* Harper Collins, London.

Glubb, J B (aka Glubb Pasha) (1969) *A Short History of the Arab Peoples,* Hodder and Stoughton, London, UK.

Gnoli, G (1987) *Manichaeism,* in The Encyclopaedia of Religion, Macmillan, N.Y., USA.

Goitein, S D, ed. (1936) *Ansab al-ashraaf,* Jerusalem.

Gold, D (2003), *Hatred's Kingdom: How Saudi Arabia Sponsors the New Global Terrorism* Regnery Publishing, Washington, USA.

Goldziher, I, *Muslim Studies* (1889-90), vol. 2.

Guillame, A (1955) *The Life of Muhammad* – *a translation of Is-haq's* Sirat arrasul Allah, Oxford University Press, Karachi, Pakistan.

Hadith, Compilations of – Bokhari and others.

Hans Wehr (1980) *A Dictionary of Modern Written Arabic,* Libraire du Liban, Beirut, Lebenon.

Hasan, Dr. M (c. 1970's) *Shahraah e Inqalaab,* Lahore, Pakistan.

Hawting, G R (1997) *John Wansbrough, Islam and Monotheism*
Haykal, M H (1976) *The Life of Muhammad,* North American Trust Publications, USA.
    - *Life of 'Umr Farooq,* Egypt.
    - *Life of Abu Bakr,* Egypt.

Bibliography

Holmes, J., *An Introduction to Sociolinguistics* (1992), p. 246, Longman, UK.

Hospers J (1973), *An Introduction to Philosophical Analysis*, London.

Humphreys, R S (1991), *Islamic History – A Framework for Inquiry*, I B Tauris & Co. Ltd., UK.

Huntingdon, S (1993) *The Clash of Civilizations?* - the journal 'Foreign Affairs', USA.

Husain, S S Azfar, *The Indianness of Rudyard Kipling: A Study in Stylistics* (1983) chapter 3: Style and Context, Cosmic Press, London.

Ibn 'Abdul Hakim (1922) *Futuh Misr*, ed. Charles C Torrey, New Haven

Ibn Hisham (1985) *Sira-tur-Rasool Allah* (an abridgement of Ibn Is-haq's book), an Urdu translation by Rafiullah Shahaab, Maqbool Academy, Lahore, Pakistan.

Ibn Warraq (ed), *The Quest for the Historical Muhammad* (2000), Prometheus Books, Amherst, New York, USA.
 - (1995) *Why I am not a Muslim*, Prometheus Books, Amherst, New York, USA.
 - ed., (2002) *What The Koran Really Says* Prometheus Books, Amherst, New York

Ilyas, A Ilyas, *Al-Qamoos al 'Asari*, Egypt.

Iqbal, M (1973) *Kulliyaat e Iqbal* (The Complete Works of Iqbal), Sheikh Ghulam Ali & Sons Publishers, Lahore, Pakistan.
 - *Tashkeel e Jadeed Elahiyaat e Islamia* (Reconstruction of Islamic Religious Thought) an Urdu translation by Syed Nazeer Niazi (1983), Bazm e Iqbal, Lahore, Pakistan.

Islam, K M (c. 1970's) *Maut ka Manzar*, Lahore, Pakistan.

Izutsu, T - (1959) *The Structure of Ethical Terms in the Koran – A Study in Semantics*, p. 20.
 - (1964) *God and Man in the Koran–Semantics of the Koranic Weltanschawung (worldview)*, Keio Institute of Cultural and Linguistic Studies, Keio University, Tokyo, Japan.

Jaleel, A (1981) *Hadith al Hadith* Riyadh, Saudi Arabia (unpublished).

Jaynes, J (1982) *The Origin of Consciousness in the Breakdown of the Bicameral Mind*, Houghton Mifflin Co., Chicago, USA.

Karl Marx, *The Communist Manifesto*.

Lammens, H (1910) *The Koran and Tradition* tr. Ibn Warraq (2000).
 - (1912), *Fatima and the Daughters of Muhammad*, tr. Ibn Warraq (2000).

Lings, M (Abu Bekr Sirajuddin) (1983) *Muhammad – his life based on the earliest sources*, George Allen & Unwin, Cambridge, UK.

The Quran's Challenge To Islam

Machiavelli, N, *The Prince*

Maudoodi, A A. (1973), article in magazine *Asia* (an organ of *Jamaat e Islami*), Lahore, Pakistan.
- *Al-khutba ath-thaania* (The second Address) from *Khutabaat,* Jamaat e Islami, Lahore, Pakistan.
- *Jihad fil Islam,* Lahore, Pakistan.
- *Khilafat aur Mulookiat* (circa '60s), Lahore, Pakistan.
- *Tafheem al Quran,* footnote on verse 24:2, Lahore, Pakistan.

Morris, D (c. 1960's) *Manwatching*, London.

Parwez, G A (1958) *Shola-e-Mastoor,* Idara Tolu-e-Islam, Lahore, Pakistan.
- (1960) *Lughaat al Quran,* Idara Tolu-e-Islam, Lahore, Pakistan
- (1972) *Taahera kay naam khutoot* ('Letters to Taahera'), pp. 49-50, Idara Tolu-e-Islam, Lahore, Pakistan.
- (1976) *Me'raaj e Insaaniyat* ('The Zenith of Humanity'), Idara Tolu-e-Islam, 25-B, Gulberg, Lahore, Pakistan.
- (1979), *Mataaleb al Furqaan,* Idara Tolu-e-Islam, Lahore, Pakistan.
- (c 1970) *Shahkaar e Risaalat,* Idara Tolu-e-Islam, Lahore, Pakistan.
- (c. 1960's) *Iblees aur Aadam,* Idara Tolu-e-Islam, Lahore, Pakistan.
- *Mazahabe Aalam ki Aasmaani Kitaaben* (Divine Books of World Religions), Idara Tolu-e-Islam, Lahore, Pakistan.
- *Lettere to Saleem,* Idara Tolu-e-Islam, Lahore, Pakistan.
- *Qurani Faiseley,* 2nd edition (1987), Idara Tolu-e-Islam, Lahore, Pakistan
- *Tabveeb al Quran,* Pervez, G A, Idara Tolu-e-Islam, Lahore Pakistan.

Plato, *The Republic.*

Potter, S and Hanks, P., *A Dictionary of English*, Beirut, Lebenon.

Rahman, F (1966) *Islam,* The University of Chicago, USA (second edition, 1979).
- *Islam* (1954), reprinted 1990, Penguin Books, London

Rashid-ud-Daula, P (c.1935) *Kufrzaar e Islam,* (The Infidel Land of Islam), Lahore/Delhi, British India.

Rodinson M (1961) *Mohammed,* translation form the French by Anne Carter, Penguin Books, UK.
- (1966) *Islam and Capitalism,* translation by Brian Pearce (1974), Penguin Books, UK.

Russell, Earl B (1971) *Why I am Not a Christian*, Unwin Books, London.
- (1973) *On Education*, Unwin Books, London.

Salman, Habib Antony, *Al-Qamoos al 'Aali lil mut'allem,* Lebenon.

Shirazi, Aytollah N M, (1412 Hijra) *Tafsir-e-Namoona,* an exposition of the Quran (tr. into Urdu by Syed Safdar Hussain Najafi), Misbaah al-Quran Trust, Lahore, Pakistan.
Shustari, Ayatollah Sheikh Ja'far (1377 AH), *Mawaaez – majlis chahaardeh* ('Sermons' – forty gatherings) - The Sixth Session, Markaz Baksh, Qum, Iran.

Bibliography

Siddiqi, A A, *Ahl e Bait e Rasool aur Tehqeeq Aal e Mohammed* ('People of the House of Messenger and Research on the Progeny of Mohammed), P O Box 81, Karachi 74200.

Smith A, *The Wealth of Nations*.

Tawney, R H (1964) *Religion and the Rise of Capitalism*, Penguin Books, UK.

Testament of Abraham, pp. 18-19, translated from the Greek by G H Box, published 1927 by The Macmillam Co. for Society for Promoting Christian Knowledge, London.

The Quran - Urdu translations of, by Shah Abdul Qadir, Shah Rafiullah and Ashraf Ali Thaanewi.

The World's Religions, A Handbook, Lion, London.

Tiefer, L (c. 1970's) *On Human Sexuality*, Penguin Publishers, London, UK

Torrey, C C (1922) *Three Difficult Passages In The Koran,* Cambridge.

Tritton, A S (1951) *Islam*, Hutchinson & Co. Ltd., London.

Ullman, W (1965) *A History of Political Thought: The Middle Ages*, Penguin Books, UK.

W St Clair-Tisdall (c.1901) *The Sources of Islam*, Society for Promoting Christian Knowledge, London.

Watt, W M & Bell, R (1970 / 1994), *Introduction to the Qur'an*, Edinburgh University Press, UK.

Webster's II, New Riverside Dictionary, 1984.

Zeldin, T. (1994), *An Intimate History of Humanity,* Vintage, London.

Index

A

Aaron (*Haroon*) 73, 148, 149, 150
Abbas (bin Abdul Muttalib) 32, 34
Abbas, Abdallah Ibn (narrator of hadith) 86, 87,
Abbas, House of /
    Abbasid period/caliphate 14, 33, 128,
Abdallah Chakraalewi 29
Abdul Wahaab, ibn, Mohammed 20, 23
Abdullah Yousuf Ali 43, 141
    in notes pp.193, 197
Abraham 14, 16, 35, 100, 158
    his lies and truthfulness 28, 29
    his 'sacrifice' of Ishmael 73, 166, 183
    and birds 146-147
    and *K'aba* 165-166
    in notes pp. 189, 204, 206, 207
Abu Bakr 24, 25, 31, 33, 34, 35, 109
Abu Dauood 21
Abu Hanifa al-Dinwari 22
Abu Hanifa, No'maan bin Thaabet 14, 22, 27
    in notes pp. 191
Abu Hurairah 30
Abu Muslim Khorasaani 33
Abu Taalib (bin Abdul Muttalib) 13, 14
Adam
    meaning of 51, 54
    the story of 82-88, 128
    in notes pp. 195, 196, 197, 200, 208
ahl al Bait [People of the House] 32
Ahl al Quran (People of the Quran) 29
    in notes pp. 191
Ahmediya (sect) 30
Ahraman 99
akhbar 22, 36
(*Al-*) *Akhbar al-Tiwal* 22
al-Asqalani, Ibn Hajar 22
Alawis 33, 34
Ali ibn Abi Talib 13, 14, 15, 21, 23, 33, 34, 35
    in notes pp. 189, 192

Ambrose, St. 98
Amili, Al-Hurr al- 21
amputation (of a thief's hand) 43-44
Anas bin Malik 130
anfaaq 90, 91, 115
angels 54, 58, 61, 62, 71, 80, 83, 84, 85, 90, 164, 172, 173
    in notes pp. 206, 208
ansaar, al (the Medinite Helpers) 33
Ansab al-Ashraaf 22
Anselm, St. 77
appointment, Quranic criterion of 110
Aquinas, St. Thomas 77
Arabic 16, 19, 39, 23, 26, 27
    brief introduction 46-47
    semantic root system 48
    some salient features 47-48
    speakers 47
    speaking countries 46
Aristotelian thought 101
Asbaab-an-nazool
    (Occasions of Revelation) 41
asmaa (names) 53, 83
    in notes 196
(al-) Athir, Ibn 22
Augustine, St. 98
authority (by inheritance) and Abraham 35, 36
Ayesha 29
    in notes 191

B

Babawayh 21
Baladhuri, al-,Ahmed bin Yahya 22
banks (banking) 120
Battles/Raids
    annals of 15, 18, 21, 33
Baz, Abdel Aziz bin Abdullah, ibn 128
Bell, Richard 31
blood 83, 87, 137, 148, 184, 185
    ties of 35
    in idiom 42
    consumption of 183
    in notes pp. 191, 209
Bokhara 20
Bokhari, Mohammed bin Ismail 14, 26, 28, 34
    in notes pp. 190, 191, 192

217

C

Capitalism 57, 113, 119
captives of war 134
Chanakiyya (Kawtalliya) 98
Charaagh Ali, Maulvi 29
chastity 125, 129, 130, 135, 137, 138, 141, 142
Christianity 6, 12, 15, 101, 103
    attributes of God 78
    status of women 86
    miracles 143, 153, 157
Clergy (priests) 98, 99, 103
    in notes pp. 198
Companions 41, 60,
    of Mohammed 14, 22, 30, 31, 34, 35
    in notes pp. 191, 192
    of Christ 60
Companions of the Fire 87
Confucius 98
Cornelius, A R Justice 43
    in notes pp. 194
Crucifixion 68, 154, 169
Crusades 11, 175, 187

D

Daniken, Eric Von 77
Darwin, Charles 26, 80
David (*Daood*) 150, 151, 152
    in notes pp. 193, 199
David, Hume 158
death
    allegorical 57, 147
    of Mohammed 13, 15, 23, 24, 25, 26, 29, 33, 34, 109
    and the hereafter 51, 58, 62, 63, 67, 71, 79, 90-92
    and the concept of life 82, 90, 114, 115
    of Jesus 154, 158
    by stoning 27
    in notes pp. 189, 192, 197, 200, 202, 204, 209
(*ad-*)*Deen* (religion) 23, 41, 52, 99, 101, 112, 153, 187
    linguistically 57,
    in notes pp. 194, 197, 200, 204
defence 112, 151
democracy
    (and) capitalistic society 104
    critique of 102-103
    Quran's view on 100-101
    UNESCO's report 102
dichotomy (of religion and state) 101
Divine Energy (*rooh*) 67, 83, 90, 115
divorce 121, 122, 123, 188
    arbiters 127
    cruelty (*nushooze*) 127
    desertion (*ae'raaz*) 127
    discord (*shiqaaq*) 127
    halaala 128
    khul' 128
    reconciliation 127
    (in) Traditional Islam 128
    waiting period (*'idda*) 127
    in notes pp. 201
dualism 99-100, 104
duniya (the mundane) 51, 72, 99

E

Earth 15, 39, 56, 63, 66, 77, 79, 85, 92, 93, 94, 95, 98, 112, 117
    linguistically and in the Quran 54-55,
    as clay 67
    creation of life on 58-59, 61, 80
    death of 147
    earthly life 42, 56, 62, 63, 72, 90, 91, 118, 119
    inheriting the earth (*tamakkun fil ard*) 112
    ownership of 118-119
    produce of 118
easy wealth 120
economy 11, 16, 57
    in Marxism 113
    the Quranic system of 113
    in Capitalism 113
    in Socialism 104
    in Arabic 114
    and *zakaa* 168
Egypt 14, 20, 23, 46
    slaughter of Israelite males in 72-73
    pharaohs 98
    in notes pp. 197
Eid al Fitr (Festival of Breaking Fast) 172

Index

equality 104, 111, 123
    of sexes 123-124
    qawwamoon 129
ethics 88,
    and morality 103-104
Eve 127
    in notes pp.196
Evolution 15
    Theory of 76
    in notes pp. 200, 205
Evolutionists 78
exhaustion (*athaama*) 140

F

fabrication (of *hadith*) 30
Fasting *(sowm)* 16, 25, 26, 29, 95, 141
    linguistically 69
    timing 173
    in the Quran 170
    in various religions 168-170
    significance of 171
    in notes pp. 198, 207, 208
Fatimids 14, 33
fatwa 5, 11, 20
Fazlur Rahman 30
    in notes pp. 191
Feudalism 98
fiqh 18, 22, 27, 128
fitra (nature/origin) 89
    in notes pp. 197
foreign (non-Muslim) nationals 110
foreign policy 112
fornication 27, 135, 137, 138, 140, 153
    in notes pp. 194, 202
free will 59, 83, 84, 90, 94, 115
    in notes pp. 209
freedom of choice 16, 54, 61, 79, 83, 94, 111
Freud, Sigmund 139
Futuh al-Buldaan 22

G

(the) Garden (Paradise) 16, 20, 80, 88, 91, 111, 118, 124, 132, 141, 155, 167
    Man's expulsion from 83-87
    figurative / metaphorical 91-92
Gaza 23
Ghazali, Al- 14, 77

gender discrimination 133
General Motors 104
Gibb, H A R 88
GOD
    attributes of 40-41, 53, 54, 55, 56, 61, 65, 67, 72, 78, 79, 89, 107
    will bare His calf 42
    Book of 23, 24, 25, 30, 35, 37, 109
    concept of 53, 76-78
    existence of 59, 76-78
    guidance from 84, 87
    His law 24, 25, 53, 54, 55, 57, 59, 60, 61, 63, 64, 65, 68, 71, 72, 84, 87, 89, 91, 101, 108, 109, 110, 112, 116, 162, 163, 164, 174, 177, 178
    His Word 19, 23, 25, 59, 63, 100, 108 (also, see Quran)
    House of (*Ka'bah*) 163, 165
    in the Quran 16, 56, 58, 69, 80, 87-89, 166
    invoking name of 140, 183 (by Jesus on the Cross) 79
    linguistically (*Allah*) 53
    love of 52
    messengers of 14, 15, 54, 63, 66, 150
    shirk (associating partners with God) 68, 89
    Son of 12
    tests (*yubla*) men 78
    vicegerent on Earth of 83
    Will of 20, 64
    worship of 57
Goldziher, Ignaz 30, 35
government
    responsibilities and obligations of 101
Greece 99, 101, 104
    in notes pp. 197

H

Hadith 5, 12, 14, 15, 18, 19
    'the Six Authentic Ones' 20
    the *Shia* hadith 21
    the earliest collection of 22
    the critique of 23-27
    as 'wisdom' (*hikma*) 23
    as the Messenger's obedience 24-25
    confusion and contradictions 27-29

unreliability of 29-32
Hagar (Abraham's wife) 165
Hajj (Pilgrimage) 26, 110, 161
   linguistically 52
   ritual of 164-166
   slaughter of sacrificial animals 183
   and Abraham 146
halaal (the Permissible) 181
   linguistically 59
   the logic of 185
halaala (of marriage) 128
Hamza (bin Abdul Muttalib) 32
Hanafi 20, 22, 27
Hanbal, Ahmed bin Muhammad 21, 23, 24, 28, 130
Hanbali (school) 20, 23
Hanifa, Imam Abu 14, 22, 27
   in notes pp. 191
haraam (the Forbidden) 181
   linguistically 51
   the logic of 185
Hashemites 33
   in notes pp. 192
head of state 110
Hegel 104
Heikel, Mohammed Hussain 34
Hejaz 19, 45, 166
   in notes pp. 189
Hereafter
   linguistically 51-52
   as 'future' 51
   and death 90
   as the next stage of human evolution 115
Hinduism 78, 79, 143, 168
history 11, 13, 14, 15, 22, 88
   annals of 12, 15, 22
   Islamic 13, 15, 18, 19, 29, 32, 34, 44
   Muslim 14, 20, 32
   their critique 34
Holy War (see *jehaad*)
Hubaab ibn Mandhar 34
Hubaysh, Ibn 22
human body (disposal of the dead) 90
human nature 88
Hume, David 158
Hussain bin Ali 33
   in notes pp. 207
hypocrite (*munaafiq*) 116

I

Iblees (Devil) 54, 63, 84, 87
   linguistically 61
   in notes pp. 205
(ibn) Is-haaq, Muhammad 21
idiom 42-44, 67, 71, 73, 88, 147, 149, 153
   in notes pp. 194
'Ilmuddin 133
   in notes pp. 188
imam 14, 23, 35,
   in notes pp. 189-190, 197
incest (forbidden relations) 134
inheritance 188, 130
   of Earth 112
   of power 72, 100, 117
interest (usury) 65, 113, 119, 120
internationalism 106
Iqbal, Mohammed 44
iqtesaad (economic system) 114
Iran 20, 33, 47, 99, 135
   in notes pp. 190, 192, 198
isnad (chain of transmitters) 26, 35-36
Istibsar, Al- 21

J

Ja'far al-Saadiq 23
jaaheliyya, al 33
Jaame al-Bayaan 'an Taweel al-Quran 22
Jacob (*Ya'aqoob*) 141
jahannum (Hell) 16, 69, 84, 91, 92, 119, 148, 155, 167
   linguistically 61-62
   the Quranic concept of 90-91
   in notes pp. 207
Jainism 168, 169
Jamaat e Islami 20, 124
janna (Paradise) 16, 20, 61, 62, 63, 69, 80, 85, 86, 87, 88, 91, 92, 111, 118, 123, 124, 132, 141, 155, 167
   linguistically 63
(al-)Jawzi, Ibn 130
jehaad 175, 178-179
   the linguistic aspect 62
Jesus 12, 14, 16, 64, 67, 69, 143, 151, 158
   his Ascension 154

on the Cross 79
his death 154
his sacrifice 79
virgin birth 153
Second Coming 153
in notes pp. 205
Jinn (genie) 62-63
Jinnah, Mohammed Ali 133
John of Salisbury 101
Johnson, Lyndon 104
Joseph (*Yousuf*) 141-142
Judgment, the Day of 16, 71, 84, 92, 182
Judgment, God's Law for 25

K

Ka'ba 13, 26, 59, 181, 182
    in notes pp. 192, 199
Kaafi, (Al-) 21
kafir (Infidel) 8, 20, 45
kalemaat -sing. *kalema* – God's words 87
kashf saaq (baring of the calf) 42
Kathir, (Ibn) 86
Kerbala, Iraq 33
    in notes pp. 207
Khabar 22 (also see *akhbar*)
khaleefa (successor)
    of the Prophet 13, 33
    of God 83
kharejee's (the Exiters) 33
khowf (fear) 63, 87
Khurasaan, Iran 21
Kindi, (Al-) 77
Kitab al-Ghazawaat (Book of Raids) 22
Kitab al-Ma'arif (Book of Information) 22
Kufa, Iraq 22, 33
Kulayni, al- 21
Kutub al-maghaazi (Annals of Raids and Battles) 18

L

labour 66, 120
    division of 41, 129
    wages of 118
labourer 49
(bin) Laden, Osama 175
laila tal qadr (the 'Night of Values') 95, 172
    in notes pp. 198
language 39-41
    and translation 42
    and culture 44
Last Day (see Judgment, the Day of)
law
    God's 24, 25, 53, 54, 55, 57, 59, 60, 61, 63, 64, 65, 71, 72, 84, 87, 89, 91, 101, 108, 109, 110, 112, 116, 162, 163, 164, 165, 177, 178
    Islamic 19, 43
    social 16
leadership 15, 33
    kinship as the basis of 35
    religious 99
    in notes pp. 189, 193
League of Nations 106
Lent 169
Life
    after death, 51, 59, 67, 82
    in notes pp. 197
    evolution of 80, 83
    origin of, 81
    spiritualistic (Quranic) concept of 89-91
    sanctity of 141
Locke, John 101

M

Maajja (ibn), Abu Abdallah 21, 28
    in notes pp.191
Machiavelli, Nicolo 98
maghaazi (raids and battles) 15, 18, 21
Malik bin Anas 21, 22
Maliki 20, 22
Man/mankind 14, 16, 39, 41, 51, 76, 92
    as God's vicegerent 83
    creation of 80, 81, 82
    destiny of 89, 93
    distribution in groups 85
    evolution of 82
    nature of 88
Mao Tse Tung 105
marriage 121-123
    age of 123
    arranged 123
    contract (*an-nikaah*) 123

dowry 124
family planning 138
freedom of choice 123
forced 123
hars (tilth) 138
in-laws 126
officiating priest for 123
objective of 98
rights and responsibilities 124-125, 126
the wedding night 136
witnesses 124
Marx, Karl 104
Mary (*Maryam*) 153
Mashriqi (Al-), Inayatullah Khan 44, 80
   in notes pp. 190, 196, 200
Masjid al-Aqsa 155
Masjid al-Haraam 59, 155, 157, 182
Masud (Ibn) 87
Masudi, Al- 22
Maudoodi, Abul A'la 20, 27, 124, 132, 134
   in notes pp. 190, 191
Mawria, Chandragupt 98
Mazdak 99, 104
   in notes pp. 199
Mecca 13, 14, 16, 26, 33, 52, 56, 59, 110, 155, 157, 163, 165, 169, 173, 182
   in notes pp. 189, 198
Medina 14, 22, 33, 59, 155, 157, 182
   in notes pp. 192
menstruation 29, 127, 129
Merv 23
[the (Divine)] Message (see Quran)
the Messenger (see Mohammed)
Messenger, the amorous 133
miracles 143
   Abraham (*Ibraheem*) and the birds 146-148
   of David and Solomon 150-153
   of Jesus Christ 153-154
   linguistic aspect 143
   Mohammad's 'miracle' 145-146
   of Moses (*Moosa*) 148-150
   Quranic standpoint 145
   nature and purpose of 158
Mishkaat al-Masaabeeh 21
Mohammed
   ascension to heaven (*me'raaj*) 155-156

moon rent asunder 154
momeneen
   [the Convinced (Believers)] 51, 118
   in notes pp. 208
monarchy 14, 98, 100, 101
   divine rights of the king 98
morality 103-104, 106
Mu'aawiya ibn Abu Sufiyaan 33
Mughals of India 98
muhaajeroon, al (the Migrants from Mecca) 33
Muhammad Ali, Maulana 30, 32
Muhammad bin Sa'd 21
Muruj al-Dhahab wa Ma'adin al-Jawher 22
Muslim bin Al-Hujjaj 21
Mut'a (temporary marriage) 27
Muwatta 21

N

Nabiru, the tenth planet 77
nafs (ego/self/personality) 90, 115
   in notes pp. 195, 200
Nahj al-Balaagha 21
nationalism 105
Nature 39, 54, 55, 59, 61, 62, 65, 80, 83, 84, 107, 116, 119, 132, 136, 143, 144, 145, 156, 158, 159, 162
   in notes pp. 196, 197
Neishapour 20, 21
Nejd 23,
Nisaa 21
nisaa (women) 35, 41, 123
Nisaaee, Abdur Rahman, Al- 21, 28

O

Officials 35, 110
Ouhud, battle of 32

P

Pahlavi, Shah Mohammed Reza 99
Pakistan 5, 20, 27, 29, 43, 86, 124, 133
   in notes pp. 189, 200, 203
Paradise 16, 20, 61, 63, 69, 80, 85, 86, 87, 88, 91, 92, 111, 118, 124, 132, 141, 155, 167

'People of the Book' 133
permanent values 95, 107, 118, 141
Persia (Iran) 13, 73, 99, 139, 170
    in notes pp. 192, 199, 205
personality (consciousness) 15, 54, 61, 66, 67, 72, 76, 89, 90, 115, 133, 167, 188
    in notes pp. 196
Pervez, Ghulam Ahmed 3, 44, 80, 155, 157
    in notes pp. 203
Pilgrimage, 16, 26, 52, 110, 146, 161, 162-166
    the Last 23
Plato 101
Platonic thought 99
political parties 110
politics (*siaasa*) 97
polyandry 133
polygamy 131
    reasons for 132
    in Traditional Islam 132-133
Prayer (*salaa*) 16, 25, 26, 28, 162
    in *hadith* 28, 29
    linguistically 55
    mode and timing 164
    supplication 58
    wudoo (preparatory ablution) 26, 163
pre-destiny 93-95, 172
    in notes pp. 209
private ownership 55, 85, 113, 118, 188
    in notes pp. 199
Prophetic biographies 32
Prophetic licence 133
Prophetic Office 183
Psalms (*Zaboor/Az-Zaboor*) 152

Q
qabr (grave) 90
(al-)qayaama (Dooms Day) 92
Quran
    charter 117
    concept of Life 114
    constitutional framework 118
    consultation, the principle of 165
    creation of Man 80
    creation of the Universe 80
    economic system of 113
    glossary of 51-73
    interpretation/exposition of 44
    language of 44
    principle of repetition 45
    political system of 97
    practicality of 108
    'those charged with authority among you' (*ool el amr minkum*) 108
    translation of 40
    universality 107
    world-view of 80
Quraish 34
Qutayba, Ibn 22
Quzwain 21

R
Rahmaan (God) 65, 79, 99
Ramadan 16, 26, 67, 95, 130, 168, 169, 170, 172
    significance of 171
    in notes pp. 198, 208
responsibility, delegation of 35
Resurrection 90
Retreat (*e'tekaaf*) 29
Ritual
    definition of 161
    in Islam 161-174
rizq (sustenance) 93, 111, 117
    linguistically 66
    in notes pp. 200
Rousseau 101
Russell, Lord Bertrand 105

S
Sa'd bin 'Ibaada 34
(*As-*) *Safaa* and (*Al-*) *Marwa* 165
    also see *Hajj*
Sahaah Sitta 20
saqeefa of Banu Sa'da 34
Sarah (Abraham's wife) 165
Satan 61, 68, 84, 85, 86
Satanic verses 11
Saudi Arabia 5, 11, 20, 23, 26, 46, 99, 128, 134, 163, 173, 175
    in notes pp. 192, 200, 202, 205
Scripture (see Quran)

sects 15, 18, 19, 20, 22, 28
secularism 99
Seestan 21
self 67, 89
    development of 90
sex 121
    and culture 140
    and society 139
    procreation 137
    recreation 137
    in notes pp. 203
sexuality 29, 121, 126, 137, 139, 140
sexual intercourse 16, 29, 57, 140
sexual urge 137, 139, 140
Shafe'i 20, 22
Shaitaan (Devil) 54, 60, 61, 68, 73, 99, 124
(ash-) shahaada (the Testimony) 173
Shaykh al-Saadiq 21
Sheba (*Sabaa*) 151, 153
Shia 15, 20, 21, 23, 32, 33, 135
    in notes pp. 192
Shiaism 34
    in notes pp. 192
Sir Syed Ahmed Khan 44, 108
    in notes pp. 199
Sira (biography of Mohammed) 12, 15, 18, 19, 21
slaughter (of animals for food) 165, 166, 183, 184
    in notes pp. 207
slave girls 132, 134
social contract 101
socialism 104, 113
Solomon (*Suleimaan*) 150, 152, 153
    in notes pp. 199
souks (market-places) 32
sovereignty 100, 101, 107, 188
Spinoza 98
stoning to death 27
story-tellers 32
Succession, the conflict of 33
Sunna (the way of the Prophet) 15, 19, 20, 25
Sunni 15, 20, 22,
    sub-sects 27
    in notes pp. 192
surplus wealth 120

T

Tabaqaat 21
Tabari, al-, Abu Ja'far Muhammad ibn Jarir 22, 33, 34, 36
tafseer (the exegeses of the Koran) 15, 18
    by Jalaalain 42
    of Ibn Katahir 86
    in notes pp. 203, 204
Taloot (Saul) 35
taqdeer (law) 70
taqwa (God-consciousness) 88
    in notes pp. 197
tareekh / tarikh (history) 12, 15
    in notes pp. 203
(*Al-*) *Tarikh al-Rusul wa al-Muluk* 22
tasreef al aayaat (the principle of repetition) 45
Tazkera tal Haffaaz Zahbi 24
temptation 87, 141, 142
terrorism 11, 175
testimony (in a Court of Law) 130
Thaanewi, Ashraf Ali 42
theocracy 99
Tibrizi, Wali ad-Din al- 21
Tirmadh 21
Tirmadhi, Abu Eesa Mohammed 21
Tower of Babel 40
transmitters (*isnad*) 26, 35
Tree, the Forbidden 85
Tusi, Mohammed bin Hasan al- 21

U

'Umr bin Al-Khattab 25, 109
Umayyad period 14, 29, 33, 128
umma 19, 20, 28, 34, 110
United Nations 47
Unwin, Dr. J. D. 140
usury 65-66, 119, 184
Uthman, the third caliph 33

V

values (*aqdaar*) 57, 92, 95, 103, 106, 107, 109, 118, 141
    Night of, 172

W

Wahaabism 20, 29
Walpole 81
Waqidi, al-, Muhammad bin 'Umar 21
Watt, Montgomery 31, 83
will of the majority 104
Wisdom (*al-hikma*) 23, 53, 83, 100, 183
    in notes pp. 190,

Y

Yamamah 31
Yaqubi, al- 22
Yazdaan 99
Yezeed bin Mu'aawiya 33

Z

Zahbi, *Imam* 24
Zakaa 26, 112, 117, 153, 166-168
    surplus wealth 167
Zamzam 165, 166
zawaaj al mut'a (temporary marriage) 135
    in notes pp. 202
Zechariah (*Zakaria*) 153
Zoroastrianism (fasting in) 168

www.ingramcontent.com/pod-product-compliance
Lightning Source LLC
LaVergne TN
LVHW011417080426
835512LV00005B/110